Charles A. Stork

**Light on the Pilgrims Way**

Charles A. Stork

**Light on the Pilgrims Way**

ISBN/EAN: 9783337290504

Printed in Europe, USA, Canada, Australia, Japan

Cover: Foto ©Lupo / pixelio.de

More available books at **www.hansebooks.com**

# LIGHT

## ON THE

# PILGRIM'S WAY:

SELECTIONS FROM THE WRITINGS

OF

Rev. CHARLES A. STORK, D. D.

---

EDITED, WITH A SKETCH OF HIS LIFE, BY HIS BROTHER,

T. B. STORK.

---

PHILADELPHIA:
LUTHERAN PUBLICATION SOCIETY.
1885.

COPYRIGHT, 1885,
BY THE
LUTHERAN PUBLICATION SOCIETY.

# PREFACE.

When a man is traveling in the same direction, over the same road, beset with the same stumbling blocks and difficulties as ourselves, it is always helpful to hear from his own lips an account of his journeying, of his troubles, his perplexities, of what helped him, of what hindered him, and in general how he fared on his way.

And this account of his experiences is all the more valuable, if the traveler in question have the gift of observing and of truthfully telling to others the result of his observations.

The writings of Dr. Charles A. Stork here collected, are nearly all of this practical every-day kind. They treat of the homely details of the Christian life such as all know in a way that reveals the writer's source of knowledge to have been in great part his own experience in traveling along the Heavenly way. It is not unreasonable therefore to expect his writings to prove not merely interesting but helpful to those who like himself are set with their faces Heavenward.

All his writings indeed are peculiarly rich in what

may be called individualized, personal teaching; they are not mere formal didactic utterances, but the life-like expression of the real feelings of his own soul. He gave himself to his pupil in Divine things, and in his writings may be traced as truthfully as in a mirror, his own spiritual history. He gave to each one the benefit of the lessons he had himself learned from the Master. Such spiritual lessons faithfully taught have a value, a life, a reality that all must feel, and seem to justify the hope that they may truly be to the Heavenly Pilgrim a light on his way, and thus make good the title which has been chosen for them.

Fully furnished as he was with theological learning, and inheriting something of his grandfather's facility in Greek and Latin letters, Dr. Stork had no fondness for learned discussions of abstruse points of doctrine; he seems to have preferred to write of the practical every-day experiences and feelings of the Christian pilgrim. In so writing he seldom failed to invest common and apparently thread-bare subjects, with a freshness that was often surprising. This originality of treatment, while by its novelty adapted to awaken and arouse, was never suffered to go one step in the direction of the sensational or the theatrical. It was a healthy originality because it was true and natural.

To this spiritual insight, suggestive and original as

it was, he added no mean skill of a purely literary kind. What he had to say was said in the best way, gracefully, simply, pointedly. Any reference to his literary workmanship, however slight, would be incomplete if it failed to touch on the artistic feeling that showed itself not only in his published writings, but even more especially in his informal letters to his friends. His enjoyment of nature was of the keenest; the form of a cloud, the foliage of a tree, the delicate tint of the surf as it flowed over the sand; for all these he had the eye of a painter, and loved to descant upon them. Indeed it was a dream of his that with time and opportunity he could have painted pictures. His writings are full of vivid allusions to natural objects, and from them he drew some of his happiest illustrations. He rejoiced to wander in the open country and to feast his eyes upon the landscape. To him one of the great pleasures of his residence at Gettysburg, was the close communion with nature that it brought him. Walking along the country roads and over the wild hills in summer, or skating across the frozen ponds backed with the dark bare woods of winter, furnished him with unbounded enjoyment, and if any one happened to be with him, with a fund of suggestive remarks and delicately appreciative comments.

Of the strictly intellectual quality of his work, little

need be said to any who had even the most casual acquaintance with him. As of Burke, it might almost be said of him that one could not be caught with him under an arch-way in a shower without recognizing the originality of his mind.

No matter what subject chanced to present itself, he generally had something to say upon it that was suggestive and stimulating to the thought of others. For whatever he said or wrote bore the marks of original thinking: he accepted no opinion or belief until he had made it his own, and saw it clearly and completely for himself. He did not look through other men's spectacles. To this gift of clear mental vision he added the still more precious gift of conferring that vision on others. Whether it were some weighty moral problem or only some pastoral beauty that attracted his attention, whether it were a saying of St. Paul or only the flowing of a mountain stream over its pebbly bed, he could by a touch open the eyes of others to his own clear vision of it. In his conversation, however, while often instructive he was never copious; he preferred the quiet company of his own thoughts to talking, and was seldom as frank and confidential in his utterance with his most intimate friends as with his pen and paper. His letters and writings reveal his individuality more clearly than any personal intercourse could.

For these reasons, therefore, it has been thought by his friends that a few selections from his writings might not be unacceptable as putting into the permanent form of a book some of the suggestive articles which fell from his pen, either as sermons or as contributions to current church literature. Such selections thus collected serve a double purpose; they are a slight memorial, and perchance they may comfort and console others long after those for whose especial comfort and consolation they were written are dead and gone.

The matter which has been used in compiling this volume, has been drawn from three sources: *first*, from his unpublished sermons; *secondly*, from his articles contributed to *The Lutheran Observer* during the last ten years; and, *thirdly*, from articles published during about the same length of time in "The Lutheran Quarterly." While the amount has not been great (owing partly to the fact that in preaching he usually used skeletons, and only wrote out in full a few of his sermons), the quality has been of such excellence as to make the work of selection one of much nicety. Where any question has arisen preference has been given to the unpublished over the published writings, and where it was inconvenient to publish an article entire, extracts of what appeared best in it have been made and placed under the head either of Extracts or of Scattered Thoughts, as the length and importance of the part extracted seemed to demand, the longer and more important being placed under the first title.

It is proper here to mention that the work of selection has been aided by the kindness of the proprietors of "The Lutheran Quarterly" and *The Lutheran Observer*, who furnished the compiler with almost complete sets of the back numbers of their respective publications.                          T. B. STORK.

*Fircôte, January, 1885.*

# CONTENTS.

|   |   | PAGE |
|---|---|---|
| I. | Sketch of Charles A. Stork . . . . . . . . . . . . . . | 11 |
|   | Recollections of Charles A. Stork . . . . . . . . . . | 29 |
| II. | Selections . . . . . . . . . . . . . . . . . . . . . . . | 36–225 |
|   | Newman on Justification . . . . . . . . . . . . . . . | 36 |
|   | The Chinese Problem . . . . . . . . . . . . . . . . . | 70 |
|   | The Secret of Christmas . . . . . . . . . . . . . . . | 96 |
|   | The Growing Life . . . . . . . . . . . . . . . . . . . | 101 |
|   | Christ's Method of Dealing With Men . . . . . . . . | 106 |
|   | The Cure of Carefulness . . . . . . . . . . . . . . . | 131 |
|   | Eternal Life . . . . . . . . . . . . . . . . . . . . . . | 146 |
|   | Bought with a Price . . . . . . . . . . . . . . . . . . | 169 |
|   | Life a Probation . . . . . . . . . . . . . . . . . . . . | 187 |
|   | Looking Unto Jesus . . . . . . . . . . . . . . . . . . | 206 |
| III. | Extracts . . . . . . . . . . . . . . . . . . . . . . . . | 226–265 |
|   | St. Paul's Love for Men . . . . . . . . . . . . . . . | 226 |
|   | The Spirit of God . . . . . . . . . . . . . . . . . . . | 228 |
|   | Purpose in Life . . . . . . . . . . . . . . . . . . . . | 232 |
|   | Letting Religion Slip . . . . . . . . . . . . . . . . . | 235 |
|   | The Fellowship of Christ's Sufferings . . . . . . . . | 238 |
|   | Worship . . . . . . . . . . . . . . . . . . . . . . . . | 243 |
|   | True Christian Patience . . . . . . . . . . . . . . . | 245 |
|   | The Scriptural View of Heaven . . . . . . . . . . . | 247 |
|   | The Main Hindrance to the Gospel . . . . . . . . . | 249 |

## CONTENTS.

| | PAGE |
|---|---|
| Abraham's Faith | 251 |
| Christ's Valuation of Men | 252 |
| Consecration | 254 |
| Christ's Knowledge and Love of Men | 257 |
| Individuality through Christ | 260 |

IV. SCATTERED THOUGHTS . . . . . . . . . . . . . . 266–341

# CHARLES A. STORK, D. D.

## HIS LIFE.

Charles A. Stork came of a line of preachers. His grandfather, Carl August Gottlieb Storch, had been sent from Germany in the year 1788, as a missionary to the Lutheran Church in North Carolina, where he labored faithfully until his death in 1831. He bequeathed his calling and his devotion to the ministry, together with his name Gottlieb (*anglice* Theophilus) to his youngest son, Theophilus Stork, who in his turn handed them down to his own eldest son, named after his grandfather, Charles Augustus Stork.

He was born September 4, 1838, at the home of his maternal grandfather, William Lynch, in Frederick county, Maryland. Two years before, his father, coming from the Theological Seminary at Gettysburg, Pennsylvania, had taken charge of the Lutheran church in Winchester, Virginia, and soon afterward had married Mary Jane Lynch, the oldest daughter of William Lynch, a substantial farmer of old Revolutionary stock, whose farm lay on the north side of the

Potomac river, not far from the little town of Jefferson, Maryland. Winchester, Virginia, where his father's church then was, lay distant as the crow flies about thirty miles southwest from his grandfather Lynch's farm.

In September, 1841, when the young Charles was three years old, his father was called to the pastorate of St. Matthew's Lutheran church in the city of Philadelphia, where he was destined to spend the longest and most active period of his ministry. In August, 1846, his mother died of consumption, leaving to her husband's care her two children, Charles, and his younger brother, William. It was about this time, and perhaps in consequence of her death, that Charles was for the first time sent off to school, to an academy kept by the Rev. Lewis Eichelberger, in Winchester, Virginia. He could read and write, and knew a little about figures at this time; but a young boy among strangers, he felt keenly, the loss of a mother's care and kindness, and the genial influences of home. Of his experience there, he himself says that his chief gain was a fine grounding in Latin.

While a boy, he usually spent his summers on his grandfather's farm in Maryland. From the first he was of a quiet, studious turn, fonder of reading than of the outdoor sports of children. Often he would steal away from his playmates to an out-of-the-way nook, with some literary treasure that he had discovered, and would there pore over it at his leisure. His grandfather took in those days a paper called, "The New World," which was filled with serial stories and other like literary wares; of this Charles was particularly fond. It was his delight to take the back numbers of this upstairs with him, spread them out on the floor, and lying down beside them, give himself up for hours to their perusal.

Having become sufficiently advanced in years and knowledge, he was sent to Gettysburg, Pennsylvania, to prepare himself for entering College, and later to Hartwick Seminary. At the latter place he came under the influence of Dr. Irving Magee, now of Rondout, New York, who was his Bible-class teacher. To a few words, fitly spoken by him after one of the cottage prayer-meetings at Hartwick, Charles attributed under God his conversion. From Hartwick Seminary he passed to Williams College, entering the class of 1857. Here he found himself one of the youngest and smallest boys in the institution, and perhaps, partly for this reason, a general favorite. During his collegiate course he was thrown in especial intimacy with Horace E. Scudder, the *litterateur*, with Dr. Irving Magee, his old Hartwick friend, with

James A. Garfield, and with Henry M. Alden, the latter of whom has furnished for this volume a short account of his life there and at Andover Theological Seminary. These intimacies were kept alive as far as circumstances of time and place would permit, during the whole of his subsequent life.

Young as he was, however, while pursuing his studies, he had not omitted to form plans and dream dreams of the future, and at one time he had thought of the law as a profession. But with such a lineage it is not difficult to understand how this idea faded away as he grew older, and how naturally he began to turn his thoughts toward that calling which, to the earnest piety of his father and his grandfather, was the most glorious possible. On this point his father says, in one of his letters written to him when the critical time of decision was drawing near: "In regard to your studying for the ministry, you know my sentiments; you know it would afford me the greatest satisfaction, and that no earthly honors, in any sphere of human station, would be as grateful to me as to see you a devoted and respectable and useful minister of Christ. But then you must be influenced not by any desire simply to gratify me."

All the letters from home to him, while pursuing his studies at Hartwick and Williams, are filled with similar expressions. In one his father writes: "I would rather be the humblest minister in the land to preach the Gospel to perishing sinners, * * * one soul won to Christ and heaven is worth more than all the world; beside which the honors and wealth of the world are but weeds and rags."

Interspersed with these earnest exclamations, that came from the deepest feelings of his father's heart, voicing the great abiding principles of his life, were bits of homely detail that showed this all-pervading belief in the sacredness of his calling to be no mere feeling, but the realized experience of his life. In these little domestic details, casually referred to in his letters to his son, may be seen how sharply at times he realized that he was himself sacrificing earthly ease and comfort to that calling of preaching the gospel to perishing sinners; and that the *res angustæ domi* were by no means unknown to him and his household.

It was while a student at Williams, that Charles took the final step, and made up his mind to study for the ministry. From this time his father's letters are filled with plans for his taking his place, and letter after letter refers to the pleasure his father feels in anticipating his assisting him in pastoral duties, which were fast becoming too heavy to be borne alone. For while Charles had been progressing in due course through school and college, some very important changes had been taking place at home. St. Matthew's, the church to which his father had come in 1841, was an old well-established Lutheran congregation, worshipping in a plain substantial building in New street, east of Fourth. As time rolled on it became evident, by reason of the fast encroaching business of the city, and the equally rapid movement of the population westward, that not only would a new church westward of the present site, and nearer their dwellings, be acceptable to many of the congregation, but that the growth of the city westward would afford a wide field for missionary work, and for the in-gathering of new members. Accordingly, in the year 1850, a new church had been organized by some of the members of St. Matthew's congregation, and under the name of St. Mark's Evangelical Lutheran church, was duly planted at the southwest corner of Thirteenth and Spring Garden streets. His father had felt it to be his duty, as it was his earnest desire, to accompany the new congregation and to assist as its pastor in the arduous undertaking of establishing itself. The hard work and anxiety entailed by his pastorate of St. Mark's, told on a constitution that had never been robust; and although crowned with success, and seeing his work prospering as highly as he could hope, he again and again felt himself on the point of being compelled to relinquish it to others. But he struggled on, buoyed up with the one hope that his son Charles might eventually be able to assist him in his pastoral duties. Occasionally his feelings would escape in his letters in some such exclamation as: "O, how I wish you were through, and could be associated with me—it would be a good school for you, and a great relief to me. Go on: perhaps I can, by God's blessing, hold on till you are ready to assist me."

After completing his collegiate course at Williams, in 1857, Charles went with his closest friend and classmate, Alden, to Andover, Massachusetts, to pursue a two years' course in Theology at the Seminary there. Of his student life here, as well as at Williams, sufficient has been said by his friend Alden in his recollections; but one incident of his stay at Andover may be added as illustrating a strongly characteristic trait, his love of and sensibility to natural beauty. It seems that during one of his vacations, he tried the boyish adventure of camping out in the woods; but being, as he himself confesses, no great woodsman, he met with indifferent success. In a letter to his father he says that he was wet to the skin with rain, he knew not how to cook the fish he caught, and was very glad to return to civilization, scorched by fire and sun, and with bruised legs and blistered hands. " There is one thing," he adds, " I learned, however, that was worth it all, and that is the grandeur and solemnity of solitude in the night. I used to lie and listen to the lapping of the waters on the shores of the lake, and the moaning of the winds in the forest, and look at the stars shining so silently and steadily, until I was really oppressed with the solemnity of the solitary night; * * * there are many things a man may learn from nature, if he will; * * * I get sometimes an overpowering sense of the careful and continual working of God through all these scenes of nature. It seems like standing in his very presence, to watch the changes and all the movement of a strong summer day, for it sets before us his immediate workings for us and to us."

Before Charles was fully prepared to give to his father that assistance in pastoral work at St. Mark's for which he was anxiously waiting, an invitation came which seemed to offer relief in a different way. In the latter part of the year 1858, Dr. Stork was offered the presidency of the Lutheran college at Newberry, South Carolina, a new institution just established there. For several reasons the offer was inviting: the work would be much lighter than that of preaching and pastoral labor in a congregation so large as St. Mark's had grown to be, while the warmer climate of the South seemed exactly calculated to restore health to one who, like Dr. Stork, was suffering from weakness of the throat and lungs.

His father, being still anxious to have Charles associated with him in his work, asked him to become a teacher in the new College. All preliminaries having been satisfactorily settled, father and son, in the following year (1859), entered upon their duties at Newberry, the one as president, the other as professor of Greek. The civil war put an end to their labors in a little less than a year after they had begun, and Charles, whose sight had been injured by too close application to crabbed Greek texts, went abroad to consult Dr. Von Graeffe, of Berlin. This great oculist effectually restored his eyesight after a treatment of some six months. Returning to the United States he took charge, for some months, of St. James' Lutheran mission, in the city of Philadelphia. Meanwhile his father had undertaken the task of building up a new St. Mark's, in the city of Baltimore. This, like its namesake and predecessor in Philadelphia, was an offshoot of an older church, and Dr. Stork was its first pastor. At his instance and desire, Charles A. Stork was called by the congregation to be his assistant. Here he spent the best years of his life and the whole of his active ministry, the few months in Philadelphia excepted. Shortly after coming to Baltimore he married Miss Maria H. Ellis, of Andover, Massachusetts. He continued to preach and labor at St. Mark's for twenty years, first as pastor, assisting his father, and afterwards, on the resignation of his father in 1865, as sole pastor of the church.

At first his preaching was characterized by its analytic and scholarly elements, rather than by those qualities of sympathy and warmth of feeling which made the peculiar charm of his father in the pulpit. But his growth in spirituality was constant. When, on the resignation of his father in 1865, he assumed sole charge of St. Mark's, the new and greater responbility, which he keenly appreciated, drove him to a deeper and stronger reliance on God, and led him to seek for sustenance in a closer communion with him.

Like his father, it was his lot to bear the constant burden of a weak and delicate body; as early as 1870 he had received a warning of his failing health; during that summer he was taken ill, and only became convalescent in time to resume his duties in the autumn. From that time it seemed as though the "shadow feared of man" was ever casting itself on his path. He recovered his health, but the precious gift was only to be kept by him at the price of continual care.

In 1874 he was advised by his physicians that his lungs were affected, and, in pursuance of their directions, he spent the winter in Egypt. He returned much improved, and took up his work at St. Mark's with fresh hope and strength. But the improvement, as he himself more than suspected, was only a postponing of the end that was slowly yet surely approaching. What an effect this prospect had upon him, may be traced not only in his public utterances, but even more distinctly in his private correspondence. It was the purifying of the gold in the furnace of affliction. The tenderness, the sympathy, the spiritual insight that are so marked in his later writings, were doubtless the fruit of that mighty spiritual chastener—physical suffering. No one can read those sermons of his, such as The Fellowship of Christ's Sufferings, True Christian Patience, and the like, and not feel that they were drawn from the writer's own experience, that he knew in his own soul whereof he spoke. Not that his life was one of acute suffering: often he enjoyed apparently robust health, but then a slight exposure, a spell of unusually hard work, would bring him down with a sharp reminder that could not be ignored in the shape of a cough or a sore throat. Then for weeks he would be compelled to discontinue preaching, and to suffer in a dull, irritating way that was more depressing to the spirit than sharp pain. After such an attack in the spring of 1877, he writes:

"I have been suffering with my throat ever since I was in Philadelphia. You will remember I had a cough then. Well, it got worse, and I have not preached for a month till last Sunday. I tried one sermon then. But it threw me back. The doctor says it will be a tedious affair. Possibly I may be laid up for the summer. I have no pain, but only a loss of voice. My cough, which was quite bad, is nearly all gone; now I must wait for strength to come back. * * * *

"But the long continuance of the weakness is beginning to make me feel a little depressed. I suppose I am to struggle as did father; now able to preach, then laid up. But the doctor tells me it is nothing; if only we could fully trust the doctors. * * * We shall have a pleasant and profitable summer; that is, if I do not get too much depressed about my throat. I know we ought to be cheerful and take gladly anything God sends, but a weight of melancholy seems to press on me sometimes, and though I am not rebellious, I do feel sad.

"Perhaps God means us to be sad. It may be good for us to be made to feel weak and dependent. I am sure I inherit from father something of a tendency to be melancholy at times."

Later in the same year he writes more cheerfully: "I am feeling very strong and able to work; I rejoice in the strength, and want to use it for the best while I have it, knowing that when the days of weakness come, as they must come to all, then God will give me just as perfect peace and satisfaction in weakness, as I have now in strength."

Every year of his later life added greatly to his duties and his responsibilities; every year he seemed to become more conspicuous in the general work of the Lutheran church, and this in the most natural way without any seeking upon his own part, but simply from the fact that for many positions he was found peculiarly fitted, and always willing whatever his strength might be. It was his desire to be spent in the Lord's service. Thus he was made President of the Board of Foreign Missions, an onerous and responsible post which he filled to the entire satisfaction of the church. In connection with this he partly edited and wrote for a mission paper, the *Missionary Journal*. He contributed frequently to the *Lutheran Quarterly* and the *Lutheran Observer*. In addition to this for several terms he lectured to the students of Pennsylvania College on History, going up from Baltimore to Gettysburg at stated times for the purpose. He was also elected Graeff Professor of English Language and Literature in the same institution: this he declined, since it would have compelled him to give up his church, which he was loth to do.

In 1881 he was elected Professor of Didactic Theology at the Lutheran Theological Seminary at Gettysburg, Pa. In October of that year he left Baltimore, and the church where he had labored for twenty years, and to which he was warmly attached, and took up his residence on Seminary Ridge, in Gettysburg, there to enter upon the duties of his professorship. His regret at leaving St. Mark's, and with it the active ministry was deep, but he felt that the call to teach theology was God's, and he went willingly. He was learning every year to look more directly to God for each step in life.

"The secret of peace, I find, is not success," he writes at this time, "nor activity, but humility and the secret of humility is the vision and felt presence of God; when we see him we are at once humbled, cast down from self and men and also exalted with the fullness of the Divine indwelling. Some will call this mysticism; and I suppose it is; but I would wish to be such a mystic as St. Paul when he said, 'I live, yet not I but Christ liveth in me,' yes, there is a mystic element in the Christian life: you know mystic means 'hidden' and there is something 'hidden' in the new life. That is what St. Paul meant when he said your life is hid with Christ in God."

But let no one suppose that teaching was distasteful to him; he had a rare gift for imparting knowledge and could, by an apt illustration, often throw a flood of light upon some dark point; he therefore thoroughly enjoyed the work at Gettysburg; but he had his father's love of the ministry and was often glad to vary his labors by preaching when occasion offered. At the close of his first year's work in the Seminary he writes:

"I am glad my first year's work is nearly over. It ends June 25th. It has been quite hard for me making lectures on new subjects. I have been kept too close in my study. But the summer vacation will mend that; and next year I shall not be pressed so hard.

I hope I am doing good here; but I find in doing work for the Lord, as in all the Christian life, we must walk by faith, not by sight. We cannot see always that we are really accomplishing anything. The only way I find is to live day by day, being sure the Lord has given us a certain work to do, and then doing it, even though we cannot see the fruit. I preached yesterday on Mary's words at the feast at Cana, 'Whatsoever he saith unto you, do it.' How simple and beautiful that rule is; to take our work from his lips, our particular work whatever it is and then faithfully and loyally to do it just because he says it."

But the period of his usefulness on earth was not to be much longer continued. His old troubles revived, his throat primarily and his lungs in a less degree began once more to distress him. It is not certain what exactly was the predisposing cause, it was thought perhaps a visit he paid to Baltimore to attend a meeting upon some church business, was the immediate occasion of his last illness. It was a winter's day, and he returned late at night to his home in a blinding snow storm. The cold he then took aggravated the disease; which, however, must long ere that have fixed its seat in his throat and lungs. This finally brought about his death from phthisis laryngitis, on the morning of Monday, December 17, 1883, in Philadelphia, whither he had gone for medical advice and treatment.

His letters at this time and while the issue was still uncertain, are pathetic; in one he says: "I feel in myself a greater desire to communicate good, a greater richness of thought and experience to communicate; and then to lie still, to be shut up in silence is a hard trial. But God knows best. When I feel restive, impatient, weary, despondent, I just fold my hands and say over those words of Jesus: 'Thy will be done,' till I feel how blessed that will is, and all the waves of strife in me go down, and a heavenly peace comes in. I was reading yesterday the words of Adolph Monod, repeated so often in the last months of his life, when he was suffering so much: 'The crucified life is the blessed life.'"

Again he writes: "My throat improves slowly, but very slowly. I am having a thorough lesson in patience. I think sometimes I have had enough, but the Master says, No, you must go over the old lesson again. * * * *

"I reproach myself often since my weakness and sickness have been so heavy on me, that I do not praise God more for the sunshine he pours so abundantly on me in it all."

As he draws near those gates of Death, so awful in their mystery, but to him so glorious in their possibility, he seems to gain a fresh and wondrous vision of spiritual things. He writes as if already the light of another world, of heaven, were illuminating the dark problems of earth, and as if he saw all things transfigured in that radiance. "The Christian," he says in one of his letters, "is not complete in Christ until not only he has received Christ as crucified for him, but is also crucified with him. That, I think, is a very deep and, though at first sight, a repelling, yet when we experience it, a very precious truth of our holy faith. To die to self, to be baptized in suffering, to receive the strokes of God, and so to rise in Christ and to be one with him—that to me of late is growing more and more a rich part of the faith."

While the death of such a man in the very ripeness of his Christian life, when fully prepared to serve Christ and his church most effectively seems mysterious to our earthly vision, yet in one of his letters he has himself suggested a solution of the mystery that may be allowed as his own epitaph to close this brief sketch:

"I believe I am one who is destined never to have any great success, nor any great failure. I jog along the foot-path way. I can't say but that I would like to have something more stirring and marked, a great crowd to preach to, many and striking conversions, large achievements. But if I am to do ordinary work in a quiet way, I hope to be satisfied. I was much struck lately by a remark made in the *Spectator* apropos of the life of a good man who with many opportunities and some fine gifts, yet failed of his chief project for doing good, and passed away depressed by the thought that he had achieved very little. His character, however, was greatly chastened and ripened as he grew old and the reviewer says his friends at last recognized in his life that the highest end of existence is neither to shine nor achieve, but to do the Divine will. That after all is the deepest truth; we fall back on that when all else fails—that we cannot be disappointed of—being one with Christ in accepting and accomplishing God's will."

## RECOLLECTIONS OF CHARLES A. STORK.

### BY A FELLOW-STUDENT.

He was my class-mate at Williams College, and afterward, at the Andover Theological Seminary; but we had nearly completed our Junior year at college before we became intimate friends—and up to that time I knew perhaps less of him than of any other of my fellow-students. Considering our near and constant intercourse during the following years, this is somewhat remarkable, and it illustrates a peculiarity of his character. He probably never did anything in his whole life with the purpose of drawing attention to himself. He entered into no competition with his fellows. With unusual power of expression, both as a writer and as a speaker, he showed no desire for such expression. He had no outward eccentricity; and even his indifference to passing affairs was negative rather than positive, and escaped observation. He was reticent without shyness, and, whatever may have been his inner life, he gave no outward sign of it.

In all that makes up the visible exterior of a man he was the same from the first to the last observation I had of him. When he entered college, he had in all these respects reached maturity, although he was almost the youngest member of his class.

Though not inviting notice, there were some peculiarities in his personal appearance that would arrest the attention of even a casual observer. His features —as large as those we note in the portraits of Beethoven—clearly indicated his Teutonic paternity; while his mobile mouth, his small hands—as delicate as a woman's—and the sensitiveness that inter-penetrated his German phlegm, as clearly showed that his mother was of the finer Southern type. His mood was that of habitual thoughtfulness, usually contemplative, but, under excitement, lambent with fire and humor.

His intellectual habits and tastes were, even at that early period, fully formed. He had read all the great books of our literature, and his literary taste was almost an instinct. He especially appreciated authors in whom humor was a prominent characteristic; but his taste was catholic, and he delighted in the keen humor of Thackeray, as well as in the broad caricature of Dickens. In history, he read those works which interpreted the great drama of human progress, caring little for those which contained annals only. The early English poets were as familiar to him as the later.

I approach, with some difficulty, the period of our nearer acquaintance. The memory of such a friendship is too sacred for expression, except in the lofty strains of a new "In Memoriam." It was the ideal friendship of my life, and its preciousness to me may be understood from the fact that at that time I had no other intimate friend. It was characteristic of his generous nature that he sought to draw me out of the solitude in which I had immured myself. He had few intimate personal friends. Among them were James A. Garfield, of the class of '56, and Horace E. Scudder, of the class of '57. Garfield's graduation was near at hand. I remember his last evening at Williams, when a number of us joined hands with him on the college green and sang "Auld Lang Syne." Scudder was especially congenial to Stork, not only because of their intellectual sympathy, but because each of them had a pure, sweet and wholesome nature—the natural basis of a manly and lasting friendship.

But one year of college life remained to Stork and myself, and we embraced every opportunity such as friends always seek for intercourse, much of our time being spent in reading together our favorite authors. Of modern writers, the poet Tennyson made the strongest impression upon our minds. His thought —moulded after the antique, mediæval, or modern type —was at once poetic and interpretative. His wonderful rhythm and classic perfection of form gave æsthetic satisfaction. And we found in his poems sympathy with currents of modern thought into which we were drifting—especially that of "honest doubt." The studies of the senior year were largely of a speculative character, and, since these were pursued under the guidance of Dr. Mark Hopkins, it is needless to add that they developed independent thinking.

But our talk was not wholly of books and metaphysics; and it is worthy of note here that Stork loved to talk about his home and about the members of his family—always in terms of the deepest affection. While then, and always, I was impressed by his sincerity, fidelity and earnestness, I could not but notice his disposition to indulge in playful humor. His dignity was natural, without any stiffness or self-consciousness. He was always companionable, and no classmate was more popular than he was.

Among his writings at that time I remember particularly an essay on Rhythm, which was published in the *Williams Quarterly*, and which displayed not only his extensive reading in English poetry, but also a critical ability of the highest order, because it was interpretative and sympathetic, as well as keen in analysis. But, as a promise of his literary future, a brief essay, entitled "Winter," written, I believe, while he was preparing for college at Hartwick Seminary, made a stronger and more lasting impression upon my mind. His winter landscape was associated with Shakespeare's *King Lear*. Nature was more to him than books, but its charms were, in his mind, inseparably connected with the creations of the master poets. He was himself a poet, having much of the virility and dramatic power that distinguish the works of Robert Browning; but he modestly regarded what he did in this field as studies made for his own satisfaction rather than as having any claim to public recognition.

In his entire college career I can recall but a single instance of any public expression on his part. It was at a meeting of the faculty, students, and friends of the College, in recognition of some important benefaction, and he had been chosen as a speaker to represent his class. He had written nothing for recitation; but, when he came to speak, it was evident that he had let his subject take full possession of his mind, and his address was natural in manner, thoughtful, eloquent and impressive.

A few months after graduation we entered the Theological Seminary at Andover. He had reached the period when youth forecasts for itself a lofty career. It is not necessary here to indicate the plans we formed. Was there ever youthful aspiration that did not grandly shape the dream of the future—a dream never to be realized? The student lives in a world of his own—a world in which nothing seems impossible. He will probably do little of all that he then so vastly determines. He soon enters another world, in which duty takes the place of aspiration, and, if he follows this new guide, he finds later on that the work really undertaken and accomplished is, after all, greater than his early dream. Yet I am sure that neither of us ever afterward regretted the studies—in Greek literature, in the History of Philosophy, and the Philosophy of History—that occupied us at the Seminary. If, in connection with these studies, the spirit and the active exercise of doubt were developed, they were naturally incident to the intellectual period upon which we had entered. All discords were afterward resolved. Until the component parts of the mind's object-glass are fitly joined together, there must be mental aberration. But those who read the selections from Stork's writings contained in this volume will find there no indication of such aberration. It will be clear to the reader that—whatever mental struggles he may have passed through, after the conflict his Saviour remained to him the one great real presence of his life.

I can add nothing to this sketch that is not told elsewhere in this volume. I have attempted simply to draw a portrait of my friend, as he appeared to me during that uneventful but important period of his student life which is included within my own personal recollection.

*New York, August 11th, 1884.*                    H. M. A.

# SELECTIONS.

### NEWMAN ON JUSTIFICATION.*

It has often occurred to the writer to ask how it happens that a theologian so distinguished as he whose name is written above should be so little known, so seldom referred to. Surely, whether for intrinsic ability, or for interest arising from a striking individual history, there are few names in the Church of this century that can outrank that of John Henry Newman.

One reason for this comparative obscurity in the theological world may be that his writings, in the main, have not been in those lines which attract general notice. For a man may have great powers and exercise them greatly, and yet, if he write in a discursive manner, or suffer his strength to play about many subjects rather than fix itself upon one, he will, despite his greatness, be passed by unregarded. The world is intensely interested in every age on a few certain fixed points, and anxious to have light thrown on these; and he who can bring the desired light is conspicuous in the public eye, not he who shows the

---

* Lectures on the Doctrine of Justification. By John Henry Newman. Sometime fellow of Oriel College. Third edition. Rivingtons: London, Oxford and Cambridge. MDCCCLXXIV.

greatest power. It is an immensely practical world, and rewards him who can best speak the word it wants, not him who speaks the best word. Thus it is that De Quincey, though of incomparable power as a master of English prose, and a critic of the first order, is known only to the few, because he trifles gracefully with a score of subjects, none of them popular, while men of half his power and knowledge get a full audience by speaking to the point in hand.

But even this would hardly account for the neglect of an author who counts among his productions a work so prolonged and exhaustive as that which we have taken for the subject-matter of this paper. There are works upon the Doctrine of Justification of greater bulk, but few that contain more matter, and none, we may make bold to say, in which the theme is handled with more vigor or originality.

A few words as to the origin of the work, and we proceed to consider its character and merits.

The Thirteen Lectures and Appendix of which it consists, were first published in 1838. They were written under the influence of that wave of doctrinal tendency which produced what is known as the Oxford or Tractarian party in the English Church, and which gave to the modern Church Keble, and Pusey and their fellows. It was intended, says the author in the advertisement to this, the third edition, to be one " of a series of works projected in illustration of what has often been considered to be the characteristic position of the Anglican Church, as lying in a supposed *Via*

*Media*, admitting much and excluding much both of Roman and of Protestant teaching."

That this *Via Media*, which it was Dr. Newman's purpose to illustrate, lay very far over toward the Roman side of the controversy, will become apparent to any one who reads the third edition of our author's treatise and notes how few, how very few, changes he as Romish priest has found occasion to make in that which he wrote thirty-seven years ago as an Anglican clergyman. This he substantially acknowledges himself: "Unless the author held in substance in 1874, what he published in 1838, he would not at this time be re-printing what he wrote as an Anglican; certainly not with so little added by way of safeguard."

This, then, we may take to be a view of the doctrine of Justification as seen from the stand-point of Rome; or, perhaps, better still, as seen by one who is nearing Rome, but yet at that distance which enables him to look down on her position, as well as that of her antagonist, and discern with friendly criticism what in her ground is weak and therefore to be amended.

To some the time and thought given to the careful consideration of a work of this character, may seem so much strength wasted. For three reasons it seems to the present writer quite otherwise.

First, because if Burke is right in his aphorism that "*Our antagonist is our helper*," then it is a positive service to learn what one of the most powerful and sincere of those who have attacked the Protestant position respecting this doctrine can say against it.

And, again, because it is no small intellectual pleasure, as well as a profitable study, to witness the dialectical skill of a master of theological controversy, probably the most skillful that the Church of this century has produced. When most thoroughly dissenting from its conclusions, the present writer has been most charmed with the powerful reasoning, the original method, the felicitous skill with which the argument of this work is conducted. To be most charmed when one's cherished opinions are most powerfully attacked, surely this is the highest compliment one can pay his antagonist. And this testimony the stoutest defender of Luther cannot withhold from this work.

And, lastly, because here we have theology imbued with the loftiest, purest piety. Whatever Dr. Newman may or may not be, neither friend nor foe has ever held him in other esteem than as the most sincere and devout of Christian men. His is a piety that fuses the intellect; so that the reproach of theology, that it brings down the discussion of religion from heaven, and makes it of the earth earthy, can never attach to him. When most polemic, he is still the devout and humble believer. The head never paralyzes the heart. And the most thorough and subtle discussion of knotty questions does, with him, but bring fuel to the flame of devotion, food for solemn and heavenly meditations.

But without further preface, to address ourselves to the work itself:

The author sums up his position with reference to the doctrine discussed in the following terse passage:

"In asking, then, what is our righteousness, I do not mean what is its *original source*, for this is God's mercy; nor what is its *meritorious cause*, for this is the life, and above all the death of Christ; nor what is the *instrument* of it, for this (I would maintain) is Holy Baptism; nor what is the *entrance* into it, for this is regeneration; nor what the *first privilege* of it, for this is pardon; nor what is the *ultimate fruit*, for this is everlasting life." (p. 132.)

Here, then, we find the point of our author's divergence from the Protestant doctrine; it is on the question, What is the *instrumental cause* in justification? What he means by the instrumental cause he defines farther, elsewhere:

"Justification, the work of God, is brought into effect through a succession of the following causes: the mercy of God the *efficient* cause, Christ offered on the Cross the *meritorious*, Baptism the *instrumental*, and the principle of renewal in righteousness thereby communicated the *formal; upon* which immediately follows justification." (p. 343.)

This "principle of renewal" constituting the "*formal* cause," communicated in Baptism as an instrument, he still farther defines as the Presence of Christ in us.

"Christ then is our Righteousness by dwelling in us by the Spirit: he justifies us by entering into us. He continues to justify us by remaining in us. *This* is really and truly our justification, not faith; not holiness, not (much less) a mere imputation; but through God's mercy the very Presence of Christ."

Here, then, we have a sufficiently clear and full view of what in our author's judgment constitutes justification. That which constitutes a man righteous in God's sight, that which makes a justified person to differ from one not justified, the distinctive state of the soul to which the designation righteous belongs and which is the criterion within us, which God sees there, and is the seal and signature of his elect, which he accepts now, which he will acknowledge at the last day, what is it? The Protestant says, it is faith; our author says, no, it is Christ our Righteousness. This last is not a new answer. Indeed, he would be the last to claim that he had introduced here anything novel, holding, as those of his school do, that novelty is one mark of departure from the rule of Catholic antiquity, which also is the rule of faith in the interpretation of Scripture. In many respects this view is like that of A. Osiander; whom, indeed, our author cites as on his side, as one who maintains "that the formal cause of our justification is somethig in us, and therefore that it is the essential righteousness of Christ as God dwelling in us." (p. 388.)

It is not our purpose, in this paper, to enter the old lists, and fight over again the battles of the Reformed Theology with Rome. That ground has been sufficiently traversed. Furthermore, our author himself disclaims the bald view of justification by obedience, as cold and open to the charge "that it views the influence of grace, not as the operation of a living God, but as a something to bargain about, and buy, and traffic with, as if religion were not an approach to things above us, but a commerce with our equals concerning things we can master." It is true, he attacks the Protestant positions with even more evident repugnance to them than he shows to the error of Rome. Luther's doctrinal teaching on this point he declares to be erroneous and even unintelligible. This he argues at length and with great subtlety, but we leave this part of the subject. We prefer to point out those features in his work in which we agree to some extent with his conclusions, or in which at least we find his strictures profitable for the correction of the errors of Protestantism or rather the narrow forms that Protestestantism has taken on in these latter days.

The point to which we would call attention is our author's declaration that the difference between Romish and Protestant divines on justification is only verbal; a difference that has, indeed, issued in very important practical results, but that in itself is not radical, fundamental. This he repeats again and again thus:

"The drift of these lectures is to show that there is little difference but what is verbal in the various views on justification, found whether among Catholic or Protestant divines; by Protestant being meant Lutheran, Calvinistic, and thirdly that dry anti-evangelical doctrine, which was dominant in the Church of England during the last century. (p. ix.)

Again:

"The cardinal question to be considered by Catholics and Protestants in their controversy about justification is, What is its *formal cause?* When this is properly examined, it will be found that there is little or no difference of views between the disputants, except when the Protestant party adheres to the paradox of Luther: '*sola fides, non fides formata charitate justificat,*' and refuses to assign a formal cause." (p. 343.)

And once more:

"The modern controversy on the subject of justification is not a vital one, inasmuch as all parties are agreed that Christ is the sole justifier, and that he makes those holy whom He justifies." (p. 400.)

Is this, then, true? Is there no difference between saying, "I am justified by the presence and indwelling 'of Christ as the formal cause of my justification,' and saying, 'I am justified by Faith apprehending Christ's righteousness and surrendering the soul to God?' Is it all one to say with the Romanist 'I am accepted because I *am* righteous,' and to say with the Protestant, 'I am accepted because I am *accounted* righteous?' Put in this way, neither Romanist nor Protestant would admit that the difference was merely verbal. There is an actual difference between the two doctrines; and that difference appears in the results the two views produce in the lives of those who are respectively moulded by them. To teach men that their righteousness has any part in obtaining acceptance for them with God has resulted, as a rule, in leading them to trust in themselves for salvation. It has increased vain confidence in the careless, and caused perplexity and anguish in those who are careful and conscientious. These are mere truisms in the mouth of a Protestant. But they are not only the conclusions at which Protestants have arrived. Our author bears testimony to this himself:

"When you teach as follows, that Christ's Atoning Death, eighteen hundred years since, and our own personal Baptism in our infancy, so changed our state in God's sight once for all, that henceforth salvation depends on ourselves, on our doing our part in the Covenant, true as all this is to the letter, yet if nothing more is added, we shall seem, in spite of whatever we say concerning the Atonement and the influences of the Holy Ghost if duly sought, to be resting a man's salvation on himself, and to be making him the centre of the whole religious system. I would not say that this doctrine will so affect men of high religious attainments; but that viewed as the multitude will view it, it does not come up to the idea of the Gospel Creed as contained in Scripture, does not fix our thoughts on Christ in that full and direct way of which Scripture sets the pattern. This seems to be the real meaning of the popular saying that 'Christ ought to be preached.'" (pp. 185, 186.)

Singularly to the point, too, is the reluctant, and therefore more weighty, testimony of that Romanist among Romanists, Bellarmin, as quoted by our author:

"'Propter incertudinem propriae justitiae et periculum inanis gloriae, tutissimum est fiduciam totam, in sola Dei misericordia et benignitate reponere.' And then he explains this by saying that he means, not that we should not pursue good works with all our might, not that they are not a true ground of confidence, are not real righteousness, or are unable to sustain God's judgment, but that it is *safer* in a manner to *forget* what we have done, and to look solely at God's mercy, because no one can know, except by revelation, whether or not he has done any good works, or whether he shall persevere, and because the contemplation of his good works, even if he could know of them, is dangerous, as being elating." (p. 356.)

Here is the practical effect of the doctrine that we are justified by our inward righteousness and good works, even in part, put into a nut-shell. To count them in as part of our acceptability with God, tends both to unduly discourage and to falsely elate.

But there is a sense in which the Romish and Protestant doctrines do approach each other. It is on the theoretical, the theological side. We are justified, says Rome, by faith *and* by works. Nay, says the Protestant, but by faith alone. What, will faith that brings forth no righteousness make you to be accepted? Nay, answers the Protestant, it must be a faith that is living, and that infallibly produces good works. What, then, the question suggests itself, is this living principle in faith which makes it a true, justifying faith, and the absence of which makes it ineffective? What, in other words, differentiates a true from a false faith? Is it not this efficacy to produce in the soul a righteous state, a true fear and love of God; and is not this, then, an essential of justifying faith that it have, at least, the seed of holiness in itself? And what is this but to declare, by implication, if no more, that an actual holiness is part of that faith which it is maintained formally and instrumentally justifies?. Thus, the antagonist of the Protestant doctrine. And, under the pressure of this line of reasoning, the Reformers found themselves often hard put to, to make it appear that they really did differ from the Romish divines. Melanchthon went so far as to write, "Concedo in fiducia inesse dilectionem, et hanc virtutem et plerasque alias adesse opertere; sed cum dicimus, Fiducia sumus justi, non intelligatur nos propter virtutis istius dignitatem, sed per misericordiam recipi propter Mediatorem quem tamen opertet fide apprehendi. Ergo hoc dicimus *correlative*." And thereupon arises the question, what is the real difference between saying with him that faith is not justifying unless love or holiness be *with* it; or with Bellarmin, that it is not so, unless love be *in* it. Here are fine shades. For an exhaustive treatment of this point let the reader consult our author. But, surely, there is no escaping the conclusion that in the last analysis of the doctrines, both Romish and Protestant, they approach so near together that in substance they do all but coincide. The saving clause of the Reformed position is expressed in that qualification of Melanchthon's, "cum dicimus Fiducia sumus justi," etc. And yet neither Melanchthon nor any one else has made it clear, how it is that faith is constituted justifying by the presence of a living principle producing righteousness, and yet that which constitutes it a living faith, have no efficacy towards constituting the formal cause of justification. So fine become the lines of difference separating the opposite scientific theological statements. It is an approximation that must have struck every one, who has deeply pondered the question for himself, and Dr. Newman's treatment is only noticeable for the exquisite skill with which he traces the gradually approaching steps of the reasoning.

We turn now to the general drift of our author's own exposition of the doctrine. After pointing out that the controversy mainly turns upon the question "whether Christians are or are not justified by observance of the Moral Law," he proceeds to show that Justification means in Scripture both *counting* us righteous, and *making* us righteous. Nothing can better introduce this section of his argument than the following luminous statement in his own words:

"That in our natural state, and by our own strength, we are not and cannot be justified by obedience, is admitted on all hands, agreeably to St. Paul's forcible statements; and to deny it is the heresy of Pelagius. But it is a distinct question altogether, whether *with* the presence of God the Holy Ghost we can obey unto justification; and, while the received doctrine in all ages of the Church has been, that through the largeness and peculiarity of the gift of grace we can, it is the distinguishing tenet of the school of Luther, that through the incurable nature of our corruption we cannot. Or, what comes to the same thing, one side says that the righteousness in which God accepts us is inherent, wrought in us by the grace flowing from Christ's Atonement; the other says it is external, reputed, nominal, being Christ's own sacred and most perfect obedience on earth, viewed by a merciful God as if it were ours."

From this general statement of the question, he goes on to make it appear that to justify, in its primary sense, means to *declare* righteous. This he does so thoroughly and luminously that one wonders as he reads how it can be shown to mean anything else. The argument is convincing and in the conclusion rises to a pitch of power that deserves to be quoted at length. We do so for its lofty eloquence and profound spirit of devotion.

"It [justification] is an act as signal, as great, as complete, as was the condemnation into which sin plunged us. Whether or not it involves renewal, it is evidently something of a more formal and august nature than renewal. Justification is a word of state and solemnity. Divine mercy might have renewed us and kept it secret; this would have been an infinite and most unmerited grace, but he has done more. He *justifies* us; he not only makes, he declares, acknowledges, accepts us as holy. He recognizes us as his own, and publicly repeals the sentence of wrath and the penal statutes which lie against us. He sanctifies us gradually; but justification is a perfect act, anticipating at once in the sight of God what sanctification does but tend towards. In it, the whole course of sanctification is summed, reckoned, or imputed to us in its very beginning. Before man has done anything as specimen, or paid anything as installment, except faith, nor even faith in the case of infants, he has the whole treasure of redemption put to his credit, as if he were and had done infinitely more than he ever can be or do. He is 'declared' after the pattern of his Saviour, to be the adopted 'Son of God with power by a' spiritual 'resurrection.' His tears are wiped away; his fears, misgivings, remorse, shame, are changed for 'righteousness, and peace, and joy in the Holy Ghost;' he is clad in white and has a crown given him. Thus justification is at first what renewal could but be at last; and therefore, is by no means a mere result or consequence of renewal, but a real, though not a separate act of God's mercy. It is a great and august deed in the sight of heaven and hell; it is not done in a corner, but by him who would show the world 'what should be done unto those whom the King delighteth to honor.' It is a pronouncing righteous while it proceeds to make righteous. * * The declaration of our righteousness, while it contains pardon for the past, promises holiness for the future." (p. 74.)

Here, too, through the body of truth so grandly enounced, run veins of error so delicately modulated into falseness as to be almost indistinguishable from the texture in which they lie. Thus our author:

"The whole cause of sanctification is summed, reckoned, or imputed to us in its very beginning."

But it is not our sanctification yet to come that is

imputed to us in justification, but Christ's perfect righteousness. Again:

"Before man has done anything as specimen, or paid anything as installment, except faith, * * he has the whole treasures of redemption put to his credit."

Most true the "treasures of redemption" are "put to his credit," but not because faith is reckoned as an installment of his debt of duty to God. And so throughout truth and error mingle.

But we read on, and presently we discover the turning point where our author and Protestant reader part company.

"Our justification is not a mere declaration of a past fact, or a testimony to what is present, or an announcement of what is to come, * * but it is the *cause* of that being which before was *not*, and henceforth *is*." (p. 78.)

And what is this which "before was *not*, and henceforth *is?*" Our author does not leave us in doubt on this point.

"Justification is an announcement or fiat of Almighty God, which breaks upon the gloom of our natural state as the Creative Word upon Chaos; it *declares* the soul righteous, and in that declaration, on the one hand, conveys *pardon* for its past sins, and on the other *makes* it actually *righteous*. * * That it involves an actual creation in righteousness has been argued from the analogy of Almighty God's doings in Scripture, in which we find His words were represented as effective." (pp. 83, 84.)

And, finally, in the most explicit manner.

"Justification renews, therefore I say it may fitly be called renewal." (p. 86.)

Here, then, we arrive at last, at the author's objective point: "Justification is renewal." And as we look back to that from which we set out, viz., "that Justification is the 'glorious voice of the Lord' declaring us to be righteous;" and that "it must mean an imputation or declaration;" and that "if it be once granted to mean an imputation, it cannot mean anything else; since it cannot have two meanings at once" (p. 67);—we say, when we look back to this point of departure, we cannot but admire the skill by which we have been led step by step without perceptible jar or false turn, through the labyrinth of the author's wonderful dialectic to his conclusion that Justification *is* something else than "declaring us to be righteous," viz.: that it is renewal. We set out from the postulate, "justification must mean an imputation," and "cannot mean anything else;" and we land in the conclusion that justification does, notwithstanding, mean something quite else, viz.: "an actual creation in righteousness." (p. 84). This is nothing short of logical legerdemain.

The nexus by which the two meanings are made to slide into each other, it will be seen, is simply this, that what God declares must actually be. If he declares us righteous, righteous we must be; and that not in any imputed sense in which a quality is reckoned to be where it actually is not; but righteous by the possession of an indwelling holiness. "God's word, I say, effects what it announces." (p. 81.)

Now this is very skilful; but their lies against it just one objection, viz.: the fact that we are not holy in the sense in which in justification we are accounted such; that confessedly, no man is thus holy. This objection our author sees and endeavors to meet in this wise.

"How," he asks, "can we, children of Adam, be said *really and truly* to be righteous, in a sense distinct from the *imputation* of righteousness? I observe, then, we become inwardly just or righteous in God's sight, upon our regeneration, in the same sense in which we are utterly reprobate and abominable by nature. * * Justification, coming to us in the power and 'inspiration of the Spirit,' so far dries up the fountain of bitterness and impurity, that we are forthwith released from God's wrath and damnation, and are enabled in our better deeds to please him. It places us above the line in the same sense in which we were before below it." (pp. 89, 90, 91).

Now, in all this there is a measure of truth. It is true that the works of righteousness which are wrought by the justified are acceptable to God. The Spirit does make our works pleasing and acceptable to God. But we are not therefore justified; neither is our righteousness indwelling such as could be accepted as a perfect righteousness. It *is* accepted, but only as a first-fruits and pledge of what shall be as the earnest of the Spirit in us; not as meeting the command of Christ, "this do and ye shall live." This our author himself confesses when he says, "not that there is not abundant evil still remaining in us," (p. 90), after justification. We are very far from being what God declares we must be, "holy even as he is holy." So that if our indwelling righteousness in and after justification is to be accounted as a perfect righteousness, and James declares none else can be accepted as meeting the demands of the holy law, then it must be by a fiction in which an imperfect obedience is, under the circumstances, counted as a perfect obedience. What difference then, in the terms of our author's argument, whether our simple trust or our imperfect obedience, as it confessedly is imperfect, be accounted to us for righteousness. In either case the argument that what God declares righteous must be actually and in itself righteous falls to the ground. And so vanishes the beautiful fabric of dialectic by which it is to be shown that to justify means only to *declare* righteous and then that it also must mean to *make* righteous.

But whilst dissenting from his conclusion one cannot but admire the masterly skill with which the argument is handled. One almost loses the sense of displeasure at the error in the charm of the consummate dialectic and rhetoric with which it is maintained. Were ever the abstractions of theology made so brilliant? There are passages in this connection that have all the effect of wit, while they are loaded with all the weight of abstract definition and distinction. Thus, for instance, in discussing the question, whether by justification we are made righteous or only accounted so, he pours forth the following strain:

"In vain does St. Paul declare again and again, that we *are* righteous; the Protestant Masters have ruled that we are not really so. They have argued that, *if* we were really made righteous, Christ would cease to be our righteousness, and *therefore* we certainly are not really made righteous; which is much the same as arguing, that Christ must cease to be our 'sanctification,' because we are made holy, or that we are not made holy because he is our 'sanctification;' in a word, that he in his infinite fulness cannot give without a loss, and we in our utter nothingness cannot be in the continual receipt of benefits without thereby ceasing to be dependent.

"Again: When our Lord says to the Scribe who had rehearsed to him the commandments, 'This do and thou shalt live,' it is replied that he spoke in a sort of irony.

"Again: When he says, that unless our righteousness exceed that of the Scribes and Pharisees, we shall in no case enter into the kingdom of heaven; and pronounces them blessed 'who hunger and thirst after righteousness,' and 'who are persecuted for righteousness' sake,' and bids us 'seek the kingdom of God and his righteousness;' it is sometimes openly, often by implication, answered, that all this was spoken by our Lord before St. Paul wrote.

"Again: When St. Paul, who is thus appealed to, says expressly, that 'the righteousness of the Law *is* fulfilled in us,' then Luther is summoned to lay it down as a first principle, that the doctrine of our justification without any inherent righteousness is the criterion of a standing or falling church.

"Again: When St. Paul says, 'I can do all things through Christ which strengtheneth me,' this is supposed to mean all things except fulfilling the Law; and when he says, in another place, that 'love *is* the fulfilling of the Law,' and that love is not only attainable, but a duty, we are arbitrarily answered by a distinction, that such love that suffices for the fulfilling of the Law is one thing, and such love as is enjoined as a Christian grace is another.

"Again: When we urge what Hezekiah says, 'Remember now, O Lord, I beseech Thee, how I have walked before Thee in truth and with a perfect heart, and have done that which is *good in Thy sight;*' or Nehemiah, "Remember me, O my God, concerning this, *and wipe not out my good deeds* that I have done for the house of my God, and for the offices thereof,' all the answer we obtain is, that, whatever comes of Hezekiah and Nehemiah, it is evidently self-righteous and a denial of the merits of Christ, and shocking to the feelings of the serious mind, to say that we *can* do anything really good in God's sight, even with the grace of Christ, anything in consideration of which God will look mercifully upon us.

"Again: St. Paul speaks of things 'just,' of 'virtue' and of 'praise,' of 'providing things honest *in the sight of the Lord*,' of being 'acceptable to *God;*' but in vain does he thus vary his expressions, as if by way of commenting on the word 'righteous,' and imprinting upon our minds this one idea of inherent acceptableness:—no, this has become a forbidden notion; it must not even enter the thoughts, though an Evangelist plead and a Prophet threaten ever so earnestly.

"Again: 'Work must have two senses; for though we are bid to work out our salvation, God working in us, this can not *really* mean 'Work out your salvation through God's working in you;' *else* justification would be, not of grace, nor of faith, but of works of the Law.

"And 'reward,' too, it seems, has two senses; for the reward which Scripture bids us labor for, cannot, it is said, be a reward in the real and ordinary sense of the word; it is not really a reward, but is merely *called* such, by way of animating our exertion and consoling us in despondency.

"Again: The 'righteousness,' which justifies, though spoken of as a quality of our souls in Scripture, cannot mean anything *in us*, because the Jews sought a justifying righteousness, *not* 'through Christ *but* by the' *external* 'works of the Law;' and therefore if we seek justifying righteousness solely from Christ, and not at all from works done in our own strength, in inward renovation, not external profession, we shall stumble and fall as did the Jews.

"Again: It is argued that justifying righteousness cannot be of the Law, because if a man 'offend in one point, he is guilty of all,' that is, since St. James says, that, when love is *away*, we offend the Law in many points, therefore when love is *present*, we cannot fulfill it consistently, however imperfectly, like Zacharias.

"Lastly: 'Righteousness' is said to have two senses, because St. Paul declares, that *as* 'Christ was made sin for us who had known no sin,' *so* 'we are made the righteousness of God in Him:' for, it is argued, since when we *were* unrighteous, Christ was imputed to us for righteousness; therefore, now that Christ *has been* imputed to us for righteousness, we *shall* ever *be* unrighteous still.

"Such is the nature of the arguments on which it is maintained that two perfectly separate senses must be given to the word 'righteousness;' that justification is one gift, sanctification another; that deliverance from guilt is one work of God, deliverance from sin another; that reward does not really mean reward, praise not really praise, availableness not really availableness, worth not really worth, acceptableness not really acceptableness; that none but St. Paul may allowably speak of 'working out our salvation;' none but St. Peter, of 'Baptism saving us;' none but St. John, of 'doers of righteousness being righteous;' that when St. Paul speaks of '*all* faith,' he means all *but* true faith; and when St. James says, *not* by faith *only*, he means nothing *but* true faith; that it is not rash to argue that justification cannot be by works, because it is by faith, though it *is* rash to conclude that Christ is not God, because he is man; and that, though it is a sin, as it surely is, to infer that Christ is not God, because Scripture calls the Father the *only* God, yet it is no sin to argue that works cannot justify, because Luther, not Scripture, says that faith only justifies." (pp. 110, 117.)

Surely, never was dialectic so sparkling, at once so weighty and so witty. To be handled by such an antagonist affords the exquisite satisfaction, one may suppose, to have been the culprit's who was so deftly decapitated, according to the Eastern story, as to be unaware when it was his head was severed from the body.

But we must not lose sight of the measure of truth solemnly enforced by Dr. Newman in urging these views: the truth that when God justifies, he *does* impart a new life to the justified man. This is one side of the truth which Protestantism, in its enforced unhappy attitude of antagonism to the ancient error, has neglected. Neglected, I say, for it has never denied it. But it has been our misfortune to be so busy repelling the notion that we are justified by the righteousness that is wrought in us, as to lose sight of the co-ordinate truth that a righteousness is wrought in us who are justified; and that not as an after-work, as something added on, but inseparable, in its initial steps, from the justifying act of God.

On this our author speaks wisely:

"The great benefit of justification, as all will allow, is this one thing,—the transference of the soul *from* the kingdom of darkness *into* the kingdom of Christ. We may, if we will, divide this event into parts, and say that it is *both* pardon *and* renovation; but such a division is merely mental, and does not affect the change itself, which is but one act. If a man is saved from drowning, you may, if you will, say he is *both* rescued from the water *and* brought into atmospheric air; this is a discrimination in words not in things. He cannot be brought out of the water which he cannot breathe, *except* by entering the air which he can breathe. In like manner, there is, in fact, no middle state between a state of *wrath* and a state of holiness. In justifying, God takes away what is past, *by* bringing in what is new. He snatches out of the fire by lifting us in his everlasting hands, and enwrapping us in his own glory." (p. 102.)

Much arises in mind that might be said on this point. It is a fruitful topic, and one that needs to be opened and enforced on the religous shallowness of the day. But we must hasten on.

Our author goes on to show that the Righteousness, which he holds is our justification, is a "gift," and, therefore, of necessity a substantial something within the soul; and, further, that this quality superadded, and in which our justification consists, is that supernatural endowment which Adam lost in the Fall.

"Whatever else, then, Adam had by creation, this seems to have been one main supernatural gift, or rather that in which all others were included, the presence of God the Holy Ghost in him, exalting him into the family and service of his Almighty Creator. This was his clothing; this he lost by disobedience; this Christ has regained for us. This then is the robe of righteousness spoken of by Isaiah, to be bestowed in its fullness hereafter, bestowed partially at once." (p. 160.)

Upon this point he says many very, as they seem to us, erroneous things; but also some that are full of the power of solemn truth. For instance beginning with a declaration so doubtful and dangerous as this, "Justification is the setting up of the Cross within us,"—he goes on in a strain of mingled sweetness and solemnity, of meditation and exposition, thus:

"Justification actually does involve a spiritual circumcision, a crucifixion of the flesh, or sanctification. The entrance of Christ's sacred presence into the soul, which becomes our righteousness in God's sight, at the same time becomes righteousness in it. * * It is very necessary to insist upon this, for a reason which has come before us in other shapes already. It is the fashion of the day to sever these two from one another, which God has joined, the seal and the impression, justification and renewal. You hear men speak of glorying in the Cross of Christ, who are utter strangers to the notion of the Cross as actually applied to them in water and blood, in holiness and mortification. They think the Cross can be theirs *without* being applied,—without its coming near them —while they keep at a distance from it, and only gaze at it. They think individuals are justified immediately by the great Atonement—justified by Christ's death, and not, as St. Paul says, by means of his Resurrection—justified by what they consider *looking* at his death. Because the Brazen Serpent in the wilderness healed by being looked at, they consider that Christ's Sacrifice saves by the mind contemplating it. This is what they call casting themselves upon Christ—coming before him simply and without self-trust, and being saved by faith. Surely we ought so to *come* to Christ; surely we must believe; surely we must look; but the question is, in what form and manner he *gives* himself to us; and it will be found that, when he enters into us, glorious as he is himself, pain and self-denial are his attendants. Gazing on the Brazen Serpent did not heal; but God's invisible communication of the gift of health to those who gazed. \* \* Christ's Cross does not justify by being looked at, but by being applied; not by as merely beheld by faith, but by being actually set up within us, and that not by our act, but by God's invisible grace. Men sit, and gaze, and speak of the great Atonement, and think this is appropriating it; not more truly than kneeling to the material cross itself is appropriating it. Men say that faith is an apprehending and applying; faith cannot really apply the Atonement; man cannot make the Saviour of the world his own; the Cross must be brought home to us, not in word, but in power, and this is the work of the Spirit. This is justification; but when imparted to the soul, it draws blood, it heals, it purifies, it glorifies." (p. 175).

So intertwined are the strands of truth and error in this eloquent passage that one hardly sees his way clear to disentangle them. How much of solemn, edifying truth is here brought home to our hearts; but with it so much, too, of error, that the first impulse is to cast it all away. But the truth is too true, too needful, to be lightly thrown aside. We seem to hear in the consecutive sentences first a chord, and then a discord. But we must bear the discord for the sake of the chord. Thus:

"Justification actually does involve a spiritual circumcision, a crucifixion of the flesh, or sanctification."

Is not this truth? But then in the next sentence jars the discord:

"The entrance of Christ's sacred presence into the soul, which becomes our righteousness in God's sight," etc.

This surely is error, though beautiful error; error in the disguise of an angel of light.

Again:

"You hear men speak of glorying in the Cross of Christ, who are utter strangers to the notion of the Cross as actually applied to them in water and blood, in holiness and mortification."

True, again; how sadly true, as is witnessed in all our churches. But in the next sentence recurs the dissonance:

"They think individuals are justified immediately by the great atonement," etc.

And so the strain alternates from a solemn utterance of the greatest of truths to the modulation of the subtlest of errors. But we may not throw away the gold because in it there is dross. "Justification is" *not* "setting up the cross within us;" but if we are justified that Cross surely must be set up in us. "The entrance of Christ's sacred presence into the soul does" *not* "become our righteousness in God's sight;" but if we would become righteous, truly that presence, with all its attendant travail and pangs, must enter.

It is truth such as this that needs to be preached to the easy-going church of these days, days when the religion of Christ has become a self-indulgent thing, the making the best as one eminent divine terms it, of both worlds. It is the neglect of this side of truth that has driven away from the evangelical churches such men as the pure and self-denying Robertson with his bitter complaint that "the Protestant penitent repents in an arm-chair, is very glad that a broken-hearted remorse is distrust of God, and is satisfied to be all *safe*, which is the great point in his religion." Surely we need to listen to teaching that points a self-indulgent religious age back to the way of the Cross once more, and reminds us that the great apostle of Justification by Faith declared solemnly of himself, "I am crucified with Christ." One passage in this connection from our author is worthy, for its solemn warning to weigh against all his mistaken doctrine: "The saving Cross crucifies us in saving."

Other passages have been marked in the work under consideration for quotation and comment, but space will not allow us to take them up.

This discussion is concluded by a general view of the Protestant position and its practical results as a system. At some length, our author retorts upon his opponents the charge of Judaism, which is so often levelled against the Romanizing schools. And here, as so often in this admirable but dangerous writer,—all the more dangerous because, both by reason of his intellectual strength and deep, pure piety, he is so admirable,—here, as throughout his writings, truth and error mingle almost inextricably. We give at length the passage that concludes his work, premising only that, as it seems to us, there is no less of error here than usually mingles with his teachings. Surely much that he says has struck many of us, though we have not been able to express it so forcibly. Does he not seem to be describing many of our modern teachers and preachers? Are there not whole classes of religious writers much in vogue, whose error he depicts to the life? For all that calls itself Protestant and Evangelical, is not therefore scriptural and wholesome.

"I would say this, then:—that a system of doctrines has risen up in which faith or spiritual-mindedness is contemplated and rested on as the end of religion instead of Christ. I do not mean to say that Christ is not mentioned as the Author of all good, but that stress is laid rather on the believing than on the Object of belief, on the comfort and persuasiveness of the doctrine rather than on the doctrine itself. And in this way religion is made to consist in contemplating ourselves instead of Christ; not simply in looking to Christ, but in ascertaining that we look to Christ, not in his Divinity and Atonement, but in our conversion and our faith in those truths.

"The fault here spoken of is the giving to our 'experiences' a more prominent place in our thoughts than to the nature, attributes, and work of him from whom they profess to come,—the insisting on them as a special point for the consideration of all who desire to be recognized as converted and elect. When men are to be exhorted to newness of life, the true object to be put before them, as I conceive, is 'Jesus Christ, the same yesterday, to-day, and forever;' the true gospel preaching is to enlarge, as they can bear it, on the person, nature, attributes, offices, and work of him; to dwell upon his recorded words and deeds on earth. * * The true preaching of the Gospel is to preach Christ. But the fashion of the day has been, instead of this, to preach conversion; to attempt to convert by insisting on conversion; to exhort men to undergo a change; to tell them to be sure they look at Christ, instead of simply holding up Christ to them; to tell them to have faith, rather than to supply its Object; to lead them to stir up and work up their minds, instead of impressing on them the thought of him who can savingly work in them; to bid them take care their faith is justifying, not dead, formal, self-righteousness, and merely moral, whereas the image of Christ fully delineated of itself destroys deadness, formality, and self-righteousness; to rely on words, vehemence, eloquence, and the like, rather than to aim at conveying the one great evangelical idea whether in words or not. And thus faith and spiritual-mindedness are dwelt on as *ends*, and obstruct the view of Christ, just as the Law was perverted by the Jews."

He then proceeds to comment at length on passages from Newton's Letters and Haweis' Sermons in illustration of what has been quoted above. This from its length we must pass over, though it is full of point. We have space only for the latter part of the extract from Haweis, with the running comment.

"For if you have never seen" (not your Saviour, but) "*your 'desperately wicked heart,'*—been united to Christ" (by his love and grace? no, but) "*by faith,— renounced* your own righteousness to be found in him, and *receive* from him newness" (receive, as if the great thing was not his giving but our taking), "if you *know not experimentally what is meant* by 'fellowship with the Father and his Son Jesus Christ;'" (observe, not "if you *have* not fellowship," but "if you *know* not you have;" and this self-seeking, as it may truly be called, is named *experimental* religion;) "if your *devotion* hath not been inspired 'by faith which worketh by love;' if your *worship* hath not been in 'spirit and truth,' from a real *sense* of your wants, and an earnest *desire* and *expectation* of receiving from him 'in whom all fulness dwells;' if this hath not been your case, your devotions have been unmeaning ceremonies." "Poor miserable captives," proceeds the comment, "to whom such doctrine is preached as the Gospel! What! is *this* the liberty wherewith Christ has made us free, and wherein we stand, the home of our own thoughts, the prison of our own sensations, the province of self, a monotonous confession of what we are by nature, not what Christ is in us, and a resting at best not on his love towards us, but in our faith towards him? This is nothing but a specious idolatry; a man thus minded does not simply think of God when he prays to him, but is observing whether he feels properly or not; does not believe and obey, but considers it enough to be conscious that he is what he calls warm and spiritual" (pp. 324, 326, 329).

It would be interesting to introduce here a remarkable contrast drawn by our author, in an extended note, of the respective modes of treating a death-bed, in the "Visitation of the Sick," and the "Dairyman's Daughter;" but our limited space forbids. We hasten to conclude these too extended quotations:

"If the doctrine of justifying faith must be taken as a practical direction, and in a certain sense it may, then we must word it, not 'justification through faith,' but, 'justification by Christ.' Thus interpreted, the rule it gives is, '*go* to Christ;' but taken in the letter, it seems to say merely, 'Get faith; become spiritual; see that you are not mere moralists, mere formalists; see that you feel. If you do not feel, Christ will profit you nothing; you must have a spiritual taste; you must see yourself to be a sinner; you must accept, apprehend, appropriate the gift; you must be conscious of a change wrought in you, for the most part going through the successive stages of darkness, trouble, error, light, and comfort. Thus the poor and sorrowful soul, instead of being led at once to the source of all good, is taught to make much of the conflict of truth and falsehood within itself as the pledge of God's love, and to picture to itself faith as a sort of passive quality which sits amid the ruins of human nature, and keeps up what may be called a silent protest or indulges a pensive meditation over its misery. True faith is what may be called colorless, like air or water; it is but the medium through which the soul sees Christ; and the soul as little really rests upon it and contemplates it, as an eye can see the air. When, then, men are bent on holding (as it were) in their hands, curiously inspecting, analyzing, and so aiming at it, they are obliged to color and thicken it, that it may be seen and touched. That is, they substitute for it something or other, a feeling, notion, sentiment, conviction, or act of reason, which they may hang over, and doat upon. They rather aim at experiences (as they are called) within them, than at him that is without them. They are led to enlarge upon the signs of conversion, the variations of their feelings, their aspirations and longings, and to tell all this to others;—to tell others how they fear, and hope, and sin, and rejoice, and renounce themselves, and rest in Christ only; how conscious they are that their best deeds are but 'filthy rags,' and all is of grace, till, in fact, they have little time left them to guard against what they are condemning, and to exercise what they think they are full of."

How exactly does all this describe some of the worst errors in practice into which our modern Evangelical Churches have fallen! Are not these the phases of religious sickliness and shallowness and poverty which one sees in religion as popularly understood and inculcated in too many of our churches? But to conclude.

"Such is the difference between those whom Christ praises and those whom He condemns or warns. The Pharisee recounted the signs of God's mercy upon him and in him; the Publican simply looked to God. The young ruler boasted of his correct life, but the penitent woman anointed Jesus' feet and kissed them. Nay, holy Martha herself spoke of her 'much service;' while Mary waited on him for the 'one thing needful.' The one thought of themselves; the others thought of Christ. To look to Christ is to be justified by faith; to think of being justified by faith is to look from Christ and to fall from grace."

Our task is done. Too much space, indeed, has been taken up with quotations, but we wished our author to speak for himself. His errors and his splendid vindication of neglected truth, are alike obvious. His errors are those which all will unite to condemn; would we could say that the truth it has been given him to bring to view will be welcomed with a ·consent as unanimous.

(Reprinted by permission from The Quarterly Review of The Evangelical Lutheran Church, for January, 1876).

## THE CHINESE PROBLEM, OR AGNOSTICISM WORKED OUT.

The practical form assumed by the religious skepticism of the day, is Agnosticism. Is there a God? has he given us a law? Shall we live after death? if we do, shall we be rewarded and punished according to our life here? To all these questions the skepticism of the times simply answers, "*ignoramus*." It does not deny that there is a God, a future life: it only says, "We do not know." As one distinguished Agnostic puts it: "Questions of theology are questions of lunar politics;" there may be a reality answering to the speculation of theology, and there may be political activity in the moon; but we do and can know nothing about either. They are beyond the scope of human faculties.

Now this is a position at once more difficult to attack, and yet more hopeful, than the old ground of dogmatic Atheism. It was not hard to show the impossibility of proving a negative as to the Divine Existence. Let men analyze the universe as they would, and show the apparent sufficiency of matter and force to account for all phenomena; let them multiply objections to the proofs of a Personal Cause and a future state; and yet there was that great realm of unexplored possibility lying behind every philosophy. Behind force and matter there might be a Personal Intelligence, the spring of everything. After all the objections to his existence, it might be that he did exist.

## THE CHINESE PROBLEM. 71

The trouble was that between them and their conclusion, lay the deep wide gulf of human ignorance. What might not be hidden there? But now skepticism has removed that unknown region to its own side. Against every argument for the truth of Theism it entrenches itself in the dark: "we do not know;" "the data are insufficient;" "it may be so, but it is not proven." And that position can never be carried by direct argument. It will probably always remain to mere philosophy an open question.

But practically it is a more hopeful position because of what it implies. And what does it imply? It seems to me it involves this, the recognition of the vastness and mystery of the Universe. The dogmatic Atheist must always be a man singularly insensible to certain facts of life. He perceives the facts that appeal to the senses, to the hard logical understanding, but he sees nothing more. The scheme of the Universe to his mind is all clear and compact: he sees to the very bounds of it and understands it. He traces the whole structure of things, animate and inanimate, from the original atoms; and when he ends, everything is accounted for, nothing is left out. He is impatient with every one who does not see how satisfactory his explanation is. But such a state of mind can exist only with a total insensibility to whole classes of feelings and experiences that are themselves real facts to be accounted for. That, at least, is not the position of the Agnostic. He recognizes the ultimate mystery, the contradictions, the unexplained stream of tendency in human nature. He does not admit the Theistic solution of the problem; but he admits the problem. Life, he says, is a riddle; only there is no answer to it. But to see the problem, to feel the mystery and weight of it, is hopeful. It shows that the soul is alive and sensible. The Theistic solution may not be accepted, but a solution is felt to be needed. And there is always hope where there is dissatisfaction. I think we may recognize in the new form which skepticism has taken an indication of returning sensibility to the spiritual facts of life.

But while the skepticism of the day acknowledges the mystery of the Universe to be intellectually insoluble, it proposes practically to solve it. The Universe can never be explained, says the Agnostic; well then, he goes on, we will ignore the part that is mysterious, and pay attention only to what we do know and can understand. And so he draws a line around the facts that are plain and intelligible, and all that lies outside of that narrow circle he gives over to neglect.

The practical solution of the problem of life, then, is *secularism*. It says, "You cannot live for both worlds, because you do not know both. You know but one. Live for the one you do know." That is very plain; though like all rules of conduct, it is a good deal easier to understand it than it is to carry it out. It may be doubted whether, as long as the intellectual problem remains, the human mind will consent entirely to go on and ignore it. There is the mystery, and a mystery in the mind is like a foreign substance in the body; you cannot isolate it and enclose it in a neutral sack, and have the functions of life go on as if it were not. You may say, I will not think about it; but not thinking about it does not destroy it: it will exert its influence. The mind will be drawn to it; and after a season of practical activity it will go back to the mystery and try at its solution. Either that must happen, or the mystery must be destroyed, or lost sight of.

But leaving that; let us suppose the mind of the race to be disengaged from the question and interests that have absorbed so much of its energy since the dawn of history. Let us grant that Agnosticism is practically made the rule of life, and that secularism becomes the religion of the race: men no longer ask of God and his character, of his will and purpose, nor of the future life; but the whole energy of mind is bent to the business of living here; the horizon is narrowed to the life of the individual or, at the widest, to the prospects of the human family for the period of the earth's continuance. What then? What may we look for as the result of that transfer and concentration of human energy?

The Agnostics have their answer. They predict that the result of such a concentration of the powers of the race on the question of making the most of this life would be to ameliorate in a wonderful degree the evils of human existence. All hope of a future state once given up, and the whole man bent on making the most of this world, there would be, they tell us, such a fund of ingenuity available for mastering the difficulties which beset human life that we might expect, if not an extinction of the miseries of earthly existence, yet such an amelioration of them as would make life a state of extraordinary felicity. So impossible is it to extirpate that hope of the perfect state which has generally been accredited to religion as one of its barren and injurious dreams. If there is to be no heaven beyond, then men will dream of a heaven here; and so the Agnostic predicts a worldly Millennium. Taking heart by the great conquests of science and civilization over many of the manifest evils of life, he sees in the future a day when a larger knowledge and a riper civilization will relieve the race from the miseries of disease and poverty, bad government and wars, famines and accidents, and the whole train of human ills. He does not even despair of a day when, by attending carefully to the laws of good conduct and by improved education, the race will get rid of vice and crime. He believes in a kingdom of God to come, without any God of course, wherein shall dwell education and a superior knowledge, and from which all evil shall cease. It is a beautiful dream; but the Agnostic hopes that some day it shall be made real.

Take only the pictures of this condition painted by two very diverse Agnostics, leaders in their respective camps, Prof. Huxley, the prophet of salvation by science, and Mr. Matthew Arnold, the preacher of salvation by culture. Prof. Huxley describes the perfect man whom secularism, when it is finished, will bring forth,—" Who has been so trained in youth that his body is the ready servant of his will, and does with ease and pleasure all the work that, as a mechanism, it is capable of; whose intellect is a clear, cold, logic engine with all its parts of equal strength, and in smooth working order; ready, like a steam-engine, to be turned to any kind of work, and spin the gossamers as well as forge the anchors of the mind; whose mind is stored with a knowledge of the great and fundamental truths of Nature and of the laws of her operations; one who, no stunted ascetic, is full of life and fire, but whose passions are trained to come to heel by a vigorous will, the servant of a tender conscience; who has learned to love all beauty, whether of nature or of art, to hate all vileness, and to respect all others as himself." A very admirable figure; "without God in the world," it is true; but not, according to Prof. Huxley, without hope. But the "trained body," and "trained passions," and "cold logic engine,"—is it not just all a little too suggestive of an automaton? Is there not the least creak in the world about the joints? Automata, however, I believe, is what Prof. Huxley says we all are at bottom. But such automaton figures secularism is to turn out, as a button-machine turns out buttons, each the fac-simile of its fellow, and all perfect after their kind.

Mr. Arnold has a vision of a future even loftier. He has got rid, it is true, of God by ignoring Him, and of a future state by turning his back on it; but he still believes in a kingdom of God;—a very earthly sort of kingdom, however, if we may be allowed to say so.

"The expression, the kingdom of God," he says, "does point to a transformation of this present world through the victory of what Butler calls virtue, and what the Bible calls righteousness, and what in general religious people call goodness; it does suggest such transformation as possible." This possibility, which he expounds to be the immortality Christ has brought to light in the Gospel, is to be realized by "coming to live, even here in this present world, with the higher impersonal life." And this "impersonal life," we are assured, men will reach some day by the agency of culture. This substitute for the grand vision of eternal life in the heavenly state, is a poor flat thing; but, such as it is, it is a kind of millennium, the millennium of culture and commonplace. Another dream!

But there is a nearer way to get at the probable effects of Agnosticism on the race than these conjectures. If we can find a people on whom the experiment of dropping out the belief in the supernatural has been tried, we shall discover in their history what we seek. And with such a people the events of our time are bringing us into close contact.

We have been brought face to face in a very practical way of late with the civilization of China; and the longer we study it the more baffling does it seem. Practically we do not know what to do with the Chinaman; and intellectually we find the explanation of the civilization he represents the hardest of problems. Here are a people who, before the civilization of the western world was born, had possessed themselves of some of the greatest of modern inventions, gunpowder, printing and the mariner's compass; and who, when Rome was yet a rude and petty republic, had organized an elaborate and powerful government. But in the midst of this advance there suddenly came a pause. For 2,500 years the fabric of Chinese society and polity has stood motionless. Since that pause the whole face of Europe has been transformed twice over: one civilization has come and gone, and a second has reached what seems its maturity; but in China not a shadow of change has intervened. Generations have come and gone, but the nation continues motionless: it is the cloud on the side of the mountain, in which the particles are ceaselessly appearing and disappearing while the whole remains unaltered.

And this is not the pause that comes between advance and decline; if it were, it would be the pause of a life too vast to be measured by any chronology known to history. But China is as vigorous to-day as she was 2,000 years ago. Her population display a vitality and tenacity equal to that of the youngest and strongest nations. They seem to have mastered the problem of how to get the most out of life with the smallest expenditure of material. It is this that makes them so odious to the people of California. As one has described them: " They can live and work hard in all climates; they take and lose life with absolute indifference; their armies in Central Asia advance with such deadly perseverance that they plant and reap corn after one campaign in order to prepare for the next, and they kill the males of conquered districts with the same calm with which they throw a bridge over a stream." Of all nations on the face of the earth, it must be conceded that they have best learned how to make the most of this world. They have reduced life, meaning by that comfortable and healthy existence here, to a science. And yet they make no progress. It is this combination of energetic, persistent vitality with an utter immobility, that makes them the puzzle of history. With us vitality has always been associated with progress. It has seemed impossible that a man or a race should be strong and not advance. But here is a nation that for nearly 3,000 years has neither advanced nor receded, and is yet one of the most persistent races on the face of the earth.

There is only one feature in their history that throws any light on the problem. It is their religion. Five centuries before Christ, Confucius fixed his hold on the nation, and penetrated the popular mind with his theories of religion and of life. It has been disputed whether he was the creator of the present mental condition of the Chinese people, or only the skillful interpreter of tendencies and dispositions that were moving disconnectedly in the general mind. Be that as it may, China since his day has maintained the attitude towards the problem of life which he took. Other religions have come and gone among them; but they have touched only the surface. Confucianism has possessed the Chinese mind, colored all its habits, and given its peculiar tone.

And what is Confucianism? In brief, it is Agnosticism: it is the only practical form Agnosticism has ever taken. In fact, we should not be far out of the way if we were to describe Chinese civilization as Agnosticism worked out.

A brief description of its principal features will suffice. Confucius, who was born B. C. 551, came on the stage at a great crisis in the history of his people. "The World," says Mencius, his follower, "had fallen into decay, and right principles had disappeared. Perverse discourses and oppressive deeds were waxen rife. Ministers murdered their rulers, and sons their fathers. Confucius was frightened by what he saw—and he undertook the work of reformation." It was the decay of a feudal civilization, a condition of things much like that of Western Europe in the 14th century. But China had this advantage: literary culture and many arts of civilization had arrived at a high pitch of eminence. But, in spite of great knowledge and much skill in arts, the period was one of thorough degeneracy. Into this chaos Confucius came as a reformer. He attempted to effect his work of regeneration at first through political means; he sought the rulers, hoping to influence them. But in this he was foiled. He traveled from city to city, trying first one great potentate and then another, but none would adopt his schemes of reform. "If any ruler," he once said, "would submit to me as his director for twelve months, I should accomplish something considerable; and in three years I should attain the realization of my hopes."

In his 69th year he gave up the attempt to carry out his ideas by any political means, and retired into seclusion, to devote his few remaining years to literary work, and the instruction of a few devoted disciples. In five years he died, his life an apparent failure. But the day of his burial was the beginning of his influence over the nation. He became at once an object of admiration; his works were studied with avidity; his ideas took hold both of the cultivated and popular mind; and from that grasp the Chinese people have never been released. Under his tuition ages ago they became a nation of Secularists, and Secularism is the system under which they have lived to this day.

He proposed that men should learn the laws of their well-being and follow them; but that well-being he restricted wholly to the present life. He considered man only in society, and that society as existing only here. And his reforms were only of a political and superficially ethical character. The highest ideal was the State; the perfection of the State was the absolute perfection, the *summum bonum;* and all his teachings were directed to securing that. His method for attaining this was very simple; it was only the regulation of manners. He collected and codified a horde of petty maxims and precepts; and these he enforced by one fundamental virtue, obedience. The first virtue was obedience to parents; the next, obedience to the powers of government; the highest stretch of perfection was devotion to the Emperor. There was, however, very little that was systematic in the teachings of

Confucius. It was no one great idea that gave him mastery over the mind of his people; but rather a practical spirit.

There are three questions, however, that test at once the spiritual character of any moral or religious system: they are these; what does it teach about God; what about a future state; what about sin? If we try Confucianism by these, it will be evident how completely Agnostic it is.

As to the teachings of Confucius about the Being of God, it is significant that it is still an open question with scholars whether he believed in a personal God at all. Arnauld and other writers broadly assert that he did not. In speaking on the subject, Confucius himself uses only the vague impersonal term, Heaven. And this stands only for a cold abstraction of the logical faculty, certainly not the personal and spiritual Being we mean by our word God. Certain it is that he had fixed his own vague and irresolute way of regarding the question on the Chinese mind; for scholars still dispute as to what word they shall use, or if indeed there be any word in the Chinese language they can use, to express the idea of God. To all inquiries as to a personal Deity and Creator he gave answers that are pure Agnosticism. "You find yourself," he says, "in the midst of a stupendous, yet most orderly piece of mechanism. That mechanism, so far as we can tell, is self-originating, self-sustaining. Change there is, but no creation: all things from eternity existed, and were subject to a flux and reflux, in obedience to initial laws impressed upon them, how and why we know not, by some stern necessity. Being warned and guided by this principle, devote yourself no longer to the fruitless study of theology; it brings, and can bring with it no practical advantage. Seek not to explore the doctrine of final causes; rather, if you speculate at all, confine your thoughts to the discussion of phenomena and the laws of phenomena. Such alone are useful and legitimate subjects of inquiry. It is possible indeed that laws may be connected somehow with forms of spiritual agency; we cannot absolutely say that they are not. You may continue, therefore, on this ground to follow the established ritual of your ancestors. Sacrifice *as if* your sacrifice were a reality; worship *shin* as if *shin* were really present. But meanwhile your chief concern is with the visible and palpable universe, and with the homely tasks of life." How familiar all this seems; but it sounds like a quotation from an article in the " *Nineteenth Century* " or the " *Fortnightly Review*." And no wonder: the hands are the hands of Confucius, but the voice is the voice of Professor Huxley.

And what of a future state? Here, too, his teachings are thoroughly Agnostic. He refuses to derive any motives of conduct from the consideration of the life beyond. Good and evil are to be recompensed by the natural results of conduct here in time. To all inquiries about the future world he turns a cold indifference. One of his followers asked him the question, "What becomes of a man when he has passed from the stage of life?" "While you do not know life," was the reply, "what can you know of death?" He does not say that death ends all; only, " we do not know." " Perhaps this present life," he says, " may be your last, your sole possession, \* \* meanwhile your chief concern is with the visible and palpable universe, and with the homely tasks of life." Well, that is Agnosticism pure and unadulterated. Mr. Holyoake himself could not put it better.

With such negations in the place of God and the hope of immortality, it is easy to see what Confucius' doctrine of sin must be. Take away God, cut down the existence of the soul to the span of seventy years, and sin loses its essential character. Right and wrong are only convertible terms with order and disorder. Sin is not a consciousness unique, solitary, mysterious, a stain that strikes through to the roots of our being; it is only a natural stage in the development of the human animal. And all this is Confucianism. He denies that human nature is bad. "Human nature," says Mencius, echoing his master, " is good, just as water has a tendency to flow downwards; men are universally inclined to virtue, just as water invariably flows downwards. Water, by beating may be made to splash over your head, and by forcing may be made to pass over a mountain; but who would ever say that this is the natural tendency of water? It is because violence is applied to it. Thus men can be made vicious; but it is by no means their nature." Sin is not a fault in the man himself, but only a result of defective education. Correct his surroundings and give him healthy teaching and sin will disappear. And of course there is no place for self-condemnation or remorse. Guilt is something of which the Chinese philosopher takes no cognizance. He lives for time: he is satisfied with the results of time. Things are disordered here it is true; but it only needs patience and careful instruction, and above all the cultivation of political economy, and all wrongs will be righted, and the kingdom of heaven, such a kingdom of heaven as is realized in the China of to-day, will come on earth.

As for the cry of man for his God, Confucius does not hear it. The longing of the soul for the infinite, the aspiration towards the perfect in character, the sense of dependence, the exercise of reverence, the craving for spiritual regeneration are to him only the imagery of fantastic dreams.

Confucianism is Agnosticism. Feature by feature it answers to that theory of life. In its refusal to consider the questions of theology, questions concerning God, the Future State, and the reality of sin, in its determination to address itself only to the present, the temporal, the earthly, it is the skeptical philosophy of our time.

And now we are ready for the question, What has Agnosticism made of the Chinese? It has had a fair field all to itself, and a sowing of many centuries: what kind of civilization does it produce, and what sort of kingdom of heaven does it set up?

Two features strike us immediately and forcibly in considering the civilization of China: *its tremendous vitality, and its dreary commonplaceness.*

For more than twenty centuries now the Chinese have addressed themselves to the problem of how to get the most out of life here. They have simplified their problem under the inspiration of Confucius by dropping clean out of mind all questions of a theological character, and have concentrated every energy on the business of living here. In this they have had a great success. They have developed a civilization that clings close to its facts, to the seen, the palpable, the ponderable, the material; and these it has mastered. An acre of ground in China supports more human life, such as it is, than an acre in any other part of the world. The human animal there can do more work on a smaller amount of nourishment than any other human animal on the face of the earth. In the competition of labor the Chinaman can beat not only the Californian, but the European, the negro, the Hindus, in a word, every rival.

And he is not unhappy in his pinched, narrow life. He works as hard as the peasant of Germany or the artisan of England, but he is incomparably more content with his lot. All writers unite in testifying to his cheerfulness. There is no enthusiasm wasted; but neither is there any melancholy. The problem before him has been to make the most of life here; and to do this he has learned to economize feeling. Why waste energy and time in unavailing wishes, in dreams of the far-off, the supernatural? As one of their admirers has described them, "they are a swarm of plodding utilitarians, sternly adherent to the actual and the positive: * * a matter-of-fact temperament without salient ideas or special enthusiasm makes the Chinaman push all work into infinitesimal detail." As he has stripped life of the imaginative element, and made religion to consist in a code of manners and the cultivation of political economy, there is no room left for unprofitable longings. Every energy of the soul is put to practical work; there is no expenditure of vitality in spiritual speculation and aspiration. The Chinaman has learned the art of economizing vital force; and that is an enormous saving. To this should be added another great economy which they have achieved, viz., their singular freedom from excess of nervous sensibility. It is noticed that the Chinese are more insensible to pain than other races; they suffer less from nervous irritability after injuries; they recover more quickly from surgical operations. And this is a natural result of the strict confinement of nervous activity to the uses of things actual and material. Confucius turned the mind of the race away from all spiritual contemplations. The result is that the great waves of feeling which come and go with the exercise of spiritual speculation and emotion, cease. Development of sensibility is checked, and you have a race fitted for the monotonous round of a life of hard toil. You have, too, a race specially qualified for meeting the hard, cold facts of life. It is noticed that no race gives and takes life with such indifference as the Chinese. They exterminate a conquered tribe, or lie down themselves to die by famine, with equal coolness and unconcern. For this they have been judged to be cruel; but it is not cruelty, it is only the stolidity that results from defective nervous sensibility.

What a persistent, tenacious, indefatigable race of workers has Agnosticism made of them! They have solved the problem of how to live cheap, work hard, submit stoically to death, and yet be cheerful under it all. They are a race of admirable animals. And thus far they have vindicated Agnosticism as a working theory of life. To lose sight of God, to have no thought of a future life, to drop out all sense of sin and guilt from the human consciousness, to concentrate the whole energy of the mind on the business of living here and now, certainly does make of man a powerful, tenacious, and cheerful animal. But is such an animal worth preserving? Would the kingdom of heaven come if the Middle Kingdom were extended over the whole earth? Will the race have reached perfection when we are all Chinese?

And this brings us to consider the other striking feature of Chinese civilization, *its commonplaceness.* Life in China is a dreary dead level of mediocrity. There are no depressions and there are no elevations. It is one flat plain of common sordid appetites and petty desires, all of the earth earthy. There is no progress in the nation. Things are there now just as they were two thousand years ago. The national mind conceives of no possible improvement; things are just as they ought to be; the ideal has been realized; it was realized twenty centuries ago. History is only a monotonous line of coming and going emperors and dynasties. And it is the same with the individual. The Chinese child becomes a man in capacity to work; but he never ceases to be childish. St. Paul's declaration that when he became a man he put away childish things, would illustrate nothing to the Chinese mind, for a Chinaman never puts away childish things. He flies kites, plays with toys, is consumed with infantile curiosity, at the age of fifty as at five. His maturity is only a hardening of muscle and a ripening of the meaner processes of the logical faculty; character seems not to develop with manhood. There is no perspective in the Chinese mind any more than there is in their art. The blue plates, familiar to our boyish eyes, in which the man in the foreground is no bigger than his fellow a mile away across the bridge, is at once an illustration and a type of Chinese civilization: it is all an eternal here and now. They know nothing of lights or shades.

They are, as might be expected, a people devoid of humor. It would be as hard to get a joke through a Chinaman's head as Sydney Smith affirmed it was to introduce it into a Scotchman's. He is, it is true, the occasion of mirth in others, but it is *at* him we smile, not with him. No mind, for instance, with the slightest touch of humor could have written the great apostrophe to duty, with its anti-climax, which is attributed to Confucius: "You constitute one little member in some mighty organism; you stand as part of some great moral order; strive to act on all occasions as such a being should act. Far from pausing to bemoan your weakness or unworthiness, remember that he who offends against heaven has no one to whom he can pray. The past is gone and is irrevocable. Be more vigilant in time to come." This is very fine: one feels his pulse beat quicker to these grand sentiments; but now for the climax: " Endeavor so to rule yourself, according to the sacred maxims, that you may be fitted first to rule a family, and lastly may attain the highest point of your ambition—an office under government." There is a noble end for the goal of life. It is worthy of the utterance of an Andrew Jackson or a Roscoe Conkling: "Strive to act as one who is part of a great moral order, and you shall have—a post-office!" A congressman might say that seriously; but how could a sage? Well, he could not if he had a spark of humor. But Confucius had none; and his followers for twenty centuries have had none either.

There is no imagination among them; that is nothing of what we know as such. A thin play of fancy flutters over their literature and art, like the shimmer of light on polished metal; but for the power that builds and weaves and projects before the mind's eye its creation of character and life, with their mysteries of light and shade, of passion and aspiration, with a movement and goal—all this is wanting to the Chinese.

And there seems to be in them no capacity for enthusiasm, except it be an enthusiasm for making money. They have a passion for trade; but religion, patriotism, even the ordinary human affections, seem to kindle in them no fire. One writer says of their humanity, "it ameliorates, but does not reconstruct: it has an apathetic and languid air, and does not rise to enthusiasm." Now humanity is the one virtue, according to the Agnostic, which above all others is to survive the decay of religion. If Secularism is to do anything for us it is to do away the miseries of man. But the most perfectly worked out Agnosticism the world has ever seen has lost all nerve or spirit for reforming men.

Of their religion mention has been made before. It is a horde of petty maxims about daily living, with the Emperor for its object of supreme reverence, and the cultivation of political economy for its highest exercise. Its heaven is an office under government, and the proper distribution of the post-offices is its ideal of the moral order of the universe. And this is the outcome of Agnosticism!

But it will be said that the immobility and dreary commonplaceness of Chinese civilization are not the result of Agnosticism, but only an accidental quality due to natural temperament, or to some agency concealed now in their remote past.

With respect to that, two facts are to be considered.

*First*, The fact that at some distant period the Chinese were possessed of a civilization progressive, highly inventive, and fertile in ideas. No one supposes that the knowledge of gunpowder, printing, and the mariner's compass, to say nothing of all the arts and elaborations of a complex social and political structure, came to them by revelation from heaven, or by inheritance from a superior race. There is the existing civilization petrified, motionless for 2000 years, but carrying in it all the marks of a former age of discovery and progress. How came this great moving tide of civilization to a standstill, to be locked up in this frost of centuries? Concede that the feudal decay of the centuries before Confucius gave a pause to the movement; so there was a pause in the civilization of Europe when western feudalism declined; but when partial order was restored progress was resumed: it was only a pause, not a petrifaction.

Then there is the other fact, that just at the moment when order began to be restored, Confucianism laid its grasp on the Chinese mind and turned it decisively away from the idea of God, the future life, sin and righteousness, in a word, from the supernatural. Chinese immobility dates from the establishment of Secularism or practical Agnosticism, in the form of Confucianism, as the religion of the nation. This may be only a coincidence; but it is the only fact that throws any light at all on this hardest of problems.

And further, it ought not to be considered an isolated fact, a mere coincidence; for it is a fact that falls in with our natural expectations. No one will suspect M. Renan of an undue bias to theological ideas, but he says in his Studies of Religious History, that the fact that the Chinese are of all people the least supernaturalist, explains to his mind "the secret of their mediocrity." That is to say, to take from man the idea of God and immortality, is to narrow his scope. Shut him up to time; roof over the heavens above him; for his infinite substitute the indefinite: and you have not merely taken from him so much future; you have really changed the character of his present. The mystery, the greatness, the immeasurable hope of existence, all that gives to life its light on the horizon, is gone. Life becomes a measured tract—an enclosed paddock—so many years, such and such possibilities, all bounded and visible—and shut in there to browse, man loses with his infinite prospect his infinite elasticity. In short, M. Renan thinks, as most of the great thinkers have thought before him, that to paralyze the religious nature, is to save the political and social animal, but to destroy the subtle, aspiring, creative soul. It was this that Tennyson meant when he wrote,

"Better fifty years of Europe than a cycle of Cathay."

He was not thinking of the contentedness of the masses, the relations of labor and capital, the material aspects, of the two civilizations; in that view the Chinaman has the better of the European; as a working animal he far surpasses his European brother. But it was the spiritual life, the out-look, the hope, the aspiration of Europe, alongside of the spiritual apathy and languor of China, that pointed the comparison. It was the mountain region with its lovely valleys and lofty peaks, its rushing streams and rugged gorges, by the side of the flat levels of the lowlands.

Attention enough, it seems to me, has not been paid

to this aspect of the transformation which must be effected in human nature by the suppression of its spiritual side. We have been told what vast energies of the intellect were wasted on the speculations of theology; the word *scholasticism* represents that terrible expenditure; for scholasticism was the gulf that for two centuries swallowed up the most of the mental force of Europe. We know, too, what a world of passionate hopes, what a treasure of enthusiasm, of lofty aspirations, and high dreams, was sunk in religious controversy. It is easy to deplore this, and to paint a picture of what might have been done if the scholars who spent centuries in going in doors only to come out of them again, had devoted their subtlety and persistence to the problems of real life. But who can tell us what the human mind itself will be when once the spiritual world is closed up as only waste land? You can calculate how much energy will be saved by ceasing to think barrenly about God and immortality; but can you tell how much spiritual energy will be left in men who do not believe in God or a future life at all?

Such a condition of things would be to the mental economy what the reduction of all the earth's mountains to plains would be to the material economy. There would be more land to plough, but a great deal less of the forces that make it worth plowing. And Agnosticism is neither more nor less than an attempt to level the highlands of human nature, its solitary peaks of faith and aspiration, to the flat level of the plains. The plea is that mountains are only barren and uninhabitable places, and that once levelled they would grow so much more corn. But reduce human nature to the plain of mere existence, to the well-being of the body, and the cultivation of the trading and social faculties, and what sort of spiritual force would you have left? The answer, it seems to me, is given in the plains of China. That huge mass of four hundred millions of human beings, with no humor, no enthusiasm, no aspiration, no progress, no faith, no hope, no future, that crowd of toiling animals eager for gain, indifferent to life, dull, monotonous, commonplace, sullen, is the answer.

Mr. Matthew Arnold finds fault with Bishop Butler for making the full coming of the *Kingdom of God* to depend on the intervention of God Himself. "Butler," he says, "decides that good men cannot now unite sufficiently to bring this better society about; that it cannot, therefore, be brought about in the present known course of nature, and that it must be meant to come to pass in another world beyond the grave." Not so, says Mr. Arnold; we do not need, for the kingdom of God to come, to have a future state, nor a personal God, nor any fathomless distinction between sin and righteousness. He thinks we may find an immortality in being generous and unselfish here; that we may have the aspiration and joy, the inextinguishable hope and spiritual longing that belong to the idea of God and eternity, without God or eternity. He bids us believe that when we have ceased to spend our energies in arguing about a God in whose existence we firmly believe, and take to living to a God in whose existence we do not believe at all, that then the kingdom of God will come.

Well, Confucius persuaded the Chinese to try that experiment: "Devote yourself," he said, "no longer to the fruitless study of theology * * your chief concern is with the visible and palpable universe, and with the homely tasks of life * * be thoughtful, therefore, be industrious; make the most of what you have; be modest, sober, grave, decorous; cultivate the qualities which mark the man of the due medium * * and at last you may attain the highest point of your ambition—an office under government." And the Chinese tried it. They gave up theology; they dropped the fairy-tale of immortality; they turned their backs on God, and gave themselves to practical things, and to culture—to the cultivation especially of political economy, that noble science, to which Mr. Andrew White, of Cornell, so ardently urges our young men to devote themselves. They realized Professor Huxley's ideal of attending only to what they could see, and know, and verify. They followed out Mr. Arnold's gospel of seeking to establish by culture a *Kingdom of God* here. And they have it. They entered it a long time ago. The Emperor, the Son and Representative of Heaven, is their substitute for God; to become a mandarin of nine buttons is their entrance into heaven. They have mastered the problem of getting rice enough for all, of being cheerful without hope and satisfied with the commonplace. They have a *kingdom of God* of mediocrity and dreary immobility.

Their New Jerusalem is a city where nothing changes, nothing happens; there are no dreams there, no future, no aspiration; nothing but rice illimitable, and the prospect of getting an office under government.

Behold the kingdom of God is among them! but who would enter it?

(Reprinted by permission from The Lutheran Quarterly for July, 1879.)

## THE SECRET OF CHRISTMAS.

Christmas has come to mean so many things that it is easy to miss what is really essential in it, the meaning which alone gives significance to all others. It is like the pealing of a bell in the hills; the valleys and ridges take it up and toss it back and forth till we can hardly distinguish the original sound from the echoes. Christmas has a great many echoes.

Go down into the thronged streets as the bright season comes near, and ask one and another its meaning. One says, "Christmas means joy: it is the pledge and the realization of what we are so apt to forget, that there is a great joy in life." Well, that is true. A Christmas without joy would be like a spring without blossom. But then the blossoms are not spring; they do not even express all the meaning of spring.

Another says, "Christmas means kindliness and the opening of human affections." To his ear, its chimes ring out, "Peace on earth, good will to men." And that is a still truer answer. Christmas does have that power: it softens men's hearts, makes us feel the need of the needy, and puts us into sympathy with all.

Others give it a wider scope. The great festival celebrated in common in so many lands, spreading every year to new peoples, tells of the growing oneness of the race. It means the breaking down of old barriers of national prejudice, race hatred. It prophesies "the federation of the nations, the parliament of the world." And what a grand, true meaning that is! for Christmas, if it is real at all, must point at last to that, the binding together of men all over the world in one company of brethren.

To some it is apologetic: it testifies to the power of Christianity. To others it is theological: a sign of the truth of Christ's redemption. And so we might go on. But in none of these, nor in all of them together, is really given the picture of what Christmas means at its very heart. That must be found in the event itself which Christmas celebrates. And that event, when once we look at it, how simple, yet how profound it is! A child is born into the world; but that child is the Divine One himself, the great God. It is the meeting of infinite power and infinite weakness. It is the coming of God to man, the drawing near and yet nearer of the Father to his lost and bewildered child.

The meaning, then, of Christmas is, God came to us; God came to man that he might be united to us and we to him: the union of God and man. In view of that great mystery, that palpable fact, all other meanings of Christmas find their true interpretation.

And now that the blessed season comes, with all its familiar brightness and hallowed memories, how can we feel that it is a real Christmas to us individually, unless we get at its very heart and are assured that God has, indeed, come to us? Christmas and its celebration ought to be a very personal matter, for it expresses a personal relation. The message to the shepherds, "Unto you is born this day a Saviour," each Christian must translate into a particular, personal message to himself. He must hear the angels saying "Unto thee," and know that it was not only to man in general, but unto him in particular, the glad tidings are sent. Unless by faith we can do that, our Christmas falls short of what Christ meant it to be. I know, as season after season comes again, it is often hard to make the message a reality. Cares and anxieties parching the dew of our youth, suffering, breaking the elasticity of the spirit, make Christ's salvation seem a very far-off thing. What are we to do then? When Christmas comes and calls us, and the world has been filling our souls with its prosperity or its bitterness, making the message an unreal, impossible thing is there any help?

I know of no better way than to do as the shepherds did. "Let us go now," they said, "and see this thing which is come to pass." And so they went and saw the Child. Christmas is really Christmas only as we come near and see Jesus.

How much the New Testament makes of that simple experience of immediate personal contact, seeing Jesus!

When Nathanael objected that one from Nazareth could not be the Messiah, Philip says, "Come and see:" if he once saw Jesus, his doubts would be dissolved. At Samaria the noblest seekers after truth were satisfied only when they saw and heard Christ for themselves. "Now we believe," they said, "for we have heard him ourselves, and know that this is the Christ, the Saviour of the world." It is that mysterious, inexplicable power which is found in personal contact that is meant here. Something came to them from the great presence, the deep eyes, the penetrating tones, which satisfied. They felt the Divine; all doubts were dissolved, all needs met. They saw him and were drawn into the great current of his life, and became one with him.

No Christmas does for us what it ought unless it renews that sense of divine touch; and no Christmas will do that for us until, first of all, we get away from the noise and laughter and gay confusion, to look alone upon Jesus. Then, when we have seen him, felt his divine touch renewing our love and faith—then, like the shepherds and the Wise Men, we can come back to rejoice. There is such a thing as making our Christmas time "dark with excess of light;" there is so much splendor in the shop windows, so much bustle on the street, so much merrymaking and jollity, so much publicity and general rejoicing, that we lose the quiet, sweet, peaceful sense of the divine life touching ours. Is it not so with many Christians? The season comes and goes and leaves them dry. Not because they are in any special way wrong, but because they have made their Christmas so much a thing of the outside. The trimming of the Christmas tree, the selection of gifts, the party going, the feasting, even the religious exercises, the decoration of the churches, the Christmas music, the Christmas benevolence, all are outward. Then at the end a bad taste is in the mouth. It is not because this outward brightness, merriment, public exercise, social hilarity is wrong; but because it has not found its true root.

Begin with the cradle in the manger, the sacred head that lies low with the beasts of the stall, the group of rude shepherds, and the seeking Wise Men worshiping before the infant Jesus, and then all the splendor and the universal joy which have flowed out from that dark stable in the inn will seem perfectly right.

First Jesus; then what he does for us, and his gifts and the flood of joy he pours out on a heavy laden world. When we see him, touch him, we come to the centre; we receive in that union and communion a divine unction that makes us able to estimate rightly all the many meanings of Christmas. Then the frolic of the children, the widespread joy, the brightness and mirth of the season fall into their proper place; then we can enjoy all, and feel the love and presence of Christ pervading all.—(*L. O., Dec., 1883.*)

## THE GROWING LIFE.

In St. Paul's life there is always apparent a struggle after something better. While he can say of all his surroundings that he is content, he is never satisfied with the progress he has made himself. It is a small thing to him whether he live coarsely or delicately, in a luxurious or plain dwelling, is at leisure or crowded with work; but that he, Paul, should not be increasing in what really makes life, is not to be borne. He must get on. And this applies not so much to his work as to his own character. It does apply to his work: he is ever seeking new fields, dreaming of new conquests of souls, planning fresh enterprises. But not dissevered from these, and yet a wholly distinct aim, is his thirst to go on in his own inner life with God.

It was so when he was yet a Pharisee. He recounts what he sacrificed and how he toiled to realize in that poor, dry way his ideal of righteousness, of being near and acceptable to God. His conversion was not a conversion from irreligion to religion, but from one kind of religion to another; not from vice or worldliness to an honest service, but from a self-chosen service to one given him from God. And when he became a Christian, after the first bewilderment of the shock was over, once on his feet again, we see him the same Paul, bracing himself for the race; only now his goal is to know perfectly a beloved Lord and friend, his ideal is to be like the lovely Christ, his thirst is to be filled with his life, the condescending Jesus, the mighty and holy God.

That, I think, describes what is most characteristic in the great Apostle; not his wonderful genius, his tireless energy, his power over men, but his impassioned longing for perfection in the fellowship of Christ. He was actually one of the most practical and busy of men. His life seemed to be all out of doors. To find him you must go into the market-place, in the thickest of the crowd. But what drove him there was the deep sense of the riches of Christ and the intense longing that the blessedness he was grasping might be put into the hands of all men. "I am debtor both to the Greeks, and to the barbarians; both to the wise, and the unwise; so, as much as in me is, I am ready to preach the gospel to you of Rome also. For it is the power of God unto salvation to every one that believeth; to the Jew first, and also to the Greek." In reality he was a mystic, a soul loving to lose itself in the communion of Christ.

Take his experience in his Epistle to the Philippians: "I count all things but loss for the excellency of the knowledge of Christ Jesus, my Lord: * * * * that I may know him." "I count not myself to have apprehended: but this one thing I do, forgetting those things which are behind, and reaching forth unto those things which are before, I press toward the mark for the prize of the high calling of God in Christ Jesus." As we read that grand passage, we see not the great preacher, the founder of churches, the converter of men, the active propagator of a new faith, but a solitary soul forgetting all else in the vision of the glory of the perfect life of Christ. For the instant, there is to him, in the universe but one being beside himself— that is Christ, the condescending, incarnate God. To be united to him, to be like him, to be filled with him, is blessedness unalloyed; he is rapt, held enchanted with this hope. Does not this tell us something of the source of his activity? At Vaucluse, in southern France, a large river, the Sorgues, flows from a single spring. At the foot of a lofty mountain cliff sleeps a pool so pure, so still, you can scarcely tell where air begins and water ends. Up from its deep basin wells the silent stream; as it rises unruffled it seems a motionless lake, but it glides till the brink is reached; then it rushes on, a mighty, growing river, down the vale, turning the wheels of factories and mills. That is a picture of what the Apostle's mystical life of contemplation of Christ and communion with him, is to his tremendous energy as a worker among men. Out of the depths of that still contemplation, wells up the power that marks the grand Apostle to the Gentiles, the most tireless of workers.

But here the likeness ceases. With many men, the active service of God begins, as with Paul, in a vision of the blessedness of the life in Christ. In them, too, out of the still depths of devotion to the Master flows the stream of activity. But with many, as the stream flows, the spring that feeds it grows shallow. How common is this experience! The life that begins with deep devotion goes forth in eager service, and then dwindles: the preacher does not preach with the same power, the layman is not so effective in work, the Christian life at home is less and less influential. It seems strange that it is assumed as almost a law of religious life that energy should lessen with time. But the secret is an open one. With St. Paul and those like him, the stream of activity is always full and mighty, because the deep reservoir of communion with God, of contemplation and ardent longing to know Christ better was welling up afresh. To the Apostle there is no bound to the depth and scope of this knowledge and communion. He recognizes this in his own case: at the end of a long life he says, "I count not myself to have apprehended." He is a discoverer who has landed on the shore of a new continent; a little way inward he has explored the rich, strange lands; but beyond, in endless reaches, stretches a new world to be explored and possessed. He cannot sit still, he must go on to know that glorious realm. He recognizes that in the nature of the case the end can never be reached; the communion of the soul with God can never grow stale, for God is always new. Go on, he says, to "know the love of Christ, which passeth knowledge, that ye might be filled with all the fullness of God."

Here, then, we have the simple plan of that great and growing life. His aim was to be more and more one with Christ; and to reach this, he knew no better way than to cherish a deepening communion with

Christ. This plan might be formed and carried out, if Christ and St. Paul were the only beings in the universe: it is a life intensely individual, personal; but it is a life, too, that is most sympathetic with all other life, and surest to do the best work for men and God.

It is very simple; but how easily we miss its essential elements! Every Christian has for his aim this union to Christ; but we are continually forgetting that the growth of this union comes from communion. We think that doing Christian work, cultivating Christian tempers, caring for our conduct, is the way to deepen this union; but it is not so. All these things come after—they are the fruit, not the root. So if we find it necessary to abridge anything, it is the mystical part we give up; it is the hour of communion, not the hour of work, that we are apt to sacrifice. We think we can do with less devotion, less communion with God, less study of the character of Christ. We can afford better to spend a day in which we have not been alone with Christ, than a day in which we have done no outward work for him. We think it better to cultivate the little strip of new life we already know, than to explore more deeply the great realm he opens to us in the knowledge and fellowship of himself. What a mistake! And the greater the stress of work calling us, the more apt we are to fall into it. The outward call is so much louder than the inward.

But if we would do work in the untiring spirit of the Apostle, we must first seek Christ, with his thirst for union and communion with Christ. As teachers, workers in the church, ministers, leaders of others, our deepest need is closer union with Christ—more communion with him. The hour when by the patient endurance of suffering, or the pondering of his Word, or the still, rapt contemplation of the soul fixed on him, we are apart from all else, is the hour when the soul grows. Then most rapidly we are going on to know Christ: then we are more filled with the power which makes life full and strong, for ourselves and for others.—(*L. O., Dec. 1883.*)

## CHRIST'S METHOD OF DEALING WITH MEN.

JOHN IV. 7, 27. There cometh a woman of Samaria to draw water: Jesus saith unto her, Give me to drink.

And upon this came his disciples, and marvelled that he talked with the woman.

These words bring before us the strangely interesting figure of the woman of Samaria. What a stained and tattered piece of humanity she is! and yet even about her rags there lingers an air of interest. It is the charm which belongs to every figure in the Gospel that has once met Jesus and helped us to see him. For a few moments she came into the circle of his special regard, and ever since a fragrance has clung to her. I suppose many of us have felt, what seemed at times, an unreasonable tenderness for this poor creature, because of her association with Christ. But after all there is something more here than mere association. She interests us, I think, because she illustrates a great truth about Christ and his revelation of God to us. It is the truth that it is only as Christ meets men, and their sin and shame call out his sympathy and salvation that we discover what a great rich Saviour he is. It is even more—it is the truth that the inscrutable God is revealed to us as a real, loving, lovable personality by the contact of man's sin and misery.

Look at that figure of Jesus sitting by the well: how inscrutable, mysterious, his being, his thoughts; and then this poor, light creature comes, and at the touch of her sin and need we see his heart unfold its treasures of wisdom and love. The great billow rolls over the deep without a sound, almost without form till it strikes the shore and then out of its bosom bursts the dazzling foam, the rainbow in the spray, the music of the surf, all the wonder and life of the breaking wave. The ugly rock has revealed to us the beauty of the sea. So man and his sin reveal to us God and his glory; this sinful Samaritan helps us to see the beauty of the spotless Saviour.

That is not a solitary case. It happens in the gospels again and again. Thomas in his reckless doubt cries "Except I shall see, . . . I will not believe," and then over that hard incredulity breaks a great rich word of Christ. "Blessed are they that have not seen, and yet have believed." Man's doubt reveals Christ's power to call forth a deep peaceful faith. We all owe these faulty men and women in the gospel a debt for what they show us of Christ. We owe a debt to this poor creature of Samaria. How many she has unconsciously helped on in their way. Many a preacher has learned from her interview with Christ how to preach. Many a teacher has looked over the head of his stupid scholars and seeing the great teacher with his stupid scholar, has learned patience.

Let us try to understand what this scene of Jesus talking with the woman of Samaria tells us. *It illustrates Christ's sweet reasonableness towards men.*

Two things appear here:

1st. Christ's feeling towards men.

2d. His treatment of men which springs out of that feeling.

First, as to Christ's feeling towards men. That lies at the root of his whole method. We can never understand Christ's dealing with men unless we catch his feeling for them. Look at them from the common sense point of view, that of the man of the world, who says he knows men, meaning that he knows their badness and meanness, knows them as sharp buyers and sellers, wasteful servants, tricky politicians, foolish neighbors—look at men so, and Christ's treatment of them will seem absurd. I have no doubt the Jews thought, Christ's going home to dine with Zaccheus, not only an uncleanness, but also a ridiculous bit of softness. A son of Abraham, indeed! What had Abraham to do with such a renegade and extortioner? We know what Simon, the Pharisee, thought of Christ's treatment of the woman who was a sinner.

Instead of exciting his admiration, it only led him to infer that Christ did not know much about human nature.

But one of Christ's blessings to us is that he has taught us that man has a nature really precious and salvable. Christ's life was continually saying, "The Son of man is come to seek and to save that which was lost;" well, then, he must be worth saving. When the great God came down to earth and lay a babe in the cradle at Bethlehem, the lesson began: "Yes, man is worth saving;" and all along to the end, to the cross on calvary, to the ascension to heaven, every new scene repeated it over and over. "Man is dear to God; he is the lost child; he is God's broken image, the beautiful although corrupted image of the glorious God." We read it in every picture of the Saviour's gentleness and pity; we hear it in every word of balm from his lips. It is the golden thread running through the story of Zaccheus, of the woman who was a sinner, of the young ruler whom Jesus loved, of the Prodigal Son, of the weeping over Jerusalem. They all tell us of some wonderful attraction to the heart of Jesus in the poor waifs and strays which drift by him along the streets and lanes of Palestine.

And now here the same story is repeated. Jesus sits weary by the well. He has traveled far, and is faint with hunger and fatigue; the dust of travel is on him: how dull life and all things seem at such times. But now a foot-step comes along the road. He looks up: it is only a poor woman of the town carrying her water-jar on her head, one of the dull toiling millions, a beast of burden, a mere lump of appetites and sordid habits. But Christ speaks to her; something in her draws his heart; and when the disciples return he has forgotten hunger and fatigue: "I have meat to eat that ye know not of." That interest overpowering the weariness of the body tells us how deep is the love of man in Christ's soul. The soul triumphs over the body again and again when it loves. The soldier forgets the long march at the sound of the bugle blown for battle. The weary mother leaps up unwearied at her child's cry of pain. And Jesus, when a wretched soul comes before him, for the love of what is in it to be, for the yearning to wake the deaf nature and make it hear the voice of God, to open the blind eyes to see the glory of goodness, feels no more the dust and toil of the way.

We need to feel deeply this preciousness of every soul to Christ in its possibilities, both to learn to love him intimately, and to learn to love our fellow men.

We need to see Christ's tender regard for men to make our admiration of his perfection near and warm and close. Take away that yearning of his heart, that ineffable pity for the Father's image defaced in men, and then Christ's perfection is very beautiful and glorious; but it is perfect as the snow-peak is perfect. It dazzles; it freezes. It is a cold, unearthly, hopeless beauty. Our hearts chill into despair as we see that immaculate whiteness over against our stains. What can such a Christ be to me but a far-off, frozen peak of glory? But now see him come near! See him bend his eye on Zaccheus; on this poor, draggled thing. Does he frown? Is he revolted at her uncleanness? No, beneath the stain and folly he sees something better. Tenderly he lifts away one layer of vileness after another, and there below all we see what he sees, the soul with its wonderful possibility of angelhood. He breathes on it, and the faded lineaments of God start out. "See," he says, "that is what you can be." And then we feel what it is that has drawn him to earth, to Bethlehem, to Calvary, to me. Then in that vision of what he sees in our future, that possible likeness to himself traced through our disguises we feel that we can love such a Saviour intimately. We have something in common with him. We are not like him, but we may become so. We are poor sinners, but we may be shining saints. The whiteness that is in him shall be ours one day, for he recognizes it, promises it. And then the far-off glittering peak softens into a flush, as the snow-peaks glow when the evening falls.

We need this knowledge of Christ, too, to learn to love our fellow-men. Sometimes when we look at the people we meet along the streets, the servants in the kitchen, the loafers on the corners, the politicians at the grocery, we wonder if it is really possible to feel a drawing to all men. We all have our poor, mean side, and sometimes that side is so conspicuous that we seem even to ourselves unlovable. I suppose we never really cease to care for ourselves in an instinctive way of benevolence, to see that all our wants are supplied; but there are times when we do not feel any particular drawing to ourselves; we see our bad qualities, we are in a state of self-disgust. We are such bad company that we would like, if possible, to get away from ourselves. I suppose we all know what that feeling is. Much more is it true with reference to those about us. How repelling they often are! Is it possible to find in them that which drew Christ to this world, to individual men, to this poor ugly soul? The only possible way is to learn how from Christ. He has made it possible. By his death for every man he has stamped a new value on every one. Sometimes old gold gets so tarnished and battered, that it is hard to tell it from brass; but if we turn it over and find the Hall mark on it we are satisfied. So Christ's cross has stamped its value in each man's soul. We may say over each, Christ tasted death for every man—for this man; and then we recognize his value. The first step, then, to learning to love men, is to see them always with the shadow of the cross on them. And the next, is to see them as Jesus meets them, to see Zaccheus going home with Christ, to see the woman weeping at the Saviour's feet in Simon's house, to see this Samaritan with Jesus at the well.

Now let us see what way of treating men springs out of Christ's feeling for them. I have described it as a method of sweet reasonableness. As we read the story sympathetically trying to let the whole scene make its own atmosphere about us, we get this general impression about the whole manner of Christ apart from the particular thing he teaches, and that is of the wonderful wisdom and truth of his dealing, and then that this wisdom and truth is bathed in an atmosphere of personal tenderness and warmth. The two together we may describe as a sweet reasonableness. The two things do not always go together. Sometimes there is a reasonableness in those who approach us which is the last refinement of aggravation. A reasonableness which is more anxious to prove me wrong than to make me right, which opens my faults, but has no pity for me who am so faulty, which, in short, lacks the personal element of sympathy, is a reasonableness that drives sinful men to be more sinful. Is there anything more exasperating than the bland, "I told you so," of one who has been wiser than we? And, then, on the other hand, there is a sweetness which is of no more help to a poor sinner struggling with sin than the fragrance of the violets on the bank, to one who is struggling in the stream. The pity which is only sorry for us, but can show us no light, puts out no strong hand, may be sweet, but what is sweetness without strength and light and hope? Now Christ's treatment of men is neither helplessly pitiful, nor coldly sagacious. The hand he puts out to us is both strong and warm. Its touch thrills with tenderness, and braces with power. All this, I think, is illustrated by his conversation with the Samaritan woman.

Observe how lofty is his appeal. He speaks to her sense of what is good and true. At first sight, what could be more unwise and hopeless? She is wretchedly ignorant, steeped in prejudice, and dull with the worst of stupidities, the dullness vice brings. And yet Jesus talks to her of a God who is a spirit; tells her of a spiritual worship; speaks of the water that is to spring up to eternal life; unveils her particular sin to her conscience. Is that the way to reach a dull sinner? But that is the very reasonableness of Christ. And is it not reasonable? If man is capable of the salvation of goodness at all, there must be something in him that will respond to the voice of truth, the voice of God. If there is not, then there is no hope for him, and it is useless to go to him at all. The wisdom of Christ shines in the fearless appeal he makes to the depths of man's nature. He says, here is a child of God, erring, blind, rebellious, corrupted, but still with some strings in the wonderful harp not yet frayed quite away, the chord of conscience, of spiritual unrest, of hunger for God; let us strike them. And then he puts his hand on them, and at his touch, lo, the poor rusted strings long unsounded answer; discordantly, harshly, but they answer. The man wonders to hear them himself. How often that happened. Think of Zaccheus, the publican, despised of all; was there anything in that covetuous heart to answer to words about salvation? But Jesus tries him; the chord answers, "Lord, the half of my goods I give to the poor, and if I have taken anything by false accusation, I restore fourfold." Take one at the other end of the social scale, that scribe above whose petty question about commandments Christ lifted the great standard of truth and let it float on the breeze, "Thou shalt love the Lord thy God with all thy soul, and thy neighbor as thyself." How the deep chord responded out of his narrow heart, "Master, thou hast said the truth, to love God with all the soul, and his neighbor as himself is more than all." You will think of many such. Christ's reasonableness, then, is that he thinks the truths of God and righteousness not too high for men.

And that has been the power of all who have come after Christ. Paul preached to Felix of righteousness, temperance, and judgment to come: did he not tremble? What had ever made the proud Roman quail before? Think of the preaching at Ephesus to the worldly crowd which made them bring their precious books to be burned. So have all the great preachers done. But how slow we are to learn that! We think we must dilute truth, make it palatable, begin with worldly consideration, appeal to the lower part of human nature first, and so educate it up. But not so is the heart reached. It is one of the paradoxes which are forever puzzling men that one man comes to a body of his fellows and appeals to the bad low motives in them, and they answer him back in badness and baseness, and then another comes and appeals to what is high and holy, and the answer of high heroism, self-denial, comes from the same men. How can it be? Why, it is because there is in man the earthly and the heavenly, what God made and does not let wholly die, and what sin has made him. Appeal to the low, sensual, devilish, and he is a low, sensual, devilish creature; and appeal to the high, holy, heroic, and the high, heroic string sounds. It appears in a congregation. One preacher comes with his low faith in men and God, his philosophy of managing men, of getting them to do right by appealing to self-interest, of making them liberal by playing on their vanity, pride, worldliness, and lo, he has presently a worldly, selfish, vain church; and there comes another man who takes Christ's method and tells them of God and goodness, of holiness and self-denial, and lo, they answer to that. You know it in yourself. You are thrown in contact with one who does not believe in anything good, a skeptic as to human virtue, and you are shocked to find how his evil sneer rouses echoes out of the lair of your soul; you feel a stirring to life of mean thoughts, selfish plans, base passions. And then God sends into your life some one who is high and holy, and as he tells of what he loves and lives in, something in you responds; better thoughts come flocking out of the dark corners of your soul. It was said of a certain army officer that he made his men better by always taking it for granted that they wanted to be better. That was the meaning of the power of Nelson's signal at Trafalgar. "England expects every man to do his duty;" and every man that day did his duty. "It is a shame," Dr. Arnold's boy at Rugby used to say, "not to study and keep the school rules, for the doctor expects it so hopefully of us." It is always so. Believe in men's capacity for good things, and you help to make them good. Believe in the power of divine truth to stir men towards God, and already you have begun to stir them. I believe half the power of men who have greatly won men to God, has been their copying of Christ in this one thing, that they came to men not only with a deep belief in God, but also in a strong faith in the power of the greatest, purest truths about him to wake an answer in lost souls. We fail, we always fail, and we ought to fail when we go to men with a low appeal; when we put out of sight the great truths of righteousness and its blessedness, and the hatefulness and guilt of sin, when we hide the cross and its pain and shame and awe, because we fear men are not high enough to respond to such things. Not so Paul. "I am not ashamed of the gospel of Christ, it is the power of God unto salvation." "I determined to know nothing among you save Jesus Christ and him crucified." What a lofty, solemn, holy preaching that was; and how men answered to it, base slaves, victims of vice, proud philosophers and self-righteous Jews. Nothing is too high to bring to men in sin, for they are made for a high destiny, the strings God strung in them are there, and our business is to strike them boldly.

But will men answer to such high appeals? That leads us to another feature of Christ's treatment of men. His appeal is high, but its approach is sympathetic. He begins, you see, with this woman on her own ground. He stoops to enter the low portal. "Jesus saith unto her, give me to drink." Then by a gradual modulation, he passes from the chord of her awakened interest to his one great theme of God and his grace, the divine life and its blessedness. He touches two of the familiar springs of her life, her daily work, and her sense of humanity. He begins where she can meet him. That is indispensable. If we are really to help men, we must go where they are, enter on their ground, see and feel what they see and feel. It is curious to observe how the highest and the lowest appeal to men come down to the same gate. One man goes to his neighbor to get out of him a dollar or a vote; another goes to win him to God; and they both come and knock at the same door. They put themselves alongside of him, find out his tastes, interests, ways. They get him to go their way by first going a little way with him. And what is the lowest baseness in one, is the highest nobleness in the other. How near together, and yet how far apart, they are. Jesus talking to the woman of her daily work and offering her a better water, looks like a trader playing on the peculiar tastes of a customer; but they are worlds apart. The trader pretends a sympathy for his own ends, while Jesus really pities the dull drudge toiling at what can never satisfy, and goes with her to the well to get her to see the deeper, truer well. It is just because under the common thought and toil of each man he meets, he sees a deeper vein, a nobler toil he is capable of, that he is really interested in what he is and does.

We ought to see clearly the difference between pretending to care for a man's individual likings to do him good, and really caring so much for him that all his genuine ways are of real interest to us. For I do not believe that any mere pretense of sympathy will ever open any man's heart to the best work for him. A politician may get a vote or a trader a dollar by pretending an interest he does not feel; but votes and dollars are cheap things. If you want to get hold of what is really precious in a man, not his vote or his dollar, but his conscience, his spiritual nature, your interest must be genuine. Ah, there is the difficulty. I think we could be capable of working up an interest in a man's ways to win him to something better, but to really have the interest, that is a different matter.

That Christ teaches us. But how? By the free play of benefit between himself and this stranger. He asks a favor: "Give me to drink." There was a barrier between the Jew and the Samaritan, a double barrier of religious bigotry and caste pride. Christ simply treats it as though it were not. He is in need, and here is a fellow-creature who can help him. He frankly asks her. At once a sympathy is established; not something pretended, but the real sympathy of the helped and the helper. We are often shut out from men by refusing to take or ask benefits from them; we are too proud, or independent, or too ticklish of our dignity, too exclusive. In Marblehead, when a stranger appeared, the people used to say, "There's a stranger; heave a brick at him." And old Herodotus tells us how in early days every foreigner along the coast of Asia Minor used to be looked on as an enemy.

In California they feel so to the Chinamen to-day. Now the root of that old feeling is deep in human nature. We are apt to think of men not sympathetically, but antipathetically. Christ teaches us the better way. He lets us see how at every chance meeting with men, he felt the attraction of a common humanity: "He also is a son of Abraham;" "I must abide at thy house." "She, too, is a child of our father;" "Give me to drink." Let us exchange good offices. And so he lets his wish of help for her go out to her. He marks her burden; she is a water-carrier, and with the thought of her life-long toil, honest, necessary toil, but that at last must leave her athirst forever, his longing goes out to her. He wishes her life was not all mere drudgery—that she knew the deep well of the divine life, the water that quenches the soul's thirst in eternal joy. How natural that is! What a real interest we see springing up. But is that not possible in us for men about us, too? Did you never, when you have seen a sharp business-man hitting the mark, enlarging his trade, and you have noted his earnestness, clear-headedness, the joy he took in his work, did you never feel a pang of pity, that after all he was only blowing golden bubbles to float awhile and then break on the grave's edge? Did you not wish you could get him to see the solid realities of eternity, and engage that bright energy to be rich towards God? Or, did you never watch a mother so anxious for her boy, so proud of him, so happy in his happiness, and not wish she could learn to love her Saviour with the same loyal, self-sacrificing affection? Or, perhaps it is a college lad, ambitious, eager for praise, set on achievement, thinking what he will do in the world. Who can see such and not long to open his eyes to see what St. Paul saw, the race of eternal life, the arena where men and angels watch the struggle, the judge who holds the crown and waits to give, "to them who by patient continuance in well-doing, seek for glory and honor and immortality—eternal life."

I am sure Jesus shows us how we may feel a real interest in the lives and thoughts of those about us. It is to recognize frankly our common human nature, to give and take, to really stop long enough by each other's side to get the flavor of one another's life. Does this seem a little thing? But it was grand enough to be one reason for Christ's taking our nature upon him. What was the incarnation for? what did the great God of eternity become a struggling, learning man for? but, as one reason, that he might have just such a sympathy for us, that he could truly have a genuine interest in all our individual concerns: "in all things it behooved him to be made like unto his brethren, that he might be a merciful and faithful high priest . . . for in that he himself hath suffered being tempted, he is able also to succor them that are tempted." What a picture to hang over the cradle at Bethlehem, over the cross on Calvary! Why is the glorious God veiled in human flesh? That he might stand close by us, feel with us.

But this is not easy, even for Christ, the master of

souls.  We are to notice, then, his patience.  Sometimes, men opened to him at once.  One word, one call, and they turned.  But this woman was a stupid, empty creature.  I think, sometimes, this story was written by the Holy Ghost, among other reasons, to show how dull, and slow, and trying, a soul that is fully worth saving may be.  Read her answers to Christ's words; they are the very quintessence of frivolity, of the flightiness which nothing apparently can sober and fix.  But even that is met.  It is met by the sweet reasonableness of Christ's patience.  Both qualities appear in that patience.

*His reasonableness.*—We are impatient with men because we do not see how thoroughly sin has poisoned their nature.  Here is a sinner.  We go to him with the remedy, but he does not care for it, thinks he is well enough, laughs, turns it off, and then we are disgusted.  But what is all that frivolity, stupidity, but the effect of his sin—nay, his sin itself?  How unreasonable to be impatient with the obstinacy we came to cure?  The clear eye of Jesus sees that continually.  Behind the flighty talk he sees the wretched soul.  He reads the dumb longing under the perverseness.  We are continually misreading the signs of character.  Dr. Arnold sharply rebuked, one day, what seemed the wilful blunders and slowness of a dull scholar.  The boy burst into tears, and said, "I am doing my best, sir."  Nothing, the Doctor said, ever cut him like that protest.  Often if the deeper nature of men could speak out to us, after some stupidity or folly that exhausts our patience, it would say, too, "I am doing my best." That is what Jesus hears behind many a perverse objection, flippant answer, and he is patient.

But most of all his sweetness appears, the sweetness of the unsullied spirit. What makes us intolerant of perverseness? Our own perverseness. Fenelon says, in one of his spiritual letters, "It is our imperfection which is impatient of the imperfection of others." The chord of obstinacy sounds in them, and the chord of pride echoes back to it in us. The absence of all such impatience tells, as nothing else can, of Christ's inward sweetness. "Perfection easily bears with the faults of others." The Prince of this world, as Christ said, cometh and findeth nothing in him. He comes in the stupidity and captiousness he works in the children of disobedience, in this woman's emptiness, but he finds nothing to answer in Jesus. But when men flout us and make foolish answers, Satan finds the old charred brand of temper ready to take fire. Is it not sad to go to cure a sick man and find, instead, that we only catch his disease? But so it is between us and men. Here is a mother with her wilful child: she is to teach it self-control, and that comes first by the lesson of obedience. Its will is a slave to passion, and the mother must set it free. But, alas! how often instead of teaching our children self-control, they make us lose control over our own selves. We fail because we are impatient, and we lose patience because sin in the little one's heart has called to the sin in ours, and that has answered back, and we are betrayed into temper. That is neither sweet nor reasonable. How can you cure the evil in your child, your scholar, your friend, if you have not cured it in yourself? But when Christ comes to the sinner, and the sinner's perverseness beats against his love, it never ruffles him. He can wait, for evil has no contagion for him. How sweet is the grace which sin opposes but can not weary. Is not this Christ's infinite reasonableness? And our impatience with men, is it not at bottom our unreasonableness and sourness of temper?

But there is still more in Christ's way with men: His Faithfulness to the Truth. When we speak of our Lord's life it is almost impossible for us to keep the balance true between his sweetness and his righteousness. When we make him gentle, we are apt to lose out the strength; or we make him holy, and efface the humanity. The cure for this is to keep close to the facts. Take the facts of this interview: See how, although so tender, he is uncompromising in truth. "He whom thou now hast is not thy husband." What an unveiling of her sin! What an unswerving hand lays open the sore in her soul! Here is a wounded man, and up rush his foolish friends: they weep over him, they kiss him, they bring opiates for his pain, but the wound is unhelped. Then comes the surgeon; not a tear, not a word; he brushes away the opiates, he swiftly goes to the wound, gently but firmly he probes it through all the pain. That is reasonableness; that is true pity, and that is Christ's way with sinful men.

Patience with men does not mean that we are to hide from them unpalatable truth; sympathy with them is not saying smooth things; and faith in their deep capacity is not a refusal to tell them their faults. But just here comes the most difficult of all things in Christ to copy: his faithfulness to the truth blended with his faithfulness of love. How tell a man his faults, and yet win him? How be reasonable, and yet sweet? St. Paul solves it in a phrase which describes Christ's way with sinful men, "speaking the truth in love."

But in love of what? Of victory over error? So some read it. Nothing is oftener confounded than the love of victory and the love of truth. Men take the grand apostolic words, "Contend earnestly for the faith once delivered to the saints," and underscore the word "contend," and then put them for a motto over their newspaper, their pulpit, their creed, and baptize their itch for mastery with the sacred name of "love of truth," "loyalty to the faith." But there is a very simple test to detect the sham: are you glad to find your antagonist holding the substance of the very truth you are contending for, only in some other phrase, or do you refuse to recognize truth in any dress but your own party uniform. Such love of truth is only the love of having our own way, and is really one of the worst enemies of truth. I suppose the reason why half the arguments we have with men on politics, tariff, questions of taste, reform, religion, what not, do not convince any one, is that we are arguing for victory, to overmatch the other man, and not for truth pure and simple. Is not that at the bottom of a great deal of the fruitlessness of the discussions of the day on religious questions? Brilliant writers confute the other side, demolish opponents, with a heat of scorn that withers up all the bloom of the truth they advocate. It seems to me, more than half the power of a book like Butler's Analogy lies in the fact so open and sweet on every page that the writer cares nothing for victory, nothing to make a good point, will not evade a difficulty, nor take advantage of an opponent's slip—cares only for the truth; no, not even for the truth so much as for something beyond mere intellectual truth, to know the life of God, to have men know and feel the worth of the great living truths that have filled and satisfied his own soul. What a sweetness breathes through such dry words as these: "Things and actions are what they are, and the consequences of them will be what they will be: why, then, should we desire to be deceived?" Ah, it is a poor thing to tell a man his faults, to tower over him and get a confession of evil out of him; but to win him to the truth he was made for, that is blessed. And that was what Christ's telling men of their faults meant.

It meant more even than a love of truth. There is something beyond truth even. It is life, life in God and his life in men, which includes in itself truth, and adds to it the living use of truth. "Speaking the truth" in love to God and man: using it as gold, not with the miser's use to get and keep it for itself, but with the wise man's use for what it can get and be fashioned into, for righteousness, holiness, for the love and life of God in the soul. There is a way of telling men their faults in a cold allegiance to truth, duty, which is not sweet and only half reasonable. A minister does it sometimes: he goes to one of his people to tell him of a wrong course, a bad habit, because it is wrong the man should live so. He speaks the truth to him in the love of the truth. I am sure that is not the high Christian way. It is better so than not at all. But there is a more excellent way. It is to see the man's evil course, his fault as a cancer eating away the soul, defacing the image of God in him, bringing blight and woe to him, making him a blot in the face of his Maker. Was it not so that Jesus said to the Samaritan woman, "He whom thou now hast is not thy husband?" Not to triumph over her, not to win a soldier to virtue's side merely, not to vindicate the truth of purity even, but to wipe away a sister's stain and bring her back to his father and her father in purity. "I preached, yesterday, of hell and sinner's desert of it," said a young minister, on Monday, to McCheyne. "Did you tell them of it with tears?" was the answer. Were there not tears in Christ's soul when he said to the woman, "He whom thou now hast is not thy husband." So have the great lovers of God and his truth ever opened the faults of men. "Of whom," says St. Paul, that ardent lover of the truth, that fearless rebuker of sinners, "of whom I tell you, even weeping, that they are the enemies of the Cross of Christ." What a power there is in such words, the power of truth, the revelation of sin's vileness and guilt, the faithful words of reasonableness charging men with their faults, but mingled with it the sweetness of love that yearns for the lost to be saved, the vile to be cleansed.

Let us sum it all up. What have we seen in Jesus talking with the Samaritan woman? The picture once more of the sweetness and reasonableness of him who came to seek and to save the lost; his lofty faith in man's capacity to answer to the highest truth; his sympathy with lowly human ways and thoughts; his patience as of the perfect with the imperfect, and above all the tender severity of his love which charges the sinner with his sin to save him from it.

Is not that a wonderful picture which St. John has drawn of Christ by the well healing the misery of a poor sinner by his sweet truthfulness?

Two lessons we draw from this study of Christ's way of dealing with men: lessons about the relation between him and men.

1. That we are to study Christ as God's Revelation, not by himself, but as he is seen among men. That is only carrying out the great truth of the Incarnation. St. John says: "No man hath seen God at any time; the only begotten Son which is in the bosom of the Father, he hath declared him." It is God manifest in the flesh who shows us God. But no solitary man tells us what man is, we must see men as friends, sons, brothers, neighbors, to open the riches of human nature. And, so to know Jesus we must see him not

only on the mount praying, but by the roadside helping. This poor Samaritan, that lonely Zaccheus, the weeping woman in Simon's house—these are the torches which throw light on the depths of Christ's character. You would see Jesus like Mary, you would sit at his feet and hear his word; but you cannot see him perfectly so. That is the one defect of that wonderful book, the "Imitation of Christ;" it pictures a Saviour followed and imitated in solitude, apart from men. But it is only as Christ is seen in contact with men that he reveals the deeper nature of God. You must see him among the poor, the sick, the heart-broken, the perplexed, the lost. And he is still going on his way among men, dealing with their hurts and miseries. What a freshness, brightness, and power appear in him as we go with him to save men. A Sunday-school teacher, patient with the poor imps and restless midgets from the alleys, a worker among the poor and diseased, a symyathetic soul open for perplexed, tired men to come and drink in comfort— these see Jesus.

2. We are to study man in the light of Christ's presence. The disciples "marvelled that he talked with the woman." But they learned there something about women and Samaritans they never knew before. Our fellow-men are the most repulsive or the most attractive of God's creation according as we visit them in Christ's company or without it. I do not wonder that so many strong natures become pessimists, cynics, misanthropes, skeptical of human good, who study

society out of the light of Christ's eye. There is no power of sympathy and pity in us that can resist the steady gravitation of human evil to draw us down either to despair of men, or else to despise them. Take such a pure and humane soul as George Eliot's: if ever any one had a natural feeling for human need and human worth it was she. But she saw men without any illuminating vision of Christ by them, and how steadily the vein of bitterness goes on increasing in her books! The only help is to take Christ with us to men, and to read them continually in the light of hope which shines on them from his eye. Our prayer must be, "Lord, lift up our eyes to see the field thou seest white to the harvest; draw us close to thy side to see men as thou seest, to love them as thou lovest, to be faithful to them as thou wert." There was an old theologian, I am sorry to say he was a Lutheran, whose daily prayer used to be, "Replenish me, Lord, with the hatred of heretics." That is just the opposite of the spirit with which Jesus, as he sat on the well, talked with the heretical Samaritan woman. Let us Lutherans of to-day pray in his own blessed temper, "Fill us, Lord, with the love of lost souls!" Then, as we see his eye bent on them with penetration and pity, we shall learn the worth of unworthy souls: then, as we mark the Divine image brought out by his creating breath, we shall see the glory of Jesus the Saviour of men!

## THE CURE OF CAREFULNESS.

PHILIP. IV: 6, 7. "Be careful for nothing; but in everything by prayer and supplication with thanksgiving let your requests be made known unto God. And the peace of God, which passeth all understanding, shall keep your hearts and minds through Christ Jesus."

One of the most distinctive marks of the Bible is its power of enlarging human nature. It is like electricity, which draws out of substances new energies. The battery is applied to a dull metal, and up starts a brilliant flame, a powerful gas. So the Bible comes to man, and he rises up a new being. Consider what the Old Testament did for the people of Israel, how under its touch a mob grew into a nation; and remember what the New Testament did for the decaying empire of Rome, how it breathed on the cowardice, the baseness, the despair of that wretched time, and there sprang up the courage and purity, the piety and hope of the Christian church. So it has always been: count on your fingers the nations that to-day are leading the van, thinking the new thoughts, giving the world its daily shove forward, and you have counted up the nations that have most deeply drunk in the spirit of the scriptures.

The secret of this singular power of the Bible is in its daring treatment of human nature. It has been said that Christianity is a religion of weakness; that it appeals only to the poorest part of man. On the contrary it is the religion of strength; its treatment of man is heroic. It is not what is crushing and emptying in the scriptures that stirs the heart; it is not Christ saying, "You are lost; you are nothing; you must give up," who brings men to a new life; but Christ saying, "Arise! you are redeemed; behold the greatness of the life you may live!" The scriptures really discover man to himself: like Columbus, they sail away from that old world we know so well, of our sin and misery, of our weakness and despair, to the broad new world of our possibilities, our redeemed nature. What a strange realization of this there is in every true conversion! When I see the change wrought in men by the truth of God; how a selfish, indolent, petty nature can suddenly rise up into a new hope, a great aim, a consecration and sweetness of which before it had nothing, it is like a star flashing out of the dark. If the Bible had taken the measure of us that we take of ourselves, and called men to do only what they could do easily, it would have failed. But God's call to a duty, a hope, is also a vision of a great possibility, and a promise that the vision shall become a reality. Whatever God commands us, brethren, we may be sure we can do.

The text sets before us one of these Divine impossibilities. It is made up of a command and a promise: the command seems impossible, "Be careful for nothing;" and the promise seems impossible, "the peace of God shall keep your hearts and minds."

1. How desperate seems the duty commanded: "Be careful for nothing." Only those who have never really grappled with the facts of life will think it easy.

As soon as we begin to live in earnest, to have real interests, then carefulness comes. Care is the shadow that cleaves to the substance of life; and by yourself you can only get rid of the shadow by getting rid of the substance. Have no strong love for anybody; desire nothing; do nothing; hope for nothing with a manly vigor—and you will escape all carefulness. But a thin, careless, uninterested life is not the fruit of the gospel. Christ does not make life unreal, but more solid, more real. It was so in the early Church: "Do you see a soldier more obedient, a mechanic more diligent, a mother more devoted? Be sure," says one of the Fathers, "that one is a Christian." It is so now: to make a real Christian of a man is to increase his force every way; it makes him more diligent, more enduring, a more real man at home, in the shop, at the polls, everywhere. Some, however, read the words, "Be careful for nothing," to mean care for nothing; and so they set to work to pare away the ordinary interests of life, shutting out the world, as they say. That used to be the old-fashioned way men escaped carefulness, by caring for nothing. And that was a kind of Christian stoicism. But our dangers to-day lie in quite another direction. We do not need to be convinced that the world must be used, that we must live in it, and live strongly in our use of it; there is no danger of any of us becoming ascetics. I only wish there were more danger of it. But the problem for us is how to take strong hold of life here, and not let it take hold of us—how to use the world to the full and not abuse it.

The text, brethren, tells us how to do that. It sets us the impossible task, and then reveals the power by which to achieve the impossibility.

The secret of getting rid of carefulness is to have all our interest in life resting on God. True; every real interest of life does at last rest there, whatever we may think about it. We often forget that: we look at men absorbed in business, in science, in art, in social life, and it seems to us as though their interests were wholly cut off from God. We think of them, we speak of them as men "without God in the world"; and so in one sense they are; but after all the real solid interest of their occupation has its support in God. It is his truth they study, his laws they are working, the relation to their fellow which he has established that furnishes their joy. The interest of life, for all of us, in the deepest sense, does rest on God. Do what we will, we cannot get away from that broad basis of life. But oh, the difference between having that basis, and consciously resting on it: it is the difference between the childlike freedom from all carefulness of the Christian, and the anxious attempt of the unbeliever to be his own providence. The secret of a quiet heart, then, is to feel that foundation all the time solid beneath us and our load. And this is the great thing the Bible does for us—it gives us a real living grasp of this knowledge of God, our Helper, our life, the soul of our being: "*This is life eternal, that they might know Thee, the only true God.*"

See, first of all, how it puts into us a positive force

with which to keep carefulness off at arm's length. Part of the secret of the power of the Bible is that it does not treat our sins and miseries with negatives. It does not merely say, "Thou shalt not"; but brings a positive life; it adds something; it says, "This is the way, walk ye in it." It never calls us to fight a sin, but it puts into our hands a sword to fight with; it never tells us to give up anything but it has a better to put in its place.

And so its cure for the misery of carefulness is to find for us a new strength to put under our burden. Call to mind for a moment how worldly friends advise you in times of anxiety: they come and hear your trouble, and then they sympathize, and that is something; even a blind, silent sympathy is some relief, so great is the power of love; but as for light, for wisdom, for effectual help they say, "Do not worry; you must not think about your troubles; you must not look forward." There they stop; they can only say "don't"; but God comes and says "do." Hear what Christ says to the anxious crowd, "take no anxious thought"; that is merely negative; it shows what we must not do; and then he goes on to give them a positive thought, a vision, a pledge that crowds out the anxious care, "*Your Father knoweth that ye have need.*" He sees the despondency of the disciples, and he says, "Let not your heart be troubled"; but to that he adds at once a positive support, "Ye believe in God; believe also in me." And now the message the Apostle brings in the text is in the same line; "Be careful for nothing"; that is only a negative; that only shuts the gate on the way we *are not* to go; but right by he opens another gate, into the way we are to go, "in everything by prayer let your requests be made known to God." God does not say merely "don't worry," but he says, "Come to me; tell me your need; rest on my strength."

So, my brother, in your anxiety about your children, your health, your business, when you feel yourself eaten up with troubled thoughts, and you are ashamed of it and wish you could get free, you are not to try to cast out these thoughts by main force. What is the use of saying to yourself, "I ought not to worry: I must not; I will not." No, you must take hold of something positive; you must grasp God's provided strength and expel carefulness by the sense of God's care for you: let it sweep over your soul as the evening breeze blows over the heated city. And this is the positive force with which you are to meet this positive evil of carefulness—"in everything let your requests be made known unto God." But this, you say, is only telling you to pray, and you do not feel sure that God will always give you just what you pray for. No, I hope we never shall have that kind of assurance, the remedy for carefulness is not an unlimited permission to draw on God for just what we fancy we want. What a superstitious idea of prayer that is, that every man is to get just what he asks for! What egotists, what stagnant creatures, such a power would make us. The savage in the South Seas suns himself in perpetual summer and plucks his bread ready made from the branch above him, and there he stagnates: and a spiritual kingdom where prayer was only a hand put up to pull the wished fruit off the ever-ready tree would make us in the kingdom of God what the South Sea islander is in the kingdom of this world, a do-nothing, a cipher. Prayer is not a charm to bring God to our side to do just what we want, as the slave of the lamp in the story, but it is the gate that brings us to God.

In the text we see how the apostle includes in his remedy all that men commonly think is the help they can get by prayer, and a great deal more. He does not say, "pray for what you want and you shall have it;" but he shows how coming to God is asking and seeing and finding and being taken up into the great peace and blessedness of God himself. It is as if a sick man, hearing of a great physician who had a certain famous medicine, should come and ask him for it, and the physician should look at him and say, "Come with me and I will cure you," and the man should make reply, "But will you not give me 'the medicine?" and the physician answers, "Yes, if the medicine is needed, that you shall have too, but you need more than that," and then should take him with him to the high hills, where he lived, and so set him in the right track and give him the benefit of his skill and cheering presence till he was strong again. Now men go to God to get a particular medicine: "Give me trade," says the harassed merchant;" "Give me health," cries the invalid;" "Give me back my child," prays the anxious mother; and they want nothing else—nothing else will do. But God is the soul's physician, the healer who has life in himself to give to all. And so the apostle sends us to him. "*Let your requests be made known unto God.*" How broad that is: "*by prayer,*" i. e., by committing our whole case to God, by casting the burden of life down at his feet; "*by supplication,*" i. e., by asking for the particular thing you think you need: that is not excluded. Go and ask; it may be the medicine you think will heal is the one God sees is good, and he is only waiting for you as a child to ask. God can, and often does in his good wisdom, give the particular thing we ask. Let us believe that with all our heart, while we still cling to the higher view of prayer, its spiritual answer. How many have gone to God with their one request, and got it! "The prayer of faith shall save the sick;" Elijah prayed for rain, and the rain came. It is good even to agonize for the desired blessing, yes although, at last it be withheld, even as Christ prayed till the bloody sweat ran down, as St. Paul prayed again and again that the thorn should go.

Just at this point, by a single word, the Apostle suggests the entirely unexpected way in which our load loses its heaviness as we are bringing it to God. "In everything let your requests be made known unto God with thanksgiving." "With thanksgiving:" how strangely that sounds here! It changes the key from complaint to praise. How impossible that seems. But that is really St. Paul's own history. "There was

## THE CURE OF CAREFULNESS. 139

given me a thorn," he says, "and I besought the Lord thrice that it might depart, and he said to me, My grace is sufficient for thee. Most gladly, therefore, will I rather glory in my infirmities. I take pleasure in them."

What a great truth there is here: the truth that God, in discovering himself to us, discovers to us our real selves; that as we touch him a new continent rises on the soul's horizon, and we are led out into a new, great experience. We go to him with a load, but as we go we come into a strange, fresh strength. In his presence something strikes through our pain that makes us half forget it is pain. It is as if a child should miss a plaything and run to its mother in another room to beg her to find it, and when it came where she was, should catch a glimpse through the open door of the garden full of flowers and birds and sunshine, and at that sight lose all care for its toy. You can not really come to God and not find how much deeper your life is than in your narrow carefulness you had felt it. This ought to blend with our prayer when we are very anxious. You go and cry to him of the one thing that troubles you; you have only a monotonous wail; but how can you really see God, and be conscious of nothing but your own little worry? Do you not see *him*? Lifted up here by his side, do you not see the great horizon of life? You are in the shadow, but can you not see the sunshine lying wide and far beyond? Is there not in your heart even now a great peaceful depth lying below this flurry of pain, as under the storm on the sea lie the deep, unmoved abysses? Surely a Christian must feel that when he is before God! Or if he does not have it now, yet that is his possibility; he may have it; it is what he should set before him as his aim.

Let us think for a moment how that experience grows. A man comes in the pain and darkness of his trouble and begins to pray. At first it is all only a dim groping in the midst of suffering, a trying to find the hand that holds the balm. But in the groping there comes a sense of all that God has done, of his patience and pity: it is like the faint coming of dawn, and then we falter out our thanks; with our complaints we mingle praise; and so with that thought of his goodness comes the vision of himself. He stands over us, and we are conscious of the great reality of God, and that of itself is balm to our hurt: the sense of it comes down like the soft light of the stars in the dark night. We seem to hear from the throne, "*Be still and know that I am God.*" Oh, my brother, if you have gone to God with your cry, and have come away only with the thought that you have or have not got your little petition, it seems to me you must have missed the real meaning of prayer. As if a man should have met General Washington, and only remember that he gave him a dinner which was or was not, as the case may be, very good. How you would wonder at such a man! Well, you ought to wonder at yourself, that you go to God and come back, and see nothing but the gift he puts into your hand.

I have tried to bring out the Apostle's cure for over-carefulness; that it is really resting our burden of life on the broad base of God's fatherly care for us. That is what is meant by "making known our requests;" it is falling back on God; it is losing our littleness in the sense of his greatness. You remember how Elisha's servant was crushed with the terror of the hostile army that suddenly surrounded their quiet home in Dothan, and how at the prophet's prayer the servant's eyes were opened, and he saw, and "behold the mountain was full of horses and chariots of fire round about Elisha." That was the end of all his anxiety. Now, that is the Apostle's message struck into actual life; the highest gift of prayer is not to bring us God's strength and help, these are always encamped about us, but to open our eyes to the heavenly vision, to throw wide our souls that the Divine peace may enter.

This brings us to consider another thought of the text, the promise of God's peace. And what a great promise that is! "Bring your anxiety," says the Apostle, "to God, with thanks for his goodness and entreaties for his deliverance; cast your carefulness on him, and then the peace of God shall possess you." The word we have in our translation, "keep," has a figure in it; it means to stand sentinel, to keep guard over. Life pictures itself to the Apostle's mind as a camp; without the foe, within is the mixed host of a great army, good and bad, loyal and mutineers; what a condition of insecurity, of alarms, of sudden changes! But round the camp march, the vigilant sentries; through the streets paces the patrol; the peace of God shall be our sentinel; God is on picket over the wild host: he "shall keep your hearts and minds." It seems almost impossible there should be such a power in our lives. It is only a dream, a beautiful vision seen by the Apostle in some high-wrought hour; or, it is for a great saint, a Paul, an Isaiah, or the Mary that sat at Jesus' feet. It cannot be for me, a common man, tossed in life's battle, soiled and troubled. That is what we say; and that is the first thin edge of a very old heresy, the heresy that there are castes and inner circles, a spiritual aristocracy in Christ's kingdom, that some truths, and graces and promises are for a chosen few. It begins in a disbelief that such truths as those of the text can be meant for ordinary men. It crops out in the apparent flattery, but real self-excuse of the layman to the minister: "Yes, you may live purely, and have such peace, for you are sheltered; but I in my work, never." It sounds from men in every calling, as when the merchant says: "One cannot do business and not worry." All this skepticism of the possibility of having a deep peace in ordinary life, grows out of our blindness to the strength there is in God. What makes it possible to have a great many things to care for and yet not be anxious about anything? Why, it is the sense of God's presence with us, the vision of life in him, the touch of his hand on us felt quieting the throbbing of the heart. And that is the very remedy the Apostle offers, "in everything by prayer and supplication with thanksgiving, let your requests be made

## THE CURE OF CAREFULNESS.

known unto God." Is this fanciful? Is it an extravagant idea of prayer which common men cannot take in? No, it is only the idea of our venerable catechism, the idea contained in the answer you gave as a child, when to the minister's question, What is prayer? You replied: "Prayer is conversation with God;" a conversation, a communion, an interchange of thought and wish and emotion. Think of it!—to come in contact with God, to see him, to hear his whisper in the soul, to be conscious of his presence, to be possessed by him. What may not that do for me? And then I read of what it has done; of Moses casting the burden of that great people on God; of the timid Jacob wrestling with God and prevailing as a prince; of Paul groaning under his thorn, and then rising from prayer to rejoice in his pains; and so down the long line of the troubled that have in prayer found the peace that could keep them, even down to my own experience, and how can I be unbelieving? If a man can really come to God and tell him his requests, really pray, then the peace of God shall keep him; it shall stand sentinel over the camp of his heart, and hold back every skulking foe, quiet every brawling passion.

We may understand, I think, from what the sympathy of men in our anxieties does for us, what God can do.

You go to some fellow-man with your cares, and you make known your anxieties: you know he can not relieve you; you do not believe he can tell you of any help; but you unfold your story. And he listens; he says a few words that really tell you nothing: he feels himself how helpless he is. But somehow or other you go away lightened; you have lost something of your heavy load simply by the telling. And it is not a mere fancied relief. You have unconsciously got hold of one of the great pillars of life: by opening your heart to a true fellow-man, you have got a real though imperfect support. In some dim way you realize that you are not alone: you are made aware that men are a brotherhood, and that the care and burden of one is the care also of all; and by your contact with this man and his sympathy, the strength of the human brotherhood has slipped into your soul. You have got a real strength, one that he is not conscious of having given, but that he has given none the less. And he is vaguely conscious of a weight that has come on his shoulders from your contact and his own sympathy: and it is true; the weight of thought, of foreboding, of feverish fret has been distributed. But the brotherhood of men is only a corollary, a consequent truth from the deeper relation of our sonship to God. Men are our brothers only because God is our common father. And what the brothers do for us by sharing our burden, that in an infinitely greater way God does for us, not by sharing the load, but by wholly taking us up into his strength.

You get some relief by going to men—a brief, temporary relief. What that ought to teach you is to go up higher; to leave the image and come at the actual; to leave the partial and grasp the complete. You say, " Oh, I have sought for human help and sympathy, and it only goes a little way." Yes, it does go only a little way, a very little way; and therefore you ought to make known your requests to God, who has given your fellowman the ability to bear even a fragment of your burden. Now turn to him. If a man had known only the light of the moon, and complained that it was too feeble, and then learned that this feeble light was the reflection of a greater, would he not seek the sun?

Believe me, when the Apostle rises from his negative of "be careful for nothing," to the direction, "let your requests be made known to God," he is really leading you to the gate which, once opened, lets in a new flood of life upon our being. Behind that lonely, seeking, unburdening hour of prayer stands the great angel of God's peace, with the soft cool hands that laid on the aching brow make it cease from throbbing, that touch the tired eyes and they see into the far, glorious vistas of the eternal, that unbar the soul and let in the presence of God himself. That is the real meaning of prayer: it is the magnetic chord that touches God's heart at one end and ours at the other, and sends down his life through us; it is the blank door, on this side of which is the darkness and the dumbness of life all to ourselves, but pushed open lets in the glory and voiceful fullness of a Divine presence.

Do not think, then, so much of God's gifts as of himself: not so much of what he may do for you as of what he is. I believe the surprised experience of thousands of souls is that they go to get something of God, and in the blessedness of being drawn to the Giver's breast, forget what they came for—as Saul went to search for his father's asses, and finding the great prophet with the kingdom that he promised, went back indifferent to what he sought. That is really a sweeping up—not to get one's desires, but to rise above them.

I would have you, then, come into the secret of the Lord, and be kept "secretly in a pavilion from the strife of tongues." What I could wish for you, my anxious brother, is not that your burden may all pass, or that God should certainly give you the one thing you are crying for, but something much larger and deeper, an eternal gift—that you may find him, that you may be able to see him and know his presence there, to tell all your need with prayer and thanksgiving; in one word, that you may really pray. And then his peace shall keep you: "the peace of God which passeth all understanding shall stand sentinel over your heart, and every foe shall flee away!"

## ETERNAL LIFE.

JOHN XIV. 19.—"Because I live, ye shall live also."

No word that Christ uses about himself is so inspiring and satisfying as this word "Life." It expresses the greatness, the fulness, the sufficiency there is in him for men. Whenever he speaks it, or it is spoken of him, there comes with it a sense of expansion, as though our horizon widened and the clouds lifted from our path. At the very sound of it we seem to feel the current of our being grow deeper and stronger.

See how it is he uses it, as he comes to one and another drooping spirit. With this word he dispels the despondency of Thomas when he puts that melancholy question of doubt: "How can we know the way?" "I" answers Jesus, "am the way, the truth. I am the life." It is with this that he cheers the despair of Martha at the tomb of Lazarus: "I am the resurrection and the life." And when he comes to the Apostle in exile in Patmos to show him things that must be, and give him the last message to the churches, it is with this word that he raises his mind to the height of the great vision to be unfolded: "I am he that liveth, and was dead; and behold, I am alive forevermore."

The text, then, gives us a great thought; the thought of essential life. That thought, apart from what that life may be to me, or may do for me, is full of inspiration and strength. For we must remember who it is that says this. It is he who in the beginning of John's gospel is set before us in that majestic vision of things Divine, as the word that was with God, and that was God; it is the Eternal Creator by whom all things were made, and without whom was not any thing made that was made, "In him," pursues the record, in him was life." Here then is the absolute life; life that depends on none but itself; a being unwasting, unchanging, ever full, ever glorious, ever overflowing. Let us say, for the moment, that it does nothing for me, that I can only gaze on it as a far-off star, whose glory and strength must always be outside of my history. And yet the influence of that vision does bring help. The very thought of such fulness and permanence of life is to the soul like the buttress to the wall, it fortifies it; it braces it up, and gives it solidity.

For this world of ours seems so unstable. It is all shifting and changing. At first, when we are young, we are struck with the permanence of things. To the boy the years are endless in length: he can hardly see from one end to the other. And everything seems to continue unaltered. It is a fixed world to him with only a few sluggish currents of movement that only make the general permanence of things the more conspicuous. But presently, as he grows older, the fixed mass begins to move. The old frame of things is changing; old faces are going and new ones coming. It is not, as he once thought, a solid mass; it is fluid. It moves faster and faster. And before he has come to middle age, life has come to seem a quicksand in which all things are being swallowed up. And that experience brings with it a depressing influence. We naturally seek for some central point which remains; we long for some foundation on which our thought of life may rest. But where shall we find it? We change: our bodies, they are not what they were a few years ago. A man in mid-life takes up a picture of himself as a lad: he can hardly find a feature there that is his now. All that is gone forever. And he feels that what he is now, in a few years more, will have gone in the same way. He feels as though his solid flesh and blood were fluid; they are shifting and changing as the water in the stream. And our thoughts and tastes are changing, too. We have not the same minds we had ten years ago. You put away a book on your shelf that greatly pleases you; you want to keep it, for it speaks your deepest, truest thought to you; and then after a few years you take it down, and as you turn over the pages you wonder where the light and power you once felt in them have gone. Well, you have got another mind; you have traveled past that; and you put back your author on the shelf sadly feeling that one strain of thought has been swallowed up. And our affections—they are going, too. You meet an old friend that once answered to you sympathy for sympathy, regard for regard; but as you talk you miss something: the fire has gone out—only ashes are there. You and he accord no more; and when you part it is as though you were coming away from the grave of an old friendship. It has gone. What tragedies these changing affections make! Many and many a brother grows away from his brother; many and many a husband and wife, who live together in peace, have buried the early love. Each has changed.

And if we turn away from ourselves to look out on things that are fixed—society, trade, politics—it is another world than that we knew when we were young. How often a man feels as though he were a stranger in a world that he has been living in all the time. The old merchant says, "I cannot do business in these days: everything has been so altered." The old politician can not accommodate himself to the new ideas of statesmanship; the new watch-words are all strange and awkward to him. The old preacher finds his sermons out of fashion. And they all feel as though the world had left them before they were dead. The very lessons of history grow useless: we turn to the old story of the struggles and problems of men in the ancient world; but we find they do not fit into the struggles and problems of to-day; new situations and needs have sprung up that the old experience does not meet. But surely something is fixed: the solid frame-work of the earth, seas, and mountains, and rivers, and valleys? And then Science unrolls her map and shows how rivers have left their beds, and valleys disappeared—how the mountains are wearing down, and the seas forsaking their shores— and then, far on, in the future she puts her finger on the spot when this old familiar earth shall have disappeared, swallowed up in the shifting of the Universe. It seems all a bitter mockery, the coming and fading of a dream.

And then, to our perplexity and sense of mockery comes the word of Christ, "I live." Men do come and go; but Christ abides. Nations rise and fall, but the life of nations is the same. Worlds are framed and decay; but he that gave them being and form is ever young. "I am the life : *Jesus Christ, the same yesterday, and to-day, and forever.*" That, I say, is a great thought: it brings strength and solidity to life.

> "It fortifies my soul to know
> That tho' I perish, truth is so;
> That howsoe'er I change and range,
> Whate'er I do, Thou dost not change.
> I steadier step when I recall
> That, if I slip, Thou dost not fall."

But the text does more than show us the abiding life: it gives us a share in it. "Because I live, ye shall live also." What a fragmentary thing our existence seems to us at times. It comes; it brightens; it holds its place for a time; and then it fails; it fades; it is gone. What is your life? "It is even a vapor that appeareth for a little time, and then vanisheth away." I am sure that picture of life drawn by the apostle has struck us in some hours with its truth; it has seemed the only truth about it. And it has seemed such a sad thing: this life that we have so carefully cherished, that we have spent such pains to cultivate, that we have been building up so laboriously—it is after all only a bubble, glowing with bright changing colors, but presently to burst and vanish. And then, with the sadness has come the reckless mood; why take such pains with what after all must presently disappear? Why toil to achieve, to subdue self? Why not enjoy what we can, and make the most of our short day?

And then comes the vision Christ unfolds in the text—the vision of the great unending existence. Your life here, he says, is a vapor; but you are not a vapor. Soon all this scene in which you are moving will vanish, but you shall not vanish with it: you shall live—"Because I live, ye shall live also." And with his great word comes the assurance of our permanence in the midst of all this that is so impermanent. We see our life lifted aloft like frail fragments which the artist has set in the enduring mosaic; there on the great cathedral wall the bit of glass caught up from the rubbish was set ages ago, and there it looks down on the fleeting generations, on kingdoms falling and cities decaying, itself unchanged. And so as we hear Jesus repeating his solemn, eternal promise, we see our little flash of being caught up and set in its niche in his own unfailing existence: "Because I live, ye shall live also."

Now, if we look carefully at this we will see, I think, that two great truths about life are affirmed here.

1. Christ declares our conscious existence is to go on because his goes on. That is, it is to go on beyond death. The text is a part of Christ's declaration to the disciples of what will befall them after his own decease. "I go to prepare a place for you," he says: "I will come again and receive you unto myself." It is of his departure that he is talking, and he would show them how that departure is really no destruction of life, but only another stage in it. He is to die and go out of their sight, but not out of existence; not even away from them. "I will not leave you comfortless: I will come to you." He saw before him the cross, the tomb, and the resurrection. He looked through the shadow of death that fell across his path, and saw how it was only

a shadow, beyond which he should presently emerge into the light again. And then he declared that just as he passed through the shadow and came out beyond, so should they. Of course, they did not understand his words then. Nothing but experience could interpret them. But when the experience came, and they had seen him die, and then after their short despair welcomed him from the tomb again, would they not remember his words and feel that they had in them a guarantee of endless life? So St. Paul understood it and used it. When some at Corinth had doubts about the life beyond the grave, he wrote urging the very truth of the text, that Christ's life it is that guarantees ours: "How," he asks, "if Christ be preached that he rose from the dead—how say some of you that there is no resurrection of the dead? But, now, Christ is risen from the dead, and become the first-fruits of them that slept." Did he go into the darkness and come up again? Then, so shall we. He is the first to break those heavy fetters of death; but after him follow an innumerable company.

And that is the answer to the deep question of Job: "If a man die, shall he live again?" What a question it is! Men are saying now, many of them, that it is a foolish question, and has nothing to do with the real business and worth of life; that whether we live again or not makes no difference about the importance and rightness of duty here and now. I do not think so: it seems to me that the answer to that question will have a very marked effect on our view of what is duty, and what the great ends of life are; it is therefore a deeply important question even from a practical point of view. But at any rate, foolish or wise, men will go on asking it. Over two thousand years ago Socrates sat pondering it, and turning it over to get light on it; and by him, listening eagerly to his discussion, sat the most serious minds of his day. Within a few hours of death it seemed to him one of the worthiest occupations for the end of life to ask once more: "If a man die, shall he live again?" And men have been asking it ever since. Have we not all felt the point of that question at one time or other going home to the soul, as if it had never occurred before? At the grave when we were taking our last look at the coffin as the mould fell and hid it away, has it not come—"Shall he live again?" Or, when suddenly from the busy scene of life some one that has been busiest has gone, and we look up to see the face vanishing, to hear the door closing, and then as we feel the empty place, we have asked, "Is he still conscious; is he busy?" Then the question: "Shall he live again?" does not seem vain.

Jesus answers that question: "Because I live, ye shall live also."

"But suppose," says one, "I cannot believe that Christ does live; how will this saying of his help me?" It will not help you. The question of our life Christ has bound up with his own so closely that while if we really believe on him we have everlasting life, the glorious vision and the thrilling sense of it. Yet if we throw away his life, we with the same act reject our own. It is the very thing the Apostle says: "If Christ be not risen, your faith is vain." And so if we cannot believe him there is nothing left for us but blank darkness. Men think sometimes they have very good arguments for life beyond the grave, apart from what Christ was and said. But it is all a delusion. Let them once but fairly give him up, and as he passes out of their sight the world beyond will fade out of sight too. He it is that "hath brought life and immortality to light:" he holds the light at the door of the tomb, and it shines through so that we see the life beyond. But if you thrust him into the tomb and shut the door on him, the light goes with him. All this is only saying what Peter said to the rulers and elders: "There is none other name under heaven whereby we must be saved." No Christ, no eternal life.

But is it possible, looking at that bright, radiant, vital figure, to help believing, however it may be with the countless generations of men, the shadowy procession that files ghost-like through the centuries, that Christ lives? "I live," he cries, and his penetrating voice comes ringing across the ages, those dim 1800 years, as though it were but yesterday. We open the Gospels, and as we read, out of the pale pages comes a form, a presence, a person, a thrilling life: we see him the strange child in the temple, we watch him meekly following his parents down to Nazareth; we see the baptism, the descending Dove; we go with him about Galilee, listening to his stirring words, seeing his works, feeling his sweetness and holy beauty, wondering and lost at the marvellous vision. He is before us the perfect one, the spotless, the mysteriously holy, and yet no far-off angel, but the tender, smiling, weeping, suffering man. "Which of you," he says, "convinceth me of sin?" What a challenge for a human being to make to his enemies! And yet it has never been taken up. In the midst of that foul, dark age, he walks a stainless form, like some white angel of God treading the vile ways of hell—and yet no angel, but a sensitive, tender-hearted man. Whence, we ask, can such a being come? And he gives the answer, "I came down from heaven." And then the hearts of men acknowledged that claim. "We know," said the reluctant Pharisee, "we know that thou art a teacher come from God." "We believe," cried the warm-hearted disciple, "and are sure that thou art the Christ the son of the living God." How they clung to him! "Let us also go," said Thomas, "that we may die with him." "He goes," thinks the despondent disciple, "to almost certain death; but if he dies what is there worth living for? He will die; then let us die with him."

And he did die: contrary to every thought of all that clung to him, the grave closed over him. In the bewilderment that seized the disciples when they saw that he was really dead, we can read the conviction Christ had wrought in the minds of all that loved him, that death was something alien to him. It had never occurred to his disciples that he could die: he was the supreme life. Those three days were days of darkness that could be felt. It was not merely that they had lost a friend, a leader; it was life itself that was buried in Joseph's tomb: if Christ could die, then death must seize everything; it had seized everything. From that tomb there rose a mist that enveloped the green earth, the blue sky, the fair faces of men, the bright sunshine, with a pall of despair. They and the race of men were all doomed, waiting a little moment till the eternal tomb should open for them. And then when he rose, when they saw him, touched his hands, heard his voice, then life leaped up again, never to leave them! The grave that had been swallowing everything had proved unable to hold him: he lived. They had not been wrong in thinking him one that could not perish: he lived, and at his touch the spell of death, that had lain so long on the hearts of men that it had congealed them into despair of life, was broken forever. He might go away into the heavens now; they might watch him vanishing into the clouds, and the awful silence and emptiness of that absence might fall upon them, but it could not touch any more their sense that he lived. Life was with them forever. *"Because he lived, they should live also."*

"Well," you say, "it might be so for them: they had seen him; they had known him before death; and they had seen him after death. That will do for them; but it will not do for us: we have *not* seen him." But if we have not the sight of him, we have what they could not have, the sense of that same vital presence coming down undiminished through eighteen centuries of the world's history. If in the gospel there shines out a personality, a living force so strong, so pure, so vivid, that the simplest account of it is that it was God manifest in the flesh; then in the history of Christ's influence for all these ages we have a continuance, a persistence of the force of that personality, that is nothing less than life itself going on across centuries, over oceans, through races. It is idle to talk of the influence of great ideas, as if the power of Christ to-day were in his teaching, his morality; or of his system, as if the Christian world were moved by the force of his logic; for what makes Jesus Christ a force in the world now is the sway he has over hearts. In every age Christianity has been the power that swayed the world because of souls that echoed Peter's cry, "Lord, to whom shall we go? Thou hast the words of eternal life. And we believe and are sure that thou art the Christ, the son of the living God." As each generation came, it found itself confronted by a life, a presence, a person that claimed love and service: some refused, disdained; some resisted, struggled against the influence; but always a certain portion yielded, obeyed, loved, and found in that love and obedience an inspiration and joy and freedom that was like the wine of a new being taking possession of them. These souls it is that have made Christianity powerful. To them Christ lived; lived as truly as he did to Peter and John and James and Mary on the shores of the Galilean lake and in the home of Bethany; yes, more truly, for it was when Christ was known no more after the flesh but in the spirit, that he became most real: his life was more real to St. Paul, more intimate and vital, more the very breath of his soul, than even to Peter or John when they walked up and down Judea with him. To these millions, then, in every age, Christ has lived: thousands have died for him, not for his sermon on the mount, nor for his doctrine of God's fatherhood, nor for his atonement, no, but for him. Myriads have given up home and friends and all that makes life sweet for him; millions have for his sake and under the breath of his loving suasion broken away from vice, from selfishness, from pride, and tamed their hearts to his hand. And these have always been the living spirit of each age of the church. For one Peter or John or Mary that believed and loved him then, there have been thousands and millions in the ages after; and instead of that personal presence growing less after spanning 1800 years of history, there are more that believe him as thoroughly as Peter did, and that love him as deeply as did John, now than ever. It is a strange credulity that admits that Jesus lived to Peter and Mary and John, was alive to them long after they saw him buried, and does not admit that he was alive to St. Paul, or to Augustine, or to Luther, or to you and me.

Does Christ live to my soul? When he says, "I live," does my heart answer, "Yes, Lord, I know it: thou art more real to me than father or mother, than the solid earth; yea, than my own being"—does the truest life of faith and love and loyalty in me throb responsive to his word? Well, there, then, is the ground of my hope for what is beyond the grave. "Because I live, thou shalt live also." I know that he lives; I can as soon doubt of my own existence. You may reason me out of it; but it is like reasoning a man out of a belief in the external world: prove to him that he knows nothing outside of his own sensation, and yet he will slip back into the old confidence of the outer world, and go on as if there had been no argument at all. And so prove to me that my confident assurance that Christ sees me, loves me, hears me, answers me, is only a fancy of my mind; and when you are done, though I have no arguments, the conviction of that life, and my life in him, rolls its tide over all reasons, and he lives to me. And if he lives, then his word comes to me again, therefore, "ye shall live also." I don't know why this irresistible conviction of Christ's life above me, about me, in me, is not as reasonable as our irresistible conviction of the reality of the external world. Neither of them can be proved, and yet we cannot help believing both when we have experienced them. To a Christian, Christ's life is as real as the world about him; at last it becomes more real; for when the sky and hills, and the faces of dear friends, are all swimming and reeling into mist, dissolving and vanishing in the valley of death, then to millions that face and voice have grown clearer and more real, that presence has been the only stable thing.

This then is our only guarantee of the life beyond: and it is enough. If we have once leaned our weight on it in some hour of anguish, we have been satisfied that it is enough. When Schliermacher stood by the grave of his only son, and tried the various philosophical arguments he had been constructing in his hours of study for the immortality of the soul, every one snapped in his grasp, but this. In the fire of that trying hour every reason was consumed but Christ's own word. He heard Christ say: "I live," and then through the darkness he saw that in that life his son lived also.

2. But there is a deeper truth in these words: Christ's life is the guarantee of our spiritual life.

Because he lives the Divine life of purity and love, so shall we. It is not only life beyond the grave that Christ promises to us, but that promise wraps up in it the assurance of a higher form of life—life in its spiritual elements. We are not simply to be conscious after death, to think, and feel and enjoy; but that consciousness is to be a holy consciousness. It is not only that we are to live, but we are to live with God. We are not only to be, but to be in heaven. That follows from the ground of our hope of immortality: we are to live because Christ lives: i. e., our life is a direct stream from his. And as the fountain is, so must the streams be: if our life eternal flows out of Christ's life, it must be of the quality of that life. We are to be holy even as he is holy.

It is singular to notice how the desire for continued existence dies out of men's souls, as the belief in God and the love of God dies out. It is a sort of testimony to the truth that the physical and lower intellectual life are only the scaffolding or material of the higher, the life of faith and spiritual love, that when men lose faith, and break off from communion with God, the desire for life lessens. What is the use of the scaffolding when there is no building to go up: let it fall. And so men do let it fall. How little men care for immortality when all their life is earthly! Take the sensualist: what a feeble interest he takes in the question of a future existence—he thinks of going out at last like a candle with almost utter indifference. The godless workman at his bench discusses with his fellow workman what death is, and agrees with a sort of dull satisfaction that to die is only to become nothing. When one dies, he says, he is like a dog, that is the end of him. And the unbelieving philospher is on the same level with the ignorant workman. When Prof. Clifford, the great atheistic mathematician, was dying, he professed that he did not know whether he would live beyond the grave, and that he did not care. When Harriet Martineau was asked in her last days if she did not wish for immortality, she answered: "No," that she had had enough of life here, and did not care to have another. And why should they?—if life is only to eat and drink, to feel and know the facts of earthly existence, why should one want to go on trying it over and over again? Man was made to live with God, and that life is endless, inexhaustible; it is like a river that deepens and widens as it goes. But if there is no God, or if a man does not love him or live with him, then life loses its power of sustained interest; an existence here uses up its capacity for enjoyment; sixty years are enough. Life without God is like the river that flows into the desert, it is drunk up by the sands, every year it narrows and shallows; and at last it has no moisture left, and the man at threescore, says, " I am weary of the world, I am weary of myself; let me sleep." Why should he want to wake, to try the weary thing over again?

We can go further: as the spiritual part withers and is paralyzed, leaving only the animal and the lower intellectual, we should expect men to lose their attachment even to this life. And so it is: what a strange fact is the indifference with which the more irreligious races of men front death! The Chinese, for instance, are the nearest to a people without a religion that can be found among the great races; they are practically atheists, with no belief in a future life; and there men are to be found who are willing to sell their lives for a paltry sum of money. Criminals can buy men for a few dollars to go to the place of execution in their stead. What does it mean but that as the soul loses its grasp on God, it loses its grasp on life?

Now turn to the other side: Where is it that life is most prized? To whom does it grow more and more precious? Surely it is among the nations that are called Christian. Just in proportion as a community receives the light of Christ's presence, does the sanctity of life grow more awful; because it is only in societies colored and possessed with the Christian idea that life reveals its deeper possibilities. And among those peoples it is to those specially who are most intimately Christian that life grows deeper and fuller on and on to the end.  Let a man love God, let him know Christ, let him live the life of faith and spiritual affection, carrying the consciousness of Christ's presence with him, and the longer he lives the more precious does this treasure of life seem to him.  The thrill of love, the blessedness of purity, the enlarging vision that charity brings, the deep incommunicable sense of the Divine presence, the brightening hope that is burning ever more ardently, all these enlarge existence; they give it infinite scope.  It seems such a great thing to be ever growing, ever loving more, serving more perfectly, adoring more devoutly: every year the man has climbed a higher range and looked out on a wider prospect; every year the treasure of the mysterious life with God has grown more unspeakably rich; and when the shadows of death begin to fall over his path, though the world does fade, and he is willing it should fade, that jewel of the Divine life in his soul shines brighter; in the darkness of the tomb it does but glow more deeply.  Ask him what he thinks of everlasting life, and his heart leaps up with an inextinguishable longing as he says, "It is to know God; it is to see his face; it is to be with Christ!"

Christ's assurance of life, then, is the assurance of deepening holiness.  "Because I live the Divine life of purity and love," he says, "ye also shall live it: because it is from me it shall go on deepening and broadening."  This assurance that our spiritual life has its root not in us but in one above us, is the very mark that distinguishes Christian righteousness from all others. There was virtue in the world before Christ came: the heathen had their saints, their exemplars, and in many qualities they attained a great perfection; courage, temperance, truth, justice—surely we find these scattered here and there through the history of paganism. And let us not fear to admit that outside the church, in men that are not conscious of any inspiration above themselves, great virtues are cultivated among us to-day. I do not believe, indeed, there is any goodness that has not its root in a Divine source: wherever there is any gleam of righteous living it is from him who, coming into the world from the beginning as the Light, lighteth every man. Of all such we may believe God says, as he said of Cyrus, "I girded thee, though thou hast not known me;" but it is a goodness unconscious of its source, it is a child that knows not its Father. And as such it is a one-sided, deeply deficient goodness: real holiness, as meekness, humility, spiritual affection, it knows nothing of; and as an orphaned goodness, having a father, but not knowing him, it is a melancholy goodness, doubtful of itself, not sure of its future.

Now the mark of the Christian character is that it knows its origin: "*by the grace of God*," it says, "*I am what I am.*" It is as though holiness were a light that revealed not only its own brightness, but also its source. Yes, that is the very truth about it: "Because I live," says Christ, "ye shall live also"; and then the heart of the believer answers back, "I live; yet not I, but Christ liveth in me."

What a sense of security and hope does that knowledge breathe into the soul! We are conscious that we are weak; we know there is much in us that is quite beyond our control; but above all distrust of the evil within, and over all the threatening roar of the tempting world without, comes the word of Christ, "Because I live, ye shall live also."

That word is not a mere figure of speech: it expresses a literal fact. It declares the life in our soul to be really the life of Christ; that to be his disciple is to be in him. How plain it is that Christ never contemplated the work of a mere teacher, the founding of a school or party, to be his mission. When Nicodemus came to him it was simply as a learner to a new instructor. "Rabbi, we know that thou art a teacher come from God." But Christ puts all his notions aside, "Except a man be born again, he cannot see the kingdom of God." What you need, he says, is not more light, a system of theology, a code of morals—not even shining examples, stirring motives, but an inner principle, a new life: "I am the life." He turns to his own disciples: "I am the vine, ye are the branches—abide in me, and I in you. As the branch cannot bear fruit of itself, except it abide in the vine; no more can ye, except ye abide in me."

Now I have tried to open this great saying of Christ to see what hope and strength it may yield. If we have really fathomed it, it seems to me, it does yield the truest strength and hope. It shows us that the life beyond the grave is safe; it is bound up in the undying existence of him that liveth, and was dead, and is alive for evermore. It shows us too, that the inner, spiritual life, for which all else is only the scaffolding and preparation, the existence of love and faith and goodness in us, is not something conjured up by our fancy, sustained by our resolution, the fruit of our conscience and will, but that it is a stream from the undying goodness, Christ himself. Every pious thought, every self-denial, every sacrifice for others, every triumph over temptation, every prayer lifting our hearts to God is a witness of Christ with us, in us. The light that is in us shows not only itself, but also the inexhaustible sun of righteousness from which it comes. What a thought that is, that every meek temper, every holy purpose, every faithful deed, has stamped on its bosom the image and presence of the invisible God! But is it not true? Look at what you are, my brother, at your consciousness that you do believe and love and serve God, at this conviction of loyalty which rises in your heart so that you can say with the Apostle, "Lord, thou knowest all things; thou knowest that I love thee"—and do you not know that this very love and trust is from above; that it is not you that live, but Christ that liveth in you?

Let us keep in mind, then, what our life is; that it issues forth from Christ's great Divine life—yea, that it is his own. We may not be always directly conscious that it is his, any more than we are conscious of the mighty force which is continually drawing the earth on in its course, bringing in their time the seasons, and the changes of day and night. Yet we have only to pause and think, and instantly we know it is so, that the earth does not move itself, nor by its own life bring summer and autumn. And so an instant's pause in the soul, and we know who it is that gives us spiritual life.

This ought to sanctify, too, and ennoble all the business of the Christian. Often, as we are conscious only of what is immediately about us, life seems a small thing, and our daily duties look sadly petty: we are buying and selling, writing and sewing, doing little things in a little place—it is all so little; so it seems to the mother, the teacher, the servant, the clerk. There is nothing great or worthy in it all: so it seems. But remember, in each small duty, if we do it faithfully, the life of the great God is beating through us. As the tiny wave laps up the beach of some narrow cove, what a little thing it seems; but it is the pulse of the great ocean rolling round the globe, it is the sweep of heavenly bodies pressing on that ocean that is pulsing in that tiny wave. What in our life of duty can be small, if only we feel it is Christ's life that is moving in us?

Finally, let this thought shine into our hearts with the light of a great hope. Life at times is like dwelling in a narrow court; no horizon beckons forth the gaze of the dweller there; no prospect, almost no sunlight appears, only sordid bounds, gloomy half-lights, and a sense of being shut in, buried in a narrow present. But if Christ lives, and I live with him, then a window opens in the dingy walls: I look beyond; the prospect of eternity sends its glory down into my narrow present.  When Jesus says, " Because I live, ye shall live also," then I look out on that eternal existence; the cramping bounds have disappeared: " It doth not yet appear what we shall be;" and the glory of the life to come shines down on my dingy to-day, as the sun shines down into the poor murky court, and lights up all its pettiness with the mystery and glory of light from heaven.  " It doth not yet appear what we shall be;" but this we know: " Because he lives, we shall live also."

## BOUGHT WITH A PRICE.

1 Cor. vi: 19, 20.—"Ye are not your own: for ye are bought with a price."

The text strikes a blow at one of the fondest dreams of the human heart—the dream of an absolute independence.  The boy dreams of the day when he will be a man, and when he comes to be a man, poverty is his master.  The poor man dreams of the day when he shall be rich, and when he is rich, society binds its fetters on him.  The rich man dreams of rank and office that shall give him independence, but in vain; and so the illusion goes floating before one and another.  Dreams, all dreams; there is no such thing as perfect independence.

We see this from the simple facts of life. Take the difference in freedom as the boy sees it looking forward, and as the man sees it who has come into it. The boy says, "When I am a man I will eat and drink what I please; I will go to bed and get up as I choose." He fancies he will have a free body and a free time. But he tries it: he does eat and drink as he pleases; he plunges into dissipation. His friends say, "That will not do; you must hold up"; and he fires up—"Am I not a free man? I am of age, independent; no one shall dictate to me." But one does dictate to him. His body dictates. It says to him after a debauch, "Lie there and ache"; and there he lies and aches till nature, that owns his body more than he, lets him up. Then, if he is not incorrigible he says, "I see my body is not my own; it will not serve me but as its Maker ordains. And my time is not my own: if I am idle in summer, then I must starve in winter." Life teaches him that much, and more than that. It teaches him that a man is not free to behave as he pleases towards others. The boy often thinks it hard that he has to learn rules of politeness, to be deferential to people he cares nothing for, to give way when he wants his own way. He thinks he will manage things differently when once he is independent. He tries that, too. He looks out only for himself; he shoulders his way through life, regardless of whom he jostles. He says, "Can I not do as I please with my own?—and my looks and words are my own." And then he finds that the man who goes alone will be left to go alone:

he has cared for no man, and no man cares for him. He finds life very cold and hard. It is reading him the stern, sharp lesson that a man is not his own: "A man that hath friends must show himself friendly." Perhaps he thinks he can be independent in religion. Why should a man be tied down to prayer and church-going and Bible-reading, to all this strictness?—and he goes his way reckless, pagan. But he finds that after all conscience is not his own: it will plague him for his reckless life; it gives him many gloomy hours; he is like a child—afraid of the dark in his soul. Independent in religion!—why, life before him and behind is hung with clouds of gloom. He finds that his conscience, his moral sense, his religious nature, call it what you will, is not his own.

I will go no further: I only say, all this means possession by another. Everywhere in life we run up against invisible barriers, but of adamant, that say, "Thus far and no farther." And it is not the Bible, prophets, and apostles that are saying this, but the common, hard facts of life. To the profligate, disease says, with every wrench of pain, "Ye are not your own; your body is not your own." To the cold and selfish, a lonely life without friends is repeating, "Ye are not your own; your behaviour is not your own." To the irreligious, the pangs of remorse, the emptiness of the soul are crying, "Ye are not your own; life is not your own!"

This, then, is natural religion, the law written in man's nature, built up in the structure of life. And this is a part of the revelation given in the Bible, as the foundation is a part of the building. "Ye are not your own," says the Apostle, "no man liveth to himself—we are members one of another." All this is natural religion. But the Apostle introduces a new element; he brings in the Christian side of the doctrine: "Ye are bought with a price." This takes us to Calvary, and bids us read the lesson in the light of the cross.

And now, what does the cross say to this dream of human independence? Whatever may be the facts about natural law, have we a right to ourselves? No, says the Apostle, for "ye are bought with a price." You were the slaves of sin, but Christ has redeemed you. You once had life and dropped it into the sea, and it has been rescued and given you again. And that has laid a great debt on you, the debt of gratitude. What a debt it is! God himself has suffered for you. You have been born to life again by a dreadful travail.

And this, says the Apostle, makes a deeper claim on us: here is something that your own heart will not let you disown.

We are not our own, because Christ's death for us has laid on us the claim of gratitude. Whatever else the cross may mean, and it does mean far more than we can ever fathom, it certainly means that. "Who loved me," says St. Paul, "and gave himself for me." He felt it: his whole life was a willing acknowledgment of the debt.

I do not pretend to show here all that Christ's sacrifice has done for us: St. Paul himself seems to stammer and stagger under the great weight of that thought of redemption; all the figures and comparisons he can gather, and he ransacks the universe for them, fail to express his sense of the greatness of the rescue: he was in darkness, and light of day had burst in on him; he was a prisoner, buried in his dungeon, and the deliverer broke open his prison-house; he was a debtor sold into slavery for his debts, and this friend ransomed him at an unspeakable price; he was an exile wandering in dreary, distant lands, and this messenger brought him home again. But one thing Christ's redemption does mean, it means restoration: one sentence of St. Peter expresses this most eloquently, "He suffered for sin that he might bring us to God." That sums up the greatness of our debt: we are restored. The gulf between us and God is bridged; the shadow is chased away; the distrust that sin distilled in the heart is abolished.

But now, suppose we have come back; suppose the barrier removed, the fear quenched, the old life with God re-knit, and that we are children in our Father's house once more. What an entirely new consciousness comes into our life. We are restored; we have lost something and got it again.

There is something in the experience of losing a blessing and then getting it back that makes the blessing doubly dear. You must part with your happiness, and receive it again, before you really know what happiness is. Suppose a man has never been sick, what does he know of the deep blessing of health? But he falls ill; he goes down into the dreary valley of nights of watching and days of pain; and then he recovers; and as he sits at the open window and sees the deep blue sky, hears the song of the birds, and scents the honeysuckle on the wall, he seems to himself never before to have known what life was. One hour now is fuller of joy than a week of his old rude health. He will never forget that experience, and he has learned it by losing a blessing and then getting it back. You think you love your child with all the sense of its preciousness it is possible to have; but if you have never watched it sicken and droop and fade away—never gone with it to the door of the tomb, and in heart given it back into the hand of God, saying, "If it be possible . . . but thy will be done"; and then received it back again as from the dead—then, I say, you have not measured all the depth of a parent's love. What must Isaac have been to Abraham when the father had seen his beloved son swallowed up as it were in the abyss, and then received him as one restored from the dead.

And now, to be a Christian is not simply to be a son of God; it is to be a restored son. Here, in our Father's house, cleansed and clothed and feasted, we remember when we were in rags and filth, and full of evil passions; and with every throb of love to God there comes to us this thought, "Ye are bought with a price." Do you think the Prodigal in the best robe, with the ring on his finger, sitting at the feast, did not have a thrill of grateful reverence as he remembered the husks he tried to eat, and the misery of that far-off land, such as the elder brother, who had never left the father's house, could not know?

But the Apostle goes farther; he impresses it on us that Christ's death was a service of love. It is difficult to find a theory of the atonement that will satisfy all minds. Perhaps we shall never agree on one that answers at all points. We cannot complete the circle. Our theory keeps up with the facts a little way, and then the lines diverge: we cannot make them fit our system. It may be we are trying to explain the inexplicable. What if we are seeking the neatness and lucidity of a geometric problem in a mystery much of the power of which is that we cannot understand it, that it fades away in the dim distance of God's impenetrable counsels? But one thing we know it does mean—it interprets to us God's unspeakable love. Christ's death is always figured in the Scriptures as :lowing from his deep pity. It expresses the love of the Father, and the love of the Son: in this the Father and the Son are one; "God so loved the world that he gave his only-begotten son that whosoever believeth in him should not perish"; . . . "he loved me and gave himself for me."

Here, then, is a great service of love rendered at a great cost. But every such service is a bond. It makes a debt; it takes hold of me. I know there are some who do not feel it so. Men may die for them, and never a throb of devotion answer back. There have been children who could let their parents toil and save and sacrifice for them, and never know one answering thought of gratitude. But that is not the natural law of the human heart. There is something in great masses of men that answers back to an unselfish devotion. This has made popular heroes along the ages of history. A man gives himself for his country, and his fellow-men recognize the debt; they sacredly cherish his name. Or a great benefactor dies for the cause of humanity, for the prisoner, the slave; and the human heart takes up his life and embalms it in loving songs and hallowed memories. What do we think of one who has had some great benefit procured for him by another's suffering, and then turns his back on his benefactor? Why, we revolt from him as from a moral monster. We wonder how he can be insensible to that bond. It is true that selfishness, worldliness, may overcome the power of such a bond: men may hear of a Saviour's death, and go away and forget it; they may refuse to feel it. But the natural thing is for them to acknowledge it, to be drawn by it. And this is what the Apostle appeals to when he says, "Ye are bought with a price." A man will often do for love what he will not do from any mere cold sense of duty. Many a young fellow when he steps on the Commencement stage cares for his success more because his father and sisters are caring for it, than for the thing itself. He struggles for them: their love and sacrifice for him are like a touch of life. What would the best of us be if that spur were taken away, if we did not feel the blessed bond of affection and service from devoted hearts drawing us to do our best? "We are bought with a price," if we may use such sacred words for the common ties of life, by our mothers and sisters and children, by our friends—by our servants, even. When the present Emperor of Germany was a prince, his coachman saved his life at the loss of his own. And now, how does the emperor remember that service? Years have passed, but at every anniversary of the servant's death the emperor spends the day with the widow and her orphaned children. He has provided for their wants; but that cannot satisfy his heart: he gives himself; and every year when the sorrowful day returns, he is with them.

So it is that Christ's death speaks to us. It appeals to our hearts. From the dropping blood, from the last cry on the cross sounds a voice, "Ye are not your own; ye are bought with a price!"

Christ's redemption of us, then, has brought us, as it were, into his possession. Gratitude, love, the great rescue, all are saying, "You are his." Perhaps there are some who revolt from this. They do not wish to be subjected to another. Those words, "bought with a price," sound to them like a bargain in the market: they are purchased; they are bound; they must obey. How many chafe against that! How many are kept from Christ because he is not only the Saviour, but also the Lord and Master. They are willing to be saved; but they want to be free. As if the greatest salvation of all were not a salvation from ourselves, from the lawlessness, the passion, the perverseness of our own wills!

I say, then, of Christ's possession of us by his purchase on the cross that it is a blessed possession. Not to be our own means something more than giving up our present life; it means the bringing of it into harmony with the life of Christ. We do not silence our will, we only set it to a higher key: "Who died for us that whether we wake or sleep, we should live together with him"—live!—mark that; not to give up, but to get; to live the great, full, satisfying life of Christ.

Here in a great hall stand a number of musical instruments. They are all silent, separate, each keeping its rigidity and key. But a musician comes in: he steps to an instrument and strikes a chord; and all through the room the silent instruments wake up; they answer; they have found a voice, and the swell of sound rolls through the hall; but it is not they that are speaking, it is the musician that by his stroke possesses them. Now man's nature is just such an instrument. It is strung for melody, but it cannot make music of itself; a man cannot chord his own life; it takes a stronger touch than his. Who is there of us that can master his own life? What a chaos of jarring passions, interests, wishes, riot in us till Christ stretches his hand over us and sets us to his own key!

Is there any true progress to our lives, anything that is built up in them, any plan other than the plan of a kaleidoscope, changing at every turn, until we submit to our Master and say, "Lord, possess me; set me right?" Suppose a man to have his own will;

he plans his life for money, or fame, or pleasure, and what comes of it? Does he go tranquilly on? Recall your own selfish plan; your purpose, and how did it work out? Did you not go forward like a ship in a sea full of currents? First this passion, then that interest, and then the other fear seized it, and drove it here and there. And if our own plan is accomplished, what a petty, unsatisfying thing it is! There is not a millionaire, or ambitious schemer, or successful man of the world, who when he gets his end does not feel it shrink and become something too small for him. He has possessed himself, and he is dissatisfied. No; himself he has never really possessed; he has had his own way, but himself he has never been able really to grasp. His nature is too great for his hand to master; none but one can set it in tune, and bring it out, and give it completion; none but he who bought us with a price that he might give us his own perfect life.

For Christ's possession of us is really an inspiration upon life. It is one thing to obey; it is altogether another to be swayed. Looked at from the outside to be not our own, to be another's, although that other be our Saviour himself, seems only a hard servitude. To be always doing another's will, forever crushing down our own, what a dreary prospect! But to be not our own, I say, is to be inspired by Christ. It is giving up tugging at the oar, to lift the sail and be borne on with the rush of the gale. For what is inspiration? It is to be breathed upon with an irresistible force. And to be Christ's is to be just so possessed, to be borne on by a new and vaster life. And that is a blessed state. What a great experience is an inspiration! a something descending on us! To be writing and feel a current of ideas breaking through our mind, so that we no longer hesitate, and erase, and rewrite, but let the pen race over the paper; to be speaking, and have a rush of emotion, of indignation, of enthusiasm, of pity, come to us, and sweep us on, so that it seems, not that we are speaking, but that another is speaking through us; to be at work, and by a sudden rush of motive to be lifted into a new strength—this is a great joy. And not to be our own is to be so inspired.

Even bad men have been able to inspire their friends with such a power. What a difference there is between the soldiers of some dull, wooden martinet of a general, and those of a great captain like Napoleon. The troops of the stupid, cold general obey him; but how lifelessly they march, how stolidly they go into the fight! It is a hard drudgery. But when the great emperor rides down the line before the battle, every soldier tingles with enthusiasm; every man is a hero; they are not their own; and when the order comes, they sweep like a living wave over the field. He inspires them. His great genius possesses the dull common men, and they have a joy and thrill in fighting his battles—even in dying for him. What a picture is that of the dying soldier on the field of Marengo, shot through the breast, painfully lifting himself from the ground as his general rode past, to shout with his last breath, fire flashing from his eyes, "Long live Napoleon." And if that great bad man could so possess men that it was a grand joy to be not their own, but his, what shall we say our great captain does for us? I say, brethren, it is a blessed thing to be not our own, to be bought by Christ's death, to be possessed by his life. So the great apostle felt when he flung away his own will, his own plan and prospect of life and cried, "I live, yet not I, but Christ liveth in me."

Let us turn back now and see how this great truth of our possession by Christ can be applied to life. For the final test of a great Christian doctrine is, How does it work? If it is only a beautiful dream, a splendid theory, a vision in the air, it is not of Christ, for he and his truth are for use. They are like the stars which shine with the glory of the infinitely far and yet guide our steps along the earth.

I say then in applying these thoughts that:

1st. This shows us how to meet the checks and disappointments of life.

Life is full of limitations; and experience is made up very largely of striking against them. Failures, losses, disappointments, blunders, wrecks—how full every man's path is of these! Look back on your way, and see how many barriers you have come to in your past; walls built right across your chosen way. I care not what your lot has been, rich or poor, high or low, gifted or feeble. Your experience has been one of having your will crossed, your plans thwarted, your purposes baffled. Think of the countless obstacles you have met, sickness, poverty, the death of loved ones, the failure of those you trusted, perverseness of children, the withdrawal of gifts. It seems sometimes as if we were in a ship that was beating against head-winds all the way across the sea of life. Of course, there are great differences in men's paths and in the temperaments of men themselves; but life to the most easy-going, I repeat, is full of hard passages. It is continually saying to our wills, "No!"

Now, what are we to do in such an experience? The best the world has ever been able to do for disappointed men is to give them the stoic philosophy; it tells us to remember that it has always been so, that it cannot be helped, that we must set our teeth and bear it. That is stoicism—cold, hard, hopeless, with no outlook, no explanation, nothing but submission; not to a kind, wise Father who sees the end from the beginning and who doeth all things well; but to fate, blind, hard, cruel fate. A man's child dies and philosophy says, "Have fortitude; you had him, and now he is gone; you must bear it." What consolation! dust and ashes for the thirsting soul! In the midst of joyful activities comes sickness, the end of one's lifework, a career wrecked; and what is the help? Only this—"It cannot be helped; bear it."

But Christ's possession of us puts another face on the disappointments of life. With the sense of that possession enfolding us, every loss and thwarting is only saying, "Ye are not your own; ye are bought."

Am I impoverished, bereaved, disappointed? This is God's use of me. My disappointment or failure is not an absolute disappointment or failure; personally, it is true, I have not done what I wished, I have not had my way; but then, that is no real evil, for I am not mine own—I am God's; and what seems waste is only God's hidden use of me. All things are in his hands; "he doeth all things well." In that *all* is my bereavement, my loss of health, my poverty—"all things well!" Am I poor? this is God's message to me: "Remember, you are not your own!" God will not have me rich; he will use me poor. Am I neglected, disappointed in the business of life? God is saying, "You are not your own;" you are to be laid aside; God wants you in obscurity. Am I lonely, friends departed, children gone—this is the solemn voice sounding out of the loneliness of life, "Ye are not your own;" God has chosen you for solitude.

But you will say, this is no help. And I answer: No, it is no help to one who does not know God. But to a child, to a believing heart, there is no greater, deeper help, than to trace its trial, its pain, back to the blessed will of God. It is not my business to find help or consolation for those who do not trust or love God. There is no help possible for such a soul; you might as well expect bloom and fragrance from a blossom that has been torn away from its parent stem. There is no consolation, no light, no joy in the wide universe outside of God. And if a man says, "But it does not help me to send me back to God; you might as well send me to fate, or to chance, or to an unconscious law"—then I can only say, " Poor soul!" If it be so, then there is no help for you; if God cannot supply your emptiness and put substance into your life, then there is none else can: "To whom else can we go?" If a man says, "Fate, law, chance, God, the Divine Father and Saviour, they are all one;"—then I say that contradicts the witness of all spiritual experience. No man ever went to fate, or to chance, or to law, when his child died, or his health failed, or his property was swept away, and was comforted, fortified. There have been thousands of stoics, but not one that was happy and peaceful in the day of trial; but there have been thousands who have gone to God at such times, and found in him refuge, light, life. You say in trouble, "Well, it cannot be helped; it is in the nature of things; I must submit;" and that is fate. Nothing answers back to that feeling, no sustaining power, no light. But say, "I am not my own; I am God's; I am bought with a price; Christ died for me, and this is his will, and I accept it; I take it for my own will;"—and then comes a flood of strength bursting in on the soul, uplifting it, inspiring it, filling it. There comes even more than this—then is felt the touch of a divine hand, the breath of an infinite pity, the warm pressure of God's own love; and we rejoice to live our disappointed, smitten, lonely life, because it is not we that live, but Christ that liveth in us.

2d. This shows us also what is the true joy of life; it is to recognize and accept the Divine Inspiration.

There is one way of happiness: it is to have our own way; to lay out our plan what we would like to have, and then go on and get it. Sometimes you hear it said, that there is no happiness in having your own will. But it is not true. We have all sinned enough to know that there is a certain fierce, terrible pleasure in the swing of a lawless will. When a man is angry and he thirsts for revenge, and seeks it and gets it, there is a wild delight in wreaking vengeance. When a man craves power and plots for it, clutches it, has it, and gives his wish full rein, there is pleasure. When a man will not brook contradiction, throws off restraint, and lets his will drive, reckless and determined, to its end, there is a satisfaction in it. If there were no pleasure in having our own way, would men seek to get it as they do? But this way of happiness is a false way; it begins well, it goes prosperously for a time; but gradually it fails. It is like the streams that flow into the desert, which begin deep and broad, and then dwindle away into the vast sands smaller and smaller, till they vanish. The other way is to be possessed of God, to have no will of our own, but to be taken up into his. And this just reverses the order of life from having our own will and way. The blessedness of being possessed by God is very small at first. "Ye are not your own"—how hard, how cruel that seems when we first say it to ourselves, and take it home in some agonizing loss, failure, misery. But it has a seed of life in it: it grows. Every submission to that divine possession opens the gate of the soul wider to God's entrance. It gives a keener hearing to the ear, a sharper seeing to the eye, and the pulse of the divine life beating through us becomes more palpable. We grow less, but God grows more. We are not having our own way, but God is having his way with us. His will is done in us, and that is the deepest of joys.

I say there is nothing in existence comparable to this experience of feeling the life of God throbbing through us, as St. Paul felt it when he cried, "I live, and yet not I, but Christ liveth in me:" it is as if one toiling along a lonely road should feel his own strength grow less, but suddenly by some new sense catch the rush of flight with which the solid globe is sweeping through space; he could afford to be weak while he felt that speed. And so to accept God's ownership of us in Jesus Christ, to say I am not mine own, I am bought with a price, is to catch the immense rush of life that issues from God; it is to be borne up on eagles' wings; this is to know God; this is life eternal. And will you not have that strength for yours? Will you not fling away that poor, weak self-will which clings so closely to its own independence, and yet is so slavish and helpless? If you would be really free and strong, if you would feel the sweep and scope of your true life, I bid you take Christ for yours. Let him possess you. Be rid of self; be filled with him. Let the love that has bought you claim its own. Be his; and then you will be most truly yourself.

## LIFE A PROBATION.

MATT. XXV: 14, 15, 19—"The kingdom of heaven is as a man traveling into a far country, who called his own servants and delivered unto them his goods. And unto one he gave five talents, to another two, and to another one; to every man according to his several ability; and straightway took his journey. After a long time the lord of those servants cometh, and reckoneth with them."

This familiar parable teaches the lesson of Probation, the truth that life here is a trial of what we are, and a preparation for what is to come hereafter. Here then is an answer to the question which every serious mind must at some time put to itself. "What is the great end of life? What am I here for? What is it all about? Some, it is true, do not ask it: they never seem to have a thought that life has any plan or meaning at all; they simply take it as it comes; they drift on with the stream.

But let us turn to the really serious, and what do they make of that question? Some say the great end of life is to enjoy. They may differ as to what makes enjoyment, but they agree in this, that we are here to get as much satisfaction and comfort out of living as we can. We are made, they say, with these appetites and desires for gaiety, excitement, gratification, and it is clear that our Maker intended we should satisfy them; and as life is short, the best thing is just to get all the pleasure we can. "Gather the rosebuds while ye may," they sing, and up to the table of life they rush, and seize the cups and brim them over. But what an end for a creature like man! It cannot be that we are here simply to enjoy each hour, to have pleasure; for if we were, why was a conscience given us? If we were made only to enjoy, then conscience lodged in each breast is a grand mistake. Conscience is always interfering with our enjoyments; it is the skeleton at the feast; it is the cold shadow that sweeps over the festal scene; it is the bit that pulls us up in the gayest hour. And our affections, too, those soft tender chords of the heart, how they interfere with pleasure. When we think how our hearts are wrung through our affections; how much more anguish comes through them than delight, who does not see how absurd the idea is that life was made for pleasure. If that were life's aim and purpose, we should have been made very differently—we should all have been made swine.

So of riches as an end of life: men go on accumulating, as if to add field to field, to be richer each succeeding year, was really a thing worth living for. But stand by the grave of some money-grubber, and as the grave-diggers shovel in the earth, think of what all that long, anxious, shrewd, active life has come to— to rake together a heap of wealth, and then at the touch of death to go and leave it all! Can that be the real end of living, is that what we are here for? Who can believe it? How absurd it seems!

Or, honor and fame; to climb upon a pedestal where all men can see us, and then when the crowd is beginning to gather, and the huzzas are about to go up, suddenly to be clutched by an iron hand and dragged away into the mist of the sepulchre, while men heap laurels on the pedestal where we stood—is that an end of life that seems satisfactory? To be a Robert Burns, and sing songs distilled out of the bitterness and frenzy of the soul, and then die in poverty and disappointment, and then years after we are gone to have the world praise us, and celebrate our birthday—is that worth living for? What good does it do him to be praised? How does it help that wretched, passionate, embittered life, that now the world knows he was a genius? Posthumous fame—what an end to live for!

Turn, now, from these theories of the end of life, and hear what the Great Teacher says, and what a difference at once we feel: we come out of mist into the clear; from the narrow, the petty, the unsatisfactory, to what is large and deep and adequate. Christ's view of life is that it is a probation, a time of trial, a preparation for something beyond. The whole of the Biblical view of life is lighted from above: it says in one way and another, the end of life is not here, it is beyond. "The kingdom of heaven is as a man traveling into a far country; he calls his servants, gives each his portion, and then he leaves them. There they are all to themselves: no one watches them, none checks them, none advises; they are free to idle, or revel, or abuse each other, or to do their duty; but it is clear enough what they are there for; they are to occupy for their lord, they are on trial.

Then after a time he returns, and he calls them to a reckoning: what have you done, where is your trust, how have you acquitted yourselves? Well, that is a picture of life; *our* Lord has given each his place and work and gifts; and he has gone away from us in the sense that we are left to choose our own way; and now what are we here for? What is the end of life? The end is the proving of us; it is something going on, incomplete, that never can be complete till we pass beyond to judgment. Life is a story of which we begin to read the first chapter; on and on we read, wondering how it will turn out, what is to come to the hero—when suddenly we turn the page, and the rest is gone, blank; death has torn it out; for the end we must wait and read the winding up in eternity. It is a problem; there the figures are set, and we are to work them out: we begin the process, we are making progress, but suddenly the slate is snatched from our hands, the problem is wiped out—we must wait for the answer till the great reckoning of God solves it. It is a building of which we see the foundations, and the half-reared walls, enough to know there is a plan and a purpose, enough to make us eager to have it explained; but midway the builder is called away, there is no completion here: the end is beyond.

But some one says, what a hard view of life that is; it is too stern and sombre! And to that we have to answer, that it is sombre: it is impossible to look at life as a probation, a trial and school to test us and fit us for a life beyond, and then enter on it as on a pleasure-excursion. But, then, look at it any way you will, and life is not a picnic, a tour of pleasure; for the rule of life is that every part of it is a probation for what comes after. It seems a hard thing to say of childhood, that gleeful, careless time, when the days chase each other like laughing ripples over the shining stream, that it is a time of probation, a trial time; but we know it is. Do we not know, those of us that are serious enough to think about our children's future at all, that now our boy is fixing what his manhood shall be? Is it not true that this happy, laughing girl of ours is making decisions each day that are reacting on her character and gradually shutting up the possibilities of her future to one path? That is why we are so anxious to put them in the right path, to lead them to choose the best things, to have them learn courage and self-control, and generosity and steadfastness; *we* know that they are on trial for manhood and womanhood. When we see the boy restive under the discipline and drudgery of school, when he comes home and throws down his books and says, "There, I wish there were no schools; theyr'e hateful, useless things; let me go out and find a place," do we not tremble to see how he is failing in his trial, because we see how his day of reckoning is coming here, the day of his sober, clear-seeing manhood, when he will look back, and say, "Ah, if only I had not been so foolish; if only I had drudged on and taken my schooling; if only I knew more;" that wretched time that so many come to as they look back and see how the school-time was their probation, and they were unfaithful. And so it is all along—every year is a trial time for the years that come after every new beginning of experience—the first year in business, the first year to the newly married pair, the first congregation of the young minister—these are all special times of trial that fix irrevocably some part of the after-life. "I am a slave, to-day," says one of the greatest of living preachers, "to ways of work that were made within two or three years after beginning to preach." Well, if each period of life is the proving of us, the fixing of us for the periods that come beyond, and we do not think it a special hardship that it is so, why is it a hard view of life to say that life as a whole is a preparation for life beyond?

On the other hand, what a clear, intelligible, serious view of life does this give! To come to a man who is fuming and fretting at the little ills and pains of living, all of them so petty and yet altogether so harassing, or to one bewildered by difficulties, the inequalities, the injustices of existence, and to say to them the end of life is not here, this existence is only preparatory, we are all on trial here, all at school, proving if we are worthy, being tested to show what is in us, being hammered into character and fitness for the great uses beyond—I say, how that clears up life! It is like a cold, bracing wind that sweeps off the languid mist on the path, that shows afar off, the track we are to pursue, climbing the hills and dropping out of sight beyond the horizon. It may be cold, but it braces us up for our work: it may be sombre, but it is clear, it is serious, it is worthy of such a creature as man. Such a view makes life worth living: it sets a high prize before us, it gives the thrill of a great aim, a purpose—in one word, it puts meaning into life. After reading that parable of the lord and his servants and accepting it, no man can go on whining that life is a riddle or a dream, or an empty purposeless thing. No, it is a race, a struggle, a work with a great and worthy end.

Let us see how it clears up the atmosphere. *First.* It explains man's freedom. The master in the parable took his journey into a far country; and he was gone a long time. What does that mean? It means freedom. And freedom is to character what air is to life; it does not make character, but it is the medium, the opportunity which character must have to form itself, to show itself. And so man has been given a great deal of freedom. I do not mean political or social freedom; these have very little to do with a man's moral trial; but the freedom of choice, to go this way or that in moral things, to follow conscience or inclination, to be true or false, to be selfish or generous. Of that kind of freedom there has always been abundance, for it is independent of all political or social conditions. St. Paul was free in that sense under Nero, as free as you or I in this Republic. God then does with us as the master did with his household. He asserts his rule and right over us, he does that by the voice of conscience in the soul; he gives us our place and work and gift, and then he leaves us very largely to ourselves. He goes into a far country. How far off for the most part he seems!—so far that it is one of the griefs of an earnest, pious soul, that he seems so distant, so hidden, so dumb. We know that he is, we know his rule is right; always that soft but powerful voice speaks strongly enough never to let us be quite in the dark about him. But his presence does not overawe us; it does not oppress and compel us to take this or that course. We are, like the servants in the household, free.

Now to this condition of being set loose from a compelling or overpowering restraint men are continually objecting as a serious fault. It would be better for us all, we hear it often said, if we were not so free; their liberty is the ruin of men. So there are whole schools of theorists who contend that what the world needs is more government, stronger rule, stricter restraints. Give us a church, they say, that binds men up, that watches and disciplines and follows its members closely; a church like that of Rome—and so it seems to such minds a puzzle, a blot on the divine government that men are morally so free. If God would only interfere more speedily, if he would arrest men in their folly, then how much better it would be: but now all things go as they will; men sin, and judgment does not overtake them; great iniquities rise and flourish, and no thunderbolt bursts on them out of the blue.

But such people forget what life is—that it is a school, a place of trial. If the end of life were enjoyment, that each one should be as happy as possible, then it would be better if there was less freedom. Then man's moral freedom ought to be restricted, and he should be allowed to do only what it was best for him to do; the Master should stand over him, as over a dumb beast, and drive him this way, and lead him that, and give him just what was best, and keep him in as a fattened swine. Or, if the great end of life is accumulation of wealth, why then, too, it would be better to tie men up and keep them in strict grooves. Then they ought to be like a hive of bees, where an irresistible instinct drives each one to do his best in the best way, so that the whole swarm produces as much honey as possible. If the business of life were to get as rich as possible, or to enjoy as much as possible, freedom would be a great mistake. But then that is not the business of life. Christ says it is not: *"a man's life consisteth not in the abundance of the things which he possesseth," "the life is more than meat;" "what shall it profit a man if he gain the whole world and lose his own soul?"*

But apply the idea of the parable that life is a trial, that God is schooling us, that we are all making ready for the life eternal; and then we see the meaning of freedom. It is the air the soul must breathe while it stretches its limbs, and unfolds its nature, and shows what it is. It makes a very confused and uncomfortable and topsy-turvy world; but you do not go to the laboratory and workshop where the workman is testing his work, proving it, to find the perfect machine. You do not go into the school-room to see harmony and finished minds.

This then is part of our trial—that we are free, that we can go wrong and no hand reaches out of the invisible world to make us go right—that we can mar our lives, waste them, stain them, and worse than that, waste and mar the lives about us—and the Master is silent. We can do it, for we are here to show what is in us to be ourselves, to make character, and the character must have room to grow in, and that room is freedom. This is going on in life up and down, in all scales. You send your boy away to school: what, have you no schools at home? Yes, plenty; but home is too much of a restraint on him: you feel he will never form a strong, individual character; he is like an oak in a flower-pot. No, he must go out in the open. But he will be in danger; what a peril to be so free! But that is his trial, his testing, the indispensable element of air for his soul to breathe in. He may not stand it; but go he must, and you cannot go with him: no, you send him out to get him away from you; you are like the man in the parable, into his hands you put the talents, the chance, the opportunity, the means of his training, and then you go away, and you stay away. Well, God is your Father, and you must go to school; you cannot be sheltered and apron-stringed into holiness; here into this wide, open school with its open windows where evil blows in on you, must you be sent, and God your dear, loving Father, must go and leave you. Not that he really deserts you, but he does stand off and say, "Go alone." You must try it; you must be tried.

Life is a serious business! It is not merely sitting down at the feast to enjoy, or scrambling in the throng to get a good place. No, it is freedom to be tested; it is the proving us whether we be true or false, for God or Satan—what we are for eternity. While therefore the fact that there is so much freedom given to man may be a very sombre, sobering fact, it is not one that need perplex. We say if man is to be tried, he ought to be free.

*Secondly.* It helps us also to understand the apparent injustice and inequalities of life. This is something which always oppresses a fair mind. It seems so unjust that men should be set as they are, some high and some low, some rich and some poor—some to whom all the good things of life are granted, and others whose whole history is but a struggle against adversity. And the sense of injustice and inequality is increased when we see how the advantages of a man's birth, and education, and surroundings, and opportunities, go very far to determine what sort of character he shall have, and what his destiny will be in another life. The protection, the training, the exemption from temptation, the incentives to a noble life of one well-born, give him not only this world, as the child of the poor, the ignorant, the vicious, cannot have it, but they seem even to smooth the way for him to be such a character as shall easiest enter the kingdom of heaven, too; while the poor, harassed, tempted, ill-fed, uneducated child of adversity finds his hard life here shoving him down to vice and sin and despair of a world beyond.

But that is all changed when we remember that life is only a probation. The rich man is on trial, and the poor man with him; the learned philosopher, and the ignorant day-laborer; he with the fine taste and delicate moral sense, and he who is dull and coarse. To each his position, his intelligence, his command of means, his natural sense of right and wrong, his opportunities, or his lack of opportunity—all are simply the talents put into his keeping that the disposition, the wish that is in him, may be tested and discovered. The question is not how much can he do?—how great advance does he make?—but, what will he do with what he has? And for that one place is as much a trial as another. Great gifts of mind, of will, of moral force; large possessions in money, or influence, or social distinction, constitute of themselves a great responsibility, a mighty temptation. Lazarus looks at Dives, and as he shivers in the cold, he says, "Oh, how easy for *him* to be good! he is never hungry; he has no temptation to steal or to lie; and how much good he can do;—it must be so easy to get to heaven when there are no temptations in the way." But then Lazarus forgets that merely to be honest, and contented, and to be thankful, and to be kind to the poor, will not fill up the measure of Dives' trial. "To whom much is given, of him is required the more." This great, strong, rich, clear-sighted man will not get off by bringing into the account just what is expected of Lazarus. The man with one talent, if he brings one talent more, is saluted, " Well done!"—but he who has had two talents and brings back but two, will be dismissed as unfaithful. And is it no trial to be put high, to be exempt from care for one's living, never to be dependent on another, to be free, never to know pain that pulls down, or poverty that hedges up the path? What a watch must that man keep over himself whom no one else watches; how hard it must be to be at the top, to be deferred to, to be flattered, to have no bar to one's will! And then remember that all this is our trial; that God has set us so free to see what we will do with our freedom. I wonder sometimes that princes ever enter the kingdom of heaven at all. Instead of all this power and wealth and freedom making their way to heaven easier, it is that which tries their courage and faith. Think of the trial of having the wealth of a Rothschild, the power of a Gladstone, and yet to feel that it is all only a trust; that our money and power over men were only our trial.

But then the low place, the hard lot, is a trial too; as much so as the higher and easier. Dives, harassed, perplexed, conscious that his gifts like unmanageable horses are beginning to endanger him, looks out at Lazarus with no cares, no responsibilities, and he says, "how simple a thing being faithful is for the poor and weak: they have only to submit and trust; they have only to pray give this day our daily bread and then take.  Lazarus' trial is easier than mine." And that too, is untrue.  It *is* a trial to be poor, to be dependent.  But what is apparent, is that in view of life as probation, all these differences, these inequalities and injustices melt away.  One lot may be more comfortable than another; but looked on as probation it is hard to see that there is much difference in men's conditions here.  They are all at school, some in high classes and some in low, some in velvet and some in home-spun, some in comfortable easy chairs, and a great many on hard, wooden benches—but the trial for all is the same.  Are you faithful or not?—Here is your task: will you do it, or will you shirk it.

*Third.* Another mystery this view helps to solve, and that is the apparent failures of life.

We call a life a failure when we cannot see it completed here.  That is, we measure it by the worldly standard.  Whatever a man sets out to do or to get, if he dies before he finishes that work or gets that possession, we have a feeling that life with him was a wreck: we say, "Well, his life was a failure."  Now, I am not saying that the sudden snapping off of what promised to be a beautiful growth is not a sad thing to see; or that to watch the clouds gather over the fair morning, and wrap it in gloom, and at last quench it in storm, is not something to make the heart ache.  There is nothing that can take the sadness out of life: Christ himself does not do that—he only shows how, in himself and for us, the sadness may be only the birth-pang to a deeper joy.  But look at life as a probation, and although it is still sad to see human plans dashed and human hopes frustrated, yet we can see that the sudden dropping of the curtain on a life but quarter played out, is not really a failure. Take a very common case: here is a young man setting out on a high career, with every gift that can promise success. He enters on a course of useful activity, friends and followers are gathering about him, love and honor are ripening for him; and then comes the fatal stroke—the career is cut short, the gifts are quenched, the hopes he had raised, the group he was leading, are scattered; and then as men stand about his grave and look at the ruin of that great career, they say, "What a wreck, what a failure; how mysterious it is, how such a history takes all meaning out of life!" But if life is a probation, we are not obliged to think that life a failure. What was that man here for? To carry out that plan he had formed: to complete a certain work? Doubtless; he had a work to do; his life and labor fitted into the great whole of God's kingdom here; but as far as that is concerned, we may leave it to God. He weaves the broken threads into his perfect fabric, and makes our half-spun webs, our ravelled-out lives and threads of purpose into completeness in his world-loom; the shattered life of a Martyn fills its place there as well as the long history of a Judson. But for the man himself, he was here to be tried, the purpose of his life reached beyond. And if God had proved him, and his probation was over, why should he go on to finish the task here? He had passed his examination, all the unfolding of his life could not prove him any more: why should he stay in the school to enjoy his easy seat and hear the murmured applause of the lookers-on? Let him pass beyond. It looks like failure here; but go round the curtain and see it on the other side, and it does not look like failure there. The same considerations apply to all those instances of plans for good which men undertake and are baffled in bringing to completion. A minister starts a church in some destitute place; a good man founds a school, or begins a reform; and after a while, although they meant well and labored hard, circumstances compel them to give it up; they must lay down the work, and see another succeed where they failed—or more perplexing still, the work itself is destroyed. And then comes despondency: they seem to have made nothing out of their life at all; or else they are irritated and angry at others for their inefficiency or opposition. But do not such men forget what life is, that it is only a probation? What are you here for? Is it to build a church, or found a school, or carry out this or that reform? Have you not been forgetting, in your anxiety and absorption in the immediate prosperity of what you are doing, why it was that God permitted you to have a hand in that work—in short, that you are being tried and educated for life beyond? Suppose this or that thing has not turned out as you hoped; do you forget that it is only part of God's great plan, and that when he takes it out of your hand he will take care of its issue and effect for good?

But you, yourself—how have you stood your trial, what use have you made of your probation? Do you not see that the great thing for you yourself is that you should have been found faithful, and whether you accomplished or did not accomplish what you set out to do, that you have been a loyal, true man through it all? Suppose the man with the one talent had put his lord's money out to the usurers to the very best of his ability, and the usurers had gone suddenly into bankruptcy, would he not have been accounted a faithful servant and had his lord's approval?

Here, then, is a solemn, a grand view of life. How does it elevate our daily living and redeem it from the pettiness that is always insinuating itself into our thoughts and feelings about our own career. For that is one of the evils of life, as most men have to pursue it; it does seem *petty*. The daily round of duty in our callings, so monotonous, so hemmed in, so remote from the heroic; the little things we have given us to do—day after day to write, write; to sew, sew, sew; to cook and serve the same round of meals; to teach the old lessons: it is hard to live in these and not feel that life is but an insignificant thing. The only way to rescue the soul from sinking into that poor slough is to remember that all this is only our probation, that the very dullness and monotony of life, its irksomeness and lack of excitement, is part of the trial. This lifts a corner of the curtain that shuts eternity from the present: then we feel in all the dryness and tedium of our lot that we are only waiting in the ante-room for the doors to open that admit us to the Judge, to know whether we are accounted worthy. The decision is making for heaven or hell: it is making here in these common duties that every day is bringing us.

Let us learn then to look at our life in this way. Let us see in our freedom a part of our trial and schooling. There are times when there come to every man solemn thoughts of eternity; a vision of God breaks through the dust of every-day. Religion is seen to be important, duty presses its claims, and the man is lifted above himself: he is not far from the kingdom. But that mood passes, those great and solemn thoughts fade out, and then the man is at ease again. And now without prayer, and having no life with God, he feels as comfortable as though he had obeyed his conscience. He says, "What does it matter whether one is religious or not? I prayed and was serious, and now 1 do not pray and am not serious, and I am quite as much at my ease: the irreligious man is just as happy as the religious." So he says. But he forgets that this is his trial, that the Master goes and leaves him undisturbed that he may be proved to the bottom. He forgets to say, my freedom is my probation.

And then when life seems dull and monotonous, and it appears as if it were of small consequence how we did our work or whether we did it at all, because it is all so insignificant, then let us lift the curtain and let in the light from the eternal world on our narrow lot. The rich evening sunlight slanting across the fields glorifies every common weed, makes every ditch and clod to glow with strange deep colors, and so to see every day's work in the light of the solemn final hour when every deed shall be weighed for eternity, that makes life great and serious.

Look at your failures and losses, too, in the same light. You have lost your friends and loved ones, and life seems only a miserable mockery of hopes and affections. Not so: you are being tried; you are being purified. You have failed in business, and men rush by you forgetting you, and you say you are of no use, you have accomplished nothing; yes, but if *you* endure, if you come forth untarnished, brave, uncomplaining, then you have accomplished something: you will be crowned. But your good work has been baffled, your church is closed, your school abandoned! Well, have you been faithful? have all these heavy strokes hammered your character into fineness? have you endured as seeing him that is invisible? Then, be of good courage, all is well.

Presently the Lord comes: nearer and nearer through these weary, monotonous days he is drawing toward us. "The Lord of those servants cometh:" when the tramp of his host is heard echoing on the road, and his trumpet is sounding at the gate, what then will be our store, our office, our success or failure, the drudgery or the joy of our work? Then the tool will fall from our hand, our wealth will be forgotten, the hand of the loved will drop from ours; for only one thought will fill all the soul—" Have I been faithful," have I endured my probation? Will he say,—

the Lord when he enters his hall and looks on me and my work—"well done"? Then am I blessed, then life is a success; then my work is crowned, whether it have been the rule of a kingdom or the sweeping of a crossing.

## LOOKING UNTO JESUS.

HEBREWS XII. 2. "Looking unto Jesus."

These words were written to encourage a company of disheartened men. They were addressed to the Hebrew Christians, who had left the old National Church to be followers of Christ.

What a picture that sets before us! We seem to see those early Christians, exiles from their old home, going out of the dignified and majestic Jewish Church and becoming members of a despised sect. Mocked, annoyed with petty persecutions, robbed, they are like emigrants who come from peaceful and venerable villages in an old land where everything is familiar, to a new land, where even the face of nature is strange. No wonder they were despondent; so much they had endured for Christ's sake, and even yet there seemed no end.

It is to encourage these, then, that the writer sends this epistle. "*Cast not away your confidence*," he says, "*ye have need of patience.*" And then he proceeds to set before them motives for encouragement; he brings them a stimulus.

He appeals to their conscience—to their sense of right. "Let us lay aside the weight," he says;—the weight of fear and despondency; and the sin which is so perculiarly besetting, this impatience, this feeling of restlessness under trial and sacrifice; for this is a sin. They know they ought to be brave, and that cowardice here is guilt. "Let us run the race," he urges; it *is* a race and a hard one, and often the temptation to slacken the pace, to throw one's self down in the luxurious shade by the wayside, where so many are enjoying themselves, seems irresistible; but then it is the right course; all the power of conscience throws itself into the utterance, "you ought to run." There is power in that appeal, for it touches the chord which runs through every human heart, the sense of duty. It is a power we might use oftener than we do. We might begin to use it earlier with our children; giving up something of our coaxing and personal influence to draw to what is right, to try oftener the naked force of conscience. It will not hurt our boys and girls to be thrown back clearly and sharply on that fundamental impulse. Let us say to them, "You ought: this is right, this is wrong;" that is, when the right and wrong are clear and unmistakable. To appeal to such motives is a part of moral education; and the response will often come with enthusiasm. So Nelson sailed into battle with but one appeal to his fleet, the signal floating from his mast-head, "England expects every man to do his duty, to-day."

He appeals also to their sense of fellowship with the

worthy dead. He takes them back through the long galleries of their ancestors that are opened to us in the tenth chapter of this epistle, that long roll of heroes. They were proud of those great names. Every Jew said, "We have Abraham for our father," and his heart swelled within him at the remembrance of Moses, and David, and the great memories that streamed down his history. Well, says the writer, these are all watching you: they fought their day, and never flinched, and now they are witnesses of how their children quit themselves: "We also are compassed about with a great cloud of witnesses;" how can we murmur, how dare we flinch? Remember Abraham and Moses, Joshua and David, and play the coward if you can. That appeal must have thrilled every nerve of manhood in them. And that too is a just appeal. It is one that has always struck a deep response out of men's hearts. How the light of a noble man's life has streamed out across the world long after he has gone, and made his sons ashamed to do mean things in its brightness; how a mother's sweet charity has shone behind her like the glow of the summer sun after it is set, and made her daughters' kindle in its light. I have sometimes thought that a great and lofty life, like Washington's for instance, does as much for men in the long succession of generations, by simply standing pillar-like along the track of men's lives, witnessing what unselfishness and nobleness are, as by all it ever accomplished in active work. When we are tempted to selfish ease, to cowardly shirking from duty, to mean thoughts of life, let us remember the great witnesses who stand over our path; the men of faith who endured and conquered, and now watch to see us endure and conquer in our day.

But there is yet another motive to be urged: it is an appeal to their loyalty to Christ. "Let us learn to be brave and faithful," he says, by "looking unto Jesus." You are discouraged, your strength is ebbing away. Well, there is yet one more inspiration for you: "Consider him that endured such contradiction of sinners against himself, that ye be not wearied and faint."

THAT MOTIVE TO DUTY, THE APPEAL TO OUR LOYALTY TO CHRIST'S PERSON, *is the deepest and strongest that can be made.* Everything else in religion leads up to that.

In order to understand how strong that appeal must have been to these Hebrew Christians, we should have to go back through the entire epistle, and see how the whole interest is centered in one figure, on Christ. Under one form and another, it is he who is the supreme object of thought and affection. "The Son," "the great High Priest," "the true Melchisedec," "the One Sacrifice," "the Captain of their Salvation," "the Mediator of the New Covenant," "the Elder Brother" —they are all one. Each name and form is the symbol of a great truth, the expression of a profound doctrine of religion; but all are blended and lost in the person of Christ, the Divine Saviour, the perfect Friend, the loving Jesus.

He was God, "the brightness of the Father's glory, and the express image of his person." He was the mighty Deliverer, "the great High Priest that has passed into the heavens." He was the suffering Man, "touched with the feeling of their infirmities, because tried in all points like as they; who had learned obedience by suffering, just as they were learning that hard lesson. And he was the loving brother, close to them, of their own nature, "not ashamed to call them brethren:" though so resplendent in perfection, though holy, harmless, undefiled and separate from sinners, yet joined to them in flesh and blood to deliver them. What a vision that was!

What the writer does, then, is to take the natural impulse of loyalty to a leader, and attach it to the person of Christ. And what a power that passion of loyalty has been in the world! How it has lifted up slaves to make them heroes; how it has put a soul of unselfishness into the hard soldier; how it has inspired with something of thought and spirituality the dull, stupid masses! It casts a redeeming color over the dark career of a Napoleon, to see how the loyalty of his men clung to him—how, from the marshal at the head of his columns down to the private in the ranks, even to the drummer boys, they served him with an idolatrous devotion: how they fought for him; died for him! One almost finds a compensation to the young men of France whom he sent so mercilessly to slaughter, that he gave them such an inspiration of loyalty; for is it not better to be devoted to a Napoleon even, than to live on in cold, contracted self-consideration all one's days?

But it does not need a Napoleon to waken loyalty. It is a part of universal human nature. It makes the child eager to do the parent's will: Many a young man goes on reading his Bible in the city crush and rush, not because he cares for the sacred book, but because of his promise to the dear mother in the far-off village. It appears in the church, even when it does not reach up to the heaven of the church. What pastor has not had members who would do for him what they would not do because it was right, nor because it was good for them, or honoring to Christ? How often have we felt like saying to some warm friend, "Ah, if you would only do for your Master's sake, what you are so ready to do for mine!" How sad to be loyal to home, and state, and earthly leader, and cold only to him who makes parent, and pastor, and captain worth loving. What we want is not less devotion to friend, and teacher, to the hero, the worthy leader, but more devotion to the Friend of friends, to the Great Teacher, to Jesus Christ, the man of men.

The lesson of the text, then, is that we ought to use this force of loyalty to Christ in our living more than we do. We should be "looking unto Jesus" much more than we are. Especially would I emphasize the necessity of making our loyalty more practical. Perhaps the reason there are not more lives devoted to Christ is that those who are loyal, shut up their loyalty from their common living. We are faithful to our

Lord in our creed, and in the closet; we insist in our creed that he is the True God, the Holy One, and True Man, the loving and lovable; and in the hour of prayer we worship that adorable life, at once so spotless and so sympathetic, so true and yet so tender, so holy and yet so human; but when we go down from our transfiguration mount to plod along the common road we are apt to leave this force of loyalty behind and take with us only that slow companion, duty. Our loyalty to Christ, I fear, is unproductive to us and dim to others, because it is kept too close in the closet, and the prayer-meeting. What it needs for strength and color is to be brought into the common air. What we want is that Christ should be to us a daily leader and inspiration. But how shall we secure that?

Let me indicate one or two ways.

*First.* The simplest of all ways is to see what he does in circumstances like our own. We must take with us into the dust of every day the inspiration of the closet. That inspiration was the vision of Christ's perfection; and what we need for our day's work, is the vision of the perfect Christ, doing *his* day's work. "Look to Jesus" not merely for the rapture of spiritual beauty, but to see how he lives, endures, meets difficulty, discouragement, pain : in short, learn obedience.

For instance: when our service to men is met by ingratitude, we must meet the chill with the vision of Christ's action under the like circumstances. We all know what it is to meet men whom we have befriended with time, money, sympathy, the best we had, and then have them pass us by as though we were strangers. And then comes the sense of failure, of bewilderment, of skepticism as to men's capacity for rescue. I doubt whether the mere sense of duty can meet that. Conscientiousness will perhaps enable us to forgive the ingrate; but it will hardly give us heart to go on doing good to others who may turn out ingrates too. But loyalty to Christ can do that. Instead of speculating about human nature, or commenting on its baseness, I turn round and "look unto Jesus;" I watch him as he gazes with wounded heart after the nine lepers that are hurrying unthankful away; and when I mark how he goes on unhesitatingly in his way of blessing, wounded, but unchilled, unembittered, I forget my depression. To watch this is to feel as the soldier who sees his captain's plume flashing before him in the thick of the fight.

Or, suppose we are depressed by the stupidity of the men we are trying to save. That depression will take one of two forms, according to what happens to be uppermost in our mood. If it is the Pharisee that is uppermost, the stupid sinner will awaken our contempt; if it is the Sadducee, then it will be our despair. In either case we are shorn of our strength: we can never follow Christ in doing men good, either despising or despairing of them. But, how can I help feeling the one or the other? Well, loyalty to Jesus must come in to help you. "Look to Jesus." Look at him as he talks with the woman of Samaria. Who could be more stupid, earthly, frivolous, than she? but he does not despise her; he does not despair of her. With what infinite patience he tries each entrance-way to her soul? When we see that, we forget how stupid men are; or, rather, we feel how stupid and earthly is our impatience; we feel how unlike him we are; and we burn to try at the copy he has set us, once more.

Or, perhaps, we are not called to active service. Ours is the passive lot, to wait, to suffer or, harder still, after a life of activity, our history is broken in two, and from the busy world we are turned aside into the silent room, simply to endure We are never to be busy again. As in heaven some at God's

> ———" bidding speed,
> And post o'er land and ocean without rest;"

whilst others

> ———" serve who only stand and wait;"

So our service here may be only to wait, to suffer, to bear pain and weariness for Christ. The incurable disease, the shut-up lot, the lost activity, the intolerable pain: how can human nature bear these and keep its sweetness? Only by the sight of Jesus bearing his anguish, drinking his cup. "How," said one to a friend who had gone through a long and painful surgical treatment, "how could you endure to meet it?" "Well, I could not; it seemed I could never submit to it, till I remembered Christ on the cross; and then I thought if he could bear that for me, I could bear this for him. When the surgeon took the knife I just thought of him, and I was not afraid." For every case of weakness, the weakness that shrinks from work and the weakness that sinks under suffering, there is but one cure: it is "looking unto Jesus," the vision of what he has done, of how he suffered.

*Secondly.* But there is another way to make loyalty to Christ practical: it is by simplifying our motive, *i. e.* by doing our work more purely with reference to him. There is such a thing as multiplying machinery till we lose all our power in overcoming the friction; we often interpose between ourselves and the thing we ought to do, so many levers of arguments and reasons for doing it, that we have not force enough to reach through to the end. Now, loyalty to Christ simplifies this. It gives our life a direct power from the personal Christ. Seek the closet of prayer, for instance, because Jesus is waiting for you there; visit the sick because they are his; forgive your enemies, because he has asked it; teach the ignorant and help the weak, because they are his special care. This is the most direct exercise of loyalty; and it is the Biblical way.

Take, for instance, the duty of visiting the sick. One way to look at it is to consider its utility. "Why," says the natural man, "should I visit the sick? There are plenty of others to do it; it is very distasteful to me—particularly so; and what does it amount to, after all, beyond a little temporary diversion?" With such questions the sense of duty is frittered away. But how soon loyalty to Christ puts all that aside. Instead of getting my motive to duty from balancing questions of utility and expediency and necessity, I "look unto Jesus." I hear him say, "I was sick, and ye visited me; inasmuch as ye have done it unto one of the least of these, ye have done it unto me." And my heart says, That sick man is Christ in disguise; whether to visit him is pleasant, or absolutely necessary, I am not sure; but that he is my Lord, I am sure; let me go quick and serve him! This was the argument Sister Dora, that ardent servant of Christ, used to make her repulsive work attractive: "Look upon nursing," she said, "as work done for Christ. As you touch each patient, think it is Christ himself, and then virtue will come out of the touch to yourself. I have felt that myself when I have had a particularly loathsome patient."

It is so, too, that we must take up the business of preaching and teaching the Word. We must do it in the spirit of personal loyalty. We must not forget, indeed, that it is the truth, the very truth, about God and man and his destiny; we may fortify ourselves by every reasoning to show that it is suited to man, that it will be useful to him; we may encourage ourselves with the delightful picture of what it will presently do for those we teach. But deepest of all, most strongly impelling, if we would be brave and effective, must be this, "It is the word of Jesus;" he is sending me; for him I speak first of all. Then when the audience is thin, or listless, when they go away without answering a word; when the class is half empty, and the children are restless and inattentive; when they go home and leave you doubting whether you have reached in to touch them at all, you will not be heart-broken; though cast down, you will not be destroyed. That loyalty to Christ will do for you, when mere utility, or the sense of duty, or the conviction of the truth of what you have to teach, would fail to give you heart for the work. It was so that the great mission work of this century, which has girdled the globe with its conquest of heathen races to Christ, began. If men had waited till the utility of preaching the gospel to cannibals could have been demonstrated, if they had gone on mere probabilities, or counted up the chances of a few missionaries overturning the hoary establishments of paganism, there would never have been any foreign missions at all. But Christians began to "look to Jesus" with reference to the heathen. They heard his last words, so long stifled or explained away, coming to their ears once more: "Go ye into all the world and preach the gospel to every creature." And then, out of pure loyalty to him, they went. I think they must have felt, when they looked at the dreadful odds, somewhat as Peter when Christ bade him cast in the net, What hope is there? "Nevertheless at thy word we will let down the net." It did seem desperate. There were the islands of the sea, with the fierce cannibals waiting on the shore to strike down the missionary; there were the great continents with their ramparts of caste and philosophy, and behind them the proud pagan sneering at the European's faith; and here were the handful of believing men setting out to convert them!

How could they go? Well, they could not, but for the deep personal loyalty which looked only to Jesus; the loyalty that said, He has said it, and it is true; he has commanded it, and I must obey; he has promised, and it cannot fail. Personal loyalty to Jesus: there is the secret of foreign missions, of all missions.

And now all we have been saying resolves itself at last into this: that our religion needs to take a more personal form. It is more of the child's religion that we need; not, indeed, less of the man's, not less of understanding and solidity, of strength and endurance, but more of the warm personal element which makes up nearly the whole of a child's life. Think how it is a child conceives of duty, of right and wrong, of fidelity, guilt, service; is it not all in relation to a person? Duty is what it owes to its mother; right and wrong are all measured by her will. Guilt is to be under her displeasure, forgiveness is her smile. And how warm and fresh and enthusiastic all its moral and religious life is! What is purer, fresher, than a child's religion; but that religion is only the purest form of loyalty to a personal Jesus. Well, we need to take the child's attitude to Christ. Something of this was what Jesus meant when, to the disciples full of rivalries about the grades and ranks of the new kingdom, he said, "Except ye be converted, and become as little children, ye shall not enter into the kingdom of heaven." It is the personal element, he seems to say, which gives religion its life and sweetness; until you learn to trust and love the person of him in whom all goodness centres, until you love God more than his gifts, until you are children again, there is no kingdom of heaven for you.

How this runs through the New Testament! What a joy and elasticity, what a freshness characterizes the experience of those early Christians!—their brightness and buoyancy, their inextinguishable hope, are at once our delight and our despair. But we need not despair; their secret is an open one. It is their personal, childlike loyalty to Jesus which gives them joy and elasticity: they are bright because always looking unto him. It is surprising to find how much the New Testament gives its duties this personal leverage. "Remember," says Jesus to the disciples when he prepares them to expect trial and distress, "remember the word that I said unto you." Well, what is it that is to fortify them?—the pride of manhood; the conviction that they suffered for truth's sake, the hope of reward? No, none of these things, but the thought that Jesus had suffered the same before them: "The servant is not greater than his Lord. If they have persecuted me, they will persecute you." It is an appeal to their loyalty, pure and simple. And how they answered to it. Remember how the Apostles went out from the scourging at the council at Jerusalem, rejoicing that they were counted worthy to suffer shame for his name; recall how Saint Peter asked to be crucified head downward, counting himself unworthy to die like his Master. But in none did the flame of this devotion burn brighter than in the great philosopher among the Apostles. Saint Paul was no mere servant of duty. He talks sometimes of doing things for conscience's sake, but the fire of his life is kindled by a personal touch. Abstract, logical, metaphysical as he is in reasoning, how inevitably in all the practical parts, in his very thought of life, he takes the child's attitude of loyalty to a person. When he writes to the whimsical, arrogant Corinthians that he is their servant—and what a hard thing it must have been for the high-minded Apostle to bend his neck to the yoke of their humors—he tells them it is for Christ's sake. He says he takes pleasure in his distresses, even, for Christ's sake. He tells the brethren at Cæsarea, when they forebode the danger he incurs in going to Jerusalem, that he is ready to die there—not for the truth, not for a principle—no, but for truth living and lovable in a personal Saviour, "*for the name of the Lord Jesus.*"

Let us learn, then, to be looking more steadily unto Jesus. Sum up in your mind, now, what a deeper loyalty to him will give.

*First.* It will infuse a warmer life into our religious experience. It will take out of our daily tasks the dryness and abstractness of mere duty-doing. We shall feel a companionship along the dusty way: the touch of a hand will be on us. Everything will be direct to Christ or from Christ. The presence of the great, near Friend will enable us to extract a blessedness even from the hard, repulsive things of life. What wearisome, disagreeable services in themselves does a mother's duty impose?—but the touch of the little hand, the tone of the quivering voice, the indescribable sense of the child's presence, appeals to something in her heart, which makes even the hard things blessed to do. Loyalty to Christ can bring just such a presence and blessedness to the hard duties in our path. How hard it is often to contribute to a charitable corporation, good though we know its object to be, and confident though we are of the wisdom of its management; but how easy, how delightful, to spend, to deny ourselves, to relieve a suffering wife, a wasting child! What we need then for powerful right living, is to live not for an organization, a church, a body of truth, a creed, for a dim, far-off duty, but for a friend, a master, a brother, the glorious Son of man, so near us, so bound to us, so one with us. It is this that gives compensation to life as it goes, so that Christian living repays itself in its daily consciousness of Christ's fellowship and smile. This was what Saint Paul meant when he said, "For me to live is Christ." Every daily duty was a service done for a present friend; every pain borne was a companionship with the suffering elder brother, every sacrifice made was for a leader who had just asked it. What a fullness and richness did this give to common life! This is to restore religion to its natural relations; to have it sweet because it flows through its true channels. For the sweetness of life, what makes it? Not physical comforts, not success and activity even; these are its subtance, but the flavor and richness of all, the delight of the senses, the pleasure of activities, the rapture of achievement, all depend at last on personal relations; on the affections of the heart. These extinguished, the best of life dies; these in vigor, with parent and child, husband and wife, brother and sister, friend and companion, meeting us, cheering us on, sharing our joys and sorrows—and life, although poor and cut down, still keeps its flavor and sweetness. Make, then, your religion natural; let it be the outcome of loyalty to a personal friend; let it flow from this perennial spring. Let it look unto Jesus.

*Secondly.* It will give us a larger sympathy. There is nothing, it seems to me, more dreadful in the aspect of our common life than the hardness which is engendered by competition. Especially is this true in great cities. The spectacle of the rushing crowd, jostling, grasping, trampling down the weak, forgetting the poor wretches that are overborne in the crush, is more cruel than the fierceness of the beasts of the wilderness and the jungle; for those are savage only when hunger compels, but the rivalry and struggle of men live on and grow fiercer when the appetites are all appeased. It is the lust to be first, to climb higher whoever is trodden down.

*Thirdly.* But let us turn from these uncongenial prospects to the great future, which by its outlook dwarfs all our present triumphs and failures. Loyalty to Jesus opens to us such a future. It is by "looking unto Jesus" that we begin to see clearly how great and rich this future is. Our anticipation of the future life, of heavenly rewards, apart from this personal relation to

Christ, are but vague and cold: all descriptions of the glory to come strike on the ear as a foreign speech; it is a life too separate from this. But if we are living the life of personal loyalty to Jesus, then this future is rich with meaning; it is fraught with possibilities so allied to present realities that our hearts throb to think of what is to come. For loyalty is a thing of degrees: it ranges from the first low flutter of the heart toward a dimly-conceived, faintly-seen form of loveliness, to the glorious vision of the blessed Son of God, which made the Apostle fall overwhelmed on the isle of Patmos. It begins with many of us in a vision of One seen in a mist. We see Jesus as the blind man first saw his fellows as trees walking: we see him as the disciples beheld him on the lake, a dim, ghostly figure, which stirred as much awe as love. Perhaps we go on for a long time doing our duty, praying our prayer, trying to serve a Master of whom we have only caught a glimpse. One of the best men I ever knew told me that for years he lived on trying to do his duty, and following in the path of Christ, without ever really seeing him, or having any personal feeling to him at all. Christ to him was only a name for the best goodness, the supremest excellence and claim on him: but to that name he was loyal. That was loyalty in its weakest form, devotion to an abstract ideal. But that grew. At last he of whom I speak fell sick; the strength with which he had been pressing on in a path after an unseen, unloved Leader, failed him. He lay helpless. And then to the weak heart, too feeble to resolve any more, too helpless to do, the vision of him who had been followed in the dark shone out; and he knew what it was to see Jesus, and to feel his personal drawing. So it may be to some of us; our loyalty is poor and faint, it comes and goes; now the vision of the great Friend is clear and winning, and then it fades. But we know what it is to have this devotion flame up and impel us for a few steps. That may tell us what it will be to come nearer. For this devotion to Christ will grow as it goes. The felt presence will be more constantly with us; the approval will fall more abidingly like sunlight on the heart; the form will be nearer, and the beauty clearer. It was this that Saint Paul meant when after recounting his sacrifices and struggles he says, "This I do, this I bear, *that I may know Christ.*" What, after so many years did he not know his Master? was not the vision ever before him? Surely; but what it had grown to be only showed him what it might yet go on to be. The glory and beauty of his past and present knowledge of Christ were only a prophecy of what he should see in him when he came nearer. And so he counted all life's treasures as so many poor counters to be paid down for the privilege of coming closer to this great, dear Friend. And then, when he had spent all the riches of life, and he had come to the last years, and now he can come no nearer this dear Lord, he can get no clearer vision, feel no closer union because of the chasm of the grave that yawns between, then he longs to die: "I have a desire to depart," he cries. What for? Is not life rich? Is it not full of opportunites of service? And he answers not that he is tired of life here, that there is no more to do or to bear; but this life now is only walking along the side of this separating chasm—that let him go on here as he will, he gets no nearer his one desire. No, he must die to come closer; and so he has a desire to depart that he may be with Christ, which is far better.

We are like the disciples in the boat on the lake in the mist of the morning. Dimly we see a form on the shore: it beckons, it calls, but we hardly know it; though we answer back its call, and obey its command. We are doing duty, we are following conscience; we are trying to keep Jesus' words, though we hardly can see him, though we do not know him for himself. But, suddenly we recognize who it is, though even then we cannot make out the features; it is still a form in the mist. But we press on toward him, some ardently plunging into the sea, some toiling in rowing to reach him; and as we go, he grows clearer through the mist; his form becomes distinct; his features grow into familiarity, we can see the smile of welcome, we can catch the low inflection of meaning in his voice. An! then at last we come out on the shore; he meets us, he leads us to the feast spread. We have him close and near, and all else is forgotten. We have looked unto Jesus until we need strain our eyes no more. He is with us, in us, and we with him forever.

# EXTRACTS.

### ST. PAUL'S LOVE FOR MEN.

In the ninth chapter of Romans the apostle Paul uses these remarkable words: "I could wish that myself were accursed from Christ for my brethren, my kinsman according to the flesh." Why does the apostle value men so highly? Because he loves them. Love is the penetrating vision that discovers the value that is hidden in common things. It is the golden light falling from heaven on coarse weeds and common clay, and bringing out their glorious colors. Is there anything in the universe so precious to the mother as the very common child on which her heart fixes? What ordinary people, what commonplace boys and girls, are transfigured by this glory of love. Love lends a precious seeing to the eye. We are right when we see this preciousness in those that are near to us; but we are wrong when we limit it, and find only commonness in ordinary men and women. The commonness is in us: the dullness is in our dim unloving eyes; as if a man should pick up a rough diamond in the dusk of evening and take it for only a common pebble. Ah, brethren, if we had learned the deepest lesson of our holy faith, the lesson of love, the commonness and dullness of life would be gone forever; men and women would everywhere be wonderful, interesting. There would be no tameness in that human life whose sublime mysteries love had revealed. It was so with the Apostle Paul: love for men had given him the keenest interest in every thing human; all men had a charm for him, rich and poor, wise and foolish, philosophers at Athens and rude mountaineers at Iconium, heathen poets, Roman soldiers—all attracted him, and the charm of each was that he was a man. His love pierced to the inner world of each soul, behind every disguise, and found wonders there. That world of men, which others sneered at and yawned over as dull and common, he entered as Aladdin entered the vault of gems: he found riches on every side; life blazed with the light of jewels: men that were capable of eternal blessedness, who had on them the stamp of God; and the thought that they might fail of their destiny, that this treasure might be spilled into the fathomless sea of eternity and be lost, that these jewels of souls might be uncrystallized and crumble back into nothingness, was too much for him: "I could wish that I was accursed from Christ for them."

This was the central thought in Paul's mind, the master-vision, in the light of which he saw everything— the vision of human nature redeemed and purified and perfected in Christ. It is because he has had a view of what a human soul can be, of the depths and heights of goodness, of blessedness which Christ can unfold in a saved man, that he has this passionate longing for the rescue of his countrymen. So the loss of a soul deepened, and blackened, and grew tragic beneath his gaze, with all the misery not only of a great suffering, but of a great extinction. "This it is to be saved," he seems to say—it is to know Christ; it is to be new made, to go back to youth, to the youth of Paradise, to be filled with all the fullness of God, to be a partaker of the divine nature; it is to share the greatness and blessedness that are God's. And so, looking out on the infinite, overwhelming prospect of life and glory that might be, and then seeing what men were, and foreseeing what they were going down to be, stupid, selfish, narrowing, growing poorer, going out into darkness, to eternal death, he is seized with an infinite pity. It was because he knew from his own experience what Christ was, that he longed for others to be made Christian.

## THE SPIRIT OF GOD.

It was the Spirit of God, we are expressly told in the Scriptures, that gave to Samson his great strength. If so, that strength was no common gift; it was sacred; and so we see it was by the use God made of it; for Samson was called to a high office, that of judge over Israel. He was called up for a peculiar crisis; and he had his gift, his peculiar gift, suited to the times. God seemed to say to Israel in every great act of Samson: "Do you see what one man may be who has the Spirit? So shall it be with your whole people, when you, like Samson, are separate, consecrated, and possessed by the Lord."

Now in view of this I say that Samson's gift, although apparently so low, was really sacred. It was just the gift Israel needed, for it was the gift they could best understand. That strength was holy and to be revered because it was the manifestation of the Spirit of God, and because it was bestowed for the purpose of saving God's people. It was indeed a sacred trust, a holy indwelling, and Samson's sin was his contempt for, or rather his irreverent use and holding of his gift. For what he did was to act as if that great strength was his own to do what he would with. All his conference with Delilah about it was a sort of trifling with his gift. It was an irreverent handling of sacred things. It was treating God's Spirit and his work as if they belonged to him, and were not a sacred trust to be held for God and to be used for him.

Now there is a deep lesson here for us. For what makes men strong to do their duty in life? What makes us vigorous to serve God and our generation? The same that made Samson strong for his work in Israel; the Holy Spirit of God. It is he that indites those prayers we daily offer; it is his touch that restrains us from sin, that teaches us what is good, that moves us toward God. It is he that forms Christ, is forming him in us daily by little duties done, by the constant round of daily service. And our special gifts for serving God are his work and indwelling. I do not mean the gifts that fit us for secular life; health, means, skill, courage; but the religious gifts in us, our graces and virtues. One has a meek spirit, another strong faith, another love and gentleness; and all these are the motions of the Holy Ghost. We are apt to forget this. We think our virtues, our views of truth, our gifts of prayer, of speech, of courage, are our own. And so we use them; we are led to trifle with them just as if they were like any common things. We do not feel the presence of the Holy Spirit in them. And this is the great sin of many Christians. They go where society makes a joke of religious things, they allow companions to rally them about their religious life. They think they can let religion and religious gifts be made light of, because it is *their* experience, *their* doings that are discussed. But it cannot be. If you are truly religious, if your work and life is for Christ at all, it is the Spirit of the Lord that is on you, and it is a grievous sin for you to trifle with him. When you have allowed that, you are like Samson in Delilah's lap. You go back to your closet and your Christian life and work, whatever it may be, thinking, perhaps, that all is as before; your trifling was only a joke. So Samson when he awoke out of his sleep said, I will go out as at other times before; but "he wist not that the Lord was departed from him."

For we must remember that when the Spirit of the Lord draws away from a man, he does so silently.

God did not thunder in Samson's ears whilst he was playing with Delilah, saying, "Beware!" No, he let him alone. This seems unreasonable, hard and unjust to you. You think you should have some warning, so that you might detain the Spirit. But our ways are not as God's ways. The Spirit of the Lord comes and goes silently, because its work is spiritual and manifests itself only by its effects. "He shall glorify me," says Christ. And how? As the wind blows; you hear the sound, you see the effects, but not the wind. You have a view of Christ: in reading the Bible, or hearing a sermon or thinking of our Lord, you see something newly beautiful and precious in him. You are drawn to him; melted, cheered, rebuked. And you think it is the great sermon, or the good book, or the passage of Scripture; but really it was the Spirit who receives the things of Christ and shows them to us. We are constantly moved by the Spirit, but we recognize him not. We see the pictures, but the painter is invisible. We hear the music, but see no trace of the musician.

So he departs. As we were under his influence and knew it not, so we pass away from under his touch. We only know that religion is a little duller than it used to be, that we are growing tired of church, and sermons and the Bible.

How then shall you prevent his flight. By doing just what Samson did not do. By recognizing every good thought, every pious feeling, every longing for salvation—everything in your religious life as his gift.

## PURPOSE IN LIFE.

To many life is but a succession of days, duties and enjoyments, not bound together with a plan, a purpose. To all such, life is dull, poor, fruitless, distracted; it is a bundle of sticks falling apart. The lesson of Christ's life is saying to them "seek a plan!" Even a child may have such a path marked out before it; and every day may be an advance along that path; he may be saying each day, "What shall I do to amuse myself to-day, to have a good time; where shall I get a new plaything?" or he may say, "To-day I am to obey the best I can, to learn my lesson as well as possible;" and then that child has got something of the movement, the independence, the joyful earnestness, of Christ's great life. Even a sick one may bring something of the current of Christ's life into the dull weariness of the sick-room, by saying, "Let me be more cheerful and patient and bright for my fellow-men than yesterday."

But if we would have the movement, the directness, the independence of Christ's life, we must have his conviction of having gotten our work, our purpose in life, from God, and not have chosen it for ourselves. It is God's providence which puts us into our true work. And when a man has settled down to the one aim of life, when he has got his course, he has with it, if he be a Christian, a deep sense that God has given him his work. This is clear to him, although he may not be able to show it to others.

How we are to find out the work which God has for us to do, is a personal question between ourselves and God. Only the most general directions can be given. To find the work he has for us we must be simple in our aims, unselfish, desirous to know the truth, willing to be led of God. Men make mistakes most generally because they are double-minded—they would look at God and at the world too, and so they see nothing clearly.

The directions of God as to our purpose and path in life are to be sought in no mysterious, miraculous way, but under the conviction that the closing and opening of paths to us in life are providential; that God means something by the ordering of the circumstances of our lives. This is a plain, homely, old-fashioned and most sensible guide to our work in life. With the single eye, with minute and particular prayer for direction, look and see what God's providence points you to. And how simple, how unmistakable the lines of those providences in their great bearings are. Providence has put you, for instance, in a home; you have ties of flesh and blood, father and mother, brother and sister, friends, social surroundings; they were all set for you before you came, and there is one line of direction fixed for you. It can never be right to refuse these duties; something for life is set you to do just by these relations.

But now, when men think of their life-work, how few think that God has set them any direction in the home, in the church of their birth and heritage.

What wonder that men go drifting across the sea when they begin by shutting their eyes to every indication that God's homely providence has marked for them. We are all too much set on choosing our duties and too little ready to believe that God has already chosen them for us. But no life can have the true movement of advance, of independence, of self-poise, which does not feel the propulsion of the Divine direction. I do not know what is greater than to feel in our hearts' core this sense of a Divine sending in our lives; to be able to say as we look along our life's path, as Christ did, "Let me go to the next * * * for therefore am I sent." I am sent: I have not chosen for myself; God has chosen for me, and I am only living to do his bidding. Can you say that? Have you been sent? Is your work and purpose in life of your own devising; or did God give it to you?

It is a humble way of life to have God choose for us. If we could choose, we should always choose great and shining things. But God knows best; and if once we can know that our path is given by him, then come the greatness and joy that always come with the clear doing of God's will; then we have a life like Christ's, a life like a strong stream, ever moving, ever widening, never ceasing until it finds the eternal sea.

## LETTING RELIGION SLIP.

In mature life men are prone to let the precious things of religion slip, through the growing dullness that comes from habit. We let slip what we have grown used to. The things we have heard slip away because we have heard them so often. The story of the cross, like any other story, wears out its first surface interest by being listened to over and over again. I do not know why we should expect this universal law of habit to be suspended here. To go on hearing the same thing over and over is to end in not hearing it at all, but only a sound of words. It is so in everything. And there is nothing magical in the words of Scripture, in the doctrines of religion, in the hymns we sing, in our forms of devotion, that they should not grow dull, too, by repeated going over and over. How trite and familiar seem the gospel lessons sometimes! The descriptions of heaven, the hymns of faith, the precepts of daily duty, even the words of Christ, how pallid they show at times! Is it that the gospel is really wearing out? No, it is but an intimation that we are letting slip the things we have heard. We are losing our hold on them; and they their hold on us, because we are only going over and over the same ground. They do not move us, they have no thrill of life, because they are old to us; and they are old because we have ceased to grow. We are holding our faith as a fixed thing: our devotion, our aspiration, all are completed. "Take heed!" You cannot feel that the Gospel is old, that worship has grown threadbare, and not be in danger of letting these things slip. The dull grasp of what is customary, the flatness of the trite, these are only the signs of a failing grasp. Unless the things of the kingdom of God grow deeper, unless praise and prayer and devout thought grow richer, they are slipping from you and growing less. Let not familiarity rob you of the power of religion.

But how, you ask, may we keep that which is so old, ever fresh? It is by life. Life is change, growth, the passing on and up, the deepening and widening of experience and character; not the throwing away of the past, but the carrying of it into a fuller, richer future. The bud is not cast off when the flower blooms, but only taken up and expanded. The child is in the man, the struggling disciple is all there in the ripened saint. We must go on from the bud to the blossom, from the blossom to the fruit. We must go on to perfection; for going on to perfection is only carrying out in life what we know as truth and accept as the ideal of life. Doctrine is made perfect in life. To know truth is one thing; to accept it is another; to have it transformed in us into character by living it is still another—and that is perfection.

For example, to know the love for Christ which the Apostle Paul describes as full of joy, simply as a feeling, a glow suffusing the soul, is one thing, and a very precious thing. But that is only the seed, the flush of the bloom. If we would keep it, we must go on to perfection, *i. e.* we must carry it into life, embody it in the common acts and duties of every day's experience. This Christ has shown us how to do: "If ye keep my commandments, ye shall abide in my love." To give up our wills to him; to sacrifice our ease at his word; to soften the harsh word; to deny the self-indulgent wish; to put ourselves aside for others: all this is to go on to perfection. This is to keep adding to what we have.

Or again, there are passages in the gospels that fall on our minds like the mother's cradle-song on the fretful, angry child; as we listen they seem to charm away our mean thoughts, our hardness, our selfish passions. We say, "Oh, that I were such!" That is the rousing in us by God's Spirit of the hunger for righteousness which Christ blessed. But to keep this vision of the beauty of goodness, to feel this hunger ever pressing us on, to make it perfect, there is but one way—to translate it into life; at first imperfectly, rudely; but to go on, seeking truth in the inward parts, struggling to resist the unhallowed thought, to give up and submit to wrong rather than to do wrong, this is to make the outwardly beautiful an inward beauty, to carry the vision of Christ's loveliness into our own hearts. This is the remedy that lies in life— in strenuous endeavor. This is the earthly side. By itself alone it is barren. No man can use it unless he feels that God is working in him to will and to do.

We must look up to God, "that we may obtain grace to help." We must pray.

Work and prayer, then, are the two oars by which we drive toward heaven.  Either one alone is useless.  The monk's ideal of religion—to pray and meditate, to meditate and pray—this is to pull at one oar, and go round and round in a fruitless circle.  The modern superficial idea of religion—to be always at work, busy here, busy there, living outward and by our own endeavor—this is to pull the other oar, and to repeat the idle round, only in another direction.  But to lay hold of both—to pray as though God must do all, and to work as though we must do all—this is to make progress; this is to keep what we have by getting more.  This is to pursue the ideal of the perfect man in Christ Jesus, that like all ideals grows grander and deeper as we go toward it.

## THE FELLOWSHIP OF CHRIST'S SUFFERINGS.

The phrase is not a vague bit of sentiment; it is an expression of Scripture.  Saint Paul uses it; when he speaks of giving up all for Christ, making a complete surrender of his inmost self, he says it is that he may know among other things, "the fellowship of Christ's sufferings."  That is, that in the sufferings he has to endure he may be made one with Christ.  Not to suffer alone in sullen submission; not to suffer bravely even as a stoic, wrapping himself in his pride of manhood; but even in pain of body, in the pang of loneliness and bereavement, in the misery of disappointment and weakness, feeling a fellowship with his Saviour, finding a sweetness in this, that he shares his anguish with the great Sufferer, that together they are walking through the furnace, that in a strange mysterious identity of sorrow, God is working through them towards his kingdom of righteousness. What a thought is that to light up the hour of anguish! Now there is comfort in the simple sense of companionship in suffering, springing not from envy or selfish pleasure in the knowledge that others are no happier than ourselves, but from the human craving for sympathy. It is the dim sense of comfort striking through pain, that we are not alone, that we are not shut out from fellowship. And this sense of fellowship in suffering may rise to a height of nobleness when we fall in with sufferers that are bearing their anguish with patience, with meekness, with cheerfulness, and for a great cause.

What shall be said, then, of the fellowship in pain we have with our Saviour! He, the Highest, has bowed himself to pass under the yoke of our sorrows: "It behooved him to be made like unto his brethren in all things;" yes, in suffering even, that he might be able to succor them that are tried. Not by compulsion, not for himself, but freely and for us, that we might have the fellowship of God in anguish and agony. "He tasted death" with us and for us. It is a comfort and a joy to know this. If you have not felt it, be assured you have not sounded the depths of God's comfort, you know not all the meanings of the cross. But you may know it: it is for you. Go, then, with your pain of heart, and seek this suffering Saviour; seek his cross; lay your sorrows by his; learn what it is to know "the fellowship of his sufferings." Learn how the heartache lessens and loses its pang at the cross.

And then, too, Christ's sufferings are an explanation of our sufferings. To feel that we suffer with him is to a certain extent to have a clearing up of the mystery of suffering. It may not explain it entirely. What can? There is a mystery about pain before which all philosophy is dumb. To look at a little child that has never known good or ill; to see it toss in agony; to hear it moan; to see it look at its mother, with the dumb entreaty in it for relief, with the wonder in it that she will not help—who has known this, and not felt himself on a shoreless sea of mystery? One sting of suffering—one of its keenest stings—is the darkness that gathers round it. "Why, oh, why?" goes up the wail of the stricken mother by the new-made grave; and there is no answer. In the chambers where the sick lie for years on a ceaseless rack of pain, we stand by and we cry out to ourselves and God, "Why, O God, why?" Now we are to seek for explanation at the cross. We read there that this law of suffering is a vast and high law. Pain is not an accident—a mischievous intruder, breaking over the wall in this province of God's kingdom, and wreaking its malice on poor, weak, insignificant creatures here and there: no, it is for all. This law reaches from the Creator on his throne to the worm that writhes in the dust. "The whole creation groaneth and travaileth in pain until now." Even he, "the brightness of the Father's glory, and the express image of his person," "learned obedience by the things which he suffered." Wonderful revelation of the universality of suffering! Its dark stain and shroud of mystery rest upon and encompass even the throne of the Highest. Not even in heaven is the memorial of it lost. John tells us that when he looked through the open door into heaven and saw the throne set, "Lo, in the midst of the throne stood a Lamb as it had been slain." Yes, the image of suffering is enthroned in the midst of the adoring elders, the ranks of bright seraphim and cherubim. And this is as far as it goes an explanation of suffering. I do not pronounce it a full explanation; it only moves the mystery a little farther off. When we say that suffering is a vast, wide law—a law of the universe—we still leave a mystery; but it is the mystery of the universe, the mystery of Being.

The fellowship of our suffering, then, is with the greatest, the Highest of sufferers, with the Head of the universe. In suffering with Christ we suffer under a vast, all-comprehending law. When he cries "trouble is near; there is none to help," his wail expresses what the whole creation feels. And when we see this, when we come into this august companionship of suffering is it not easier to say: "Even so, Father, for so it seemed good in thy sight?" This fellowship of suffering unites us with Christ. It constitutes a veritable bond of union and communion. We not only suffer *as* Christ, but *with* Christ, so that we go through a common experience; and in our suffering we become identified with him. This, too, is a mystery; but it is a fact. How pain unites men! The soldiers that have marched and stood watch together; that have lain wounded side by side, and shared a common prison—the sailors that have buffeted the seas, and suffered shipwreck and famine together— are not these companions ever after as no joys shared could have made them fellows? Yes, there is a welding under the strokes of affliction that knits heart to heart; as the iron on the anvil beaten and crushed grows to its fellow iron one bar of steel, so hearts under the blows of misery grow one: this is the fellowship of suffering. "I bear in my body," says Paul, "the marks of the Lord Jesus:" blows of the scourge, wounds of stoning, the galling of the prison chain— marks of his suffering for Christ—yes, of his suffering with Christ; for he calls these the marks of Christ himself, as though he and his Master had been made one in the sharp hours of anguish that these witnessed. Oh, fellowship of the hour of pain, when the flesh fainted and the heart failed, has there not come to us in that loss when so much of life was torn from us, an approach to the mind and heart of Christ, such as no happy experience had ever given? "I" says Paul, "am crucified with Christ," and so made dead to the world and alive to the indwelling Saviour—dead? yes;—but what anguish is it so to die! And yet who knows all the meaning of the cross till it is planted in his own heart? Who knows the full union of the life with

Christ till he has known "the fellowship of the sufferings of Christ?"

## WORSHIP.*

What is the great business of the soul with God? You can think of much, of religion as we know it, here that will be left behind when we go out into eternity, just as the husk and shell drop from the ripening fruit. How many duties, labors, ordinances, will fall off with the stripping of death! But one great part will remain: we will worship and adore, we will trust and praise, there as here. Heaven as St. John saw it in his vision is full of worship. By many the importance of worship in God's eyes is forgotten: "Only live right," they say, "and you need not trouble yourself about devotion." But it is clear, I think, that God expects something more from us than merely good conduct. You say that you are an honest, well-behaved man, who do your duty to your fellow-man:—suppose you are; but Christ says "The Father seeketh worshippers" and your description of yourself does not meet that. You say "I will work," but God says, "I seek worship." You say, "I believe in duty, that is the true way to heaven,"

---

* This extract is from a sermon preached at the dedication of The Messiah Evangelical Lutheran Church in the city of Philadelphia, April 27th, 1879, on the text from John iv: 23. This church had in its infancy been under the pastoral care of the Rev. Theophilus Stork, D. D., the father, and hence the son had been requested to preach the dedication sermon upon the completion of the church building.

but in heaven they are absorbed in devotion. Poor soul, struggling to the right with no inspiration but your own purpose! What a dreary path is the path of duty with no vision of God in it!

But it is precisely because men do not look up to God that it seems easy to them to fulfill the standard of right living. They lose sight of the true goodness, and then their motives of goodness dwindle, and they are satisfied with a poor, narrow ideal of life. The poor mechanical artist goes on making his pictures in his dingy garret, painting from some dull sketch, and he thinks he does well enough, till one day he takes his work out into the fields and sees it against the blaze of the sky and the loveliness of hill and dale, and then how wretched it all is! So men look down on their earthly path and plod on, honest, they think, and true, and really meritorious; but if only they had one hour of worship—if they but looked up and saw the glory of God to praise him, could they talk of their good conduct? "Now mine eye seeth thee," cried Job, "wherefore I abhor myself and repent in dust and ashes." We need to worship God to be ready to work with him. We must always be going back to see him, or we forget how high and bright and perfect goodness is. It must always be a coarser kind of conduct that puts worship into the background. "Prophecies, (preaching) shall fail, tongues, (teaching) shall cease, knowledge shall vanish away;" but the love that beholds and adores, that communes and praises—this never faileth. The deepest in you is that which links you to God. He is the beginning and the end, the sweetness, and brightness, and life of all that is good. The fragrance of a flower, the sweet face of a child, a strain of music—what a joy and brightness come from them to our souls; but they only give what they have received from their Maker. It is his beauty and perfection that breathe from them. To know God, this is life eternal. To behold him, to worship him—this is heaven.

## TRUE CHRISTIAN PATIENCE.

Patience in a Christian is not mere endurance. It is not simply taking pain and setting our teeth, and saying, "It can't be helped, I must just bear it!" That is merely a passive state of mind—it is simply the soul coiling itself up in itself, and trying not to feel; or, if it does feel, not to cry out. But passive endurance is not the true godly patience—a grace of the Holy Spirit.

Take bodily pain, for instance, that great trial of the soul, one of the greatest of trials when long continued. What is patience under that? Is it simply not to cry out, not to blaspheme or blame God? No; but under it still to praise God, to go on thanking him, obeying him, doing our daily duty as far as we are able. There is a positive side to patience under suffering— and that positive side is what makes it Christian, spiritual. Such a Christian patience is a great developing force in character. Simply to lie still and do nothing, to empty ourselves of feeling, thought, activity—and that is what many people understand by patience under affliction—develops nothing: that is death; it is healing pain by narcotizing the soul. The patience of some people is nothing but a sort of spiritual opium. The more they have of it the weaker the soul gets. By saying to themselves "be still;" by suppressing thought and emotion, by numbing themselves, they gradually sink below their suffering; but that can never be the end of God's dealing. His way is to have us rise above, not sink below, our pain. And an active patience, so to call it, does that. It meets the force of suffering by another force and overcomes it. And that force is faith: "This is the victory that overcometh the world," says the Apostle, "even our faith." Misery, anguish, the sharp blows that sever us from our joys and comforts, these have in them the tempting power of the world. Job's wife speaks the mind of the world when she comes to her husband in the hour of darkness with her bitter despair: "Curse God and die." That is the voice of the world. How potent it is! And that is to be resisted—to be met face to face and overcome by faith. This is the triumph of patience, of an active patience, that endures because it sees the Invisible.

But it does not triumph without a struggle. The book of Job is a record of such a struggle. Job comes forth from the conflict by a sheer lift of faith and is resigned, not because he understands God's way, not because he has grown numb to his pain, but simply because he commits all to God. And out of such a struggle, what inward strength rises in the soul!

## THE SCRIPTURAL VIEW OF HEAVEN.

So much has been said of late about the meanness of encouraging ourselves with the prospect of a blessed hereafter that we have to go back to the Scriptures to refresh our sense of the reality and worthiness of the heavenly hope. "You ought to be brave and cheerful and dutiful without thinking about heaven," the philosophers tell us. "Indeed," they say, "you cannot be really brave and noble until you get rid of these sneaking hopes of future happiness, and do your duty just for right's sake." Now, I think, we ought always to be suspicious of any moral teaching which finds the motives to right living which Christ and his Apostles put forward too coarse. I do not deny the apparent magnanimity of the goodness which expects no hereafter. But this superfine unselfishness which dispenses with the heaven Christ reveals and is going to be good without any God; what is it after all but the hectic flush of virtue in the consumptive—the beacon of fast approaching death. For surely goodness which has no hereafter is on its way to death. It may seem very noble and lofty to abjure all hope of heaven, to be good with no prospect but of extinction in the grave; but that is the beginning of moral paralysis. If I am only a mote in the sun-beam, a midge born in the morning to die at night, what does it matter whether I am good or not? If there are no eternal consequences from my conduct, to me or to any one else—if character is only a hut built in the forest to shelter the traveler for a single night, and then left to decay, and not an eternal habitation—what can it really matter what character I have? In such an atmosphere the thirst for the life with God in Christ, the desire for the supreme goodness, must at last die away.

It is not so the Bible speaks; the great serious minds there as they look on life and speak of it by the inspiration of God's Spirit do not disdain the hope of the great life beyond. St. Paul takes up the sorrows of life and weighs them in the scale of eternity. He looks across the grave, into eternity, through the gate of heaven; he sees the coming glory, "our light affliction which is but for a moment, worketh for us a far more exceeding and eternal weight of glory." And again he says: "Mortality shall be swallowed up of life."

That, after all, is the key to the .problem of life, God is the Eternal One; he can never cease to be; and his righteousness is an eternal righteousness; it can never fail to be glorious and satisfying. And you, the child of God, have in you by your very childhood the seed of an eternal being; you are to live forever. It is not a question of your liking or disliking; the child of God made in his image is a child of eternity, and his character is an eternal thing. "He that is holy let him be holy still, and he which is filthy let him be filthy still"—these sentences echo down the corridors of endless being. It is in the light of eternal destiny, then, that the Bible shows the solemn significance of sin and righteousness; it is this penetrating, searching light which makes all life here start out into such tremendous importance.

There is no conception of life, its duties, aims, consolations, true to God's idea of it, which does not include this vision of the perfection and consummation of our being in heaven. The artist cannot paint to the height of his art without the light from the infinite heavens streaming on his canvas, and we cannot paint our life pictures but in this light of the eternal world.

## THE MAIN HINDRANCE TO THE GOSPEL.

Let us put it into one word—*Earthliness.* It is the insensibility of the soul, its stupidity to spiritual ideas and influences. The Apostle sums it up when he says "dead in trespasses and sins." It is as if you came to a man to show him a glorious landscape and found him blind; or to tell him of a wonderful discovery in science or a startling event in history, and he had lost his mind. We talk of the difficulties skepticism puts in the way of religion, of the influence science has in unsettling men's faith; but these to the vast weight of indifference, of stolid insensibility, which presses on men's souls, are as nothing. . . . Here is the real anti-Christ; it is the carnal heart, the earthly temper, the callous soul that dreams of no heaven, hears no divine voice, looks only down on the earth at its feet.

But what is meant by *Earthliness?* it may be asked. I think the answer is given in that picture of the multitude seeking Christ for bread: to whom he said: "Ye seek me not because ye saw the miracles, but because ye did eat of the loaves and were filled."

What is it that is so wrong, so hopeless in them? Not that being hungry, they sought for bread; not that being poor they were anxious for a living, or that being weak they ran instinctively to One that was so strong. But that having met Christ and known him, nothing in them should answer to him but appetite. Let us recall the day's experience. They had gone out into the wilderness and had spent many hours with Jesus. He had healed their sick; he had taught them spiritual truths; he had spoken of sin and goodness, of God and heaven; and at last his pity had ministered to their hunger. And now only one thing vibrates in the memory of the crowd. They have forgotten miracles and teaching, they only remember that they were fed. As if a harp should be put into the hand of a player and only one low bass string should answer to his touch. What a ruin is there! They have been tested and failed. Christ has come to them, and they have made their choice—not goodness, not heaven, not Christ, but bread. And thus is earthliness, spiritual stupidity, revealed in their hearts.

## ABRAHAM'S FAITH.

It was faith, simple unshaken faith in the Word of God, that made him all his life homeless yet hopeful. He had only God's Word, "I will bring thee unto a land that I will shew thee;" and so "he looked for a city which hath foundations, whose builder and maker is God."

What a simple, childlike faith, but how sublime! Only a few plain words of God; but that was enough. He saw the eternal city, not near, but afar off; not vivid and glorious, but dim and undefined. But God had said it, and he girds himself to go forth a pilgrim and a stranger on the earth. Great, heroic soul!— faithful Abraham, who chose his portion above and beyond. He walked by faith. Oh, mighty soul, with the far-seeing vision of trust; the vague, impalpable, elusive things of the Spirit, these were thy realities— not what the hand grasped, what the ear heard, what the eye saw; not pomps and powers, luxuries and flatteries of the sense, but the solemn verities of the soul, of eternity, of God. This is what is meant by that great saying which arches over the Bible, sweeping like a vast bow from Genesis to Revelation, "The just shall live by faith."

When once a soul has been possessed by the thought of eternity—an eternity of joy or woe beyond the grave—and has begun to live with the eye fixed on that, then he is another man. He sees the schemes, and interests, and great absorbing engagements of life here as so many booths that are put up for a few days, but will presently be taken down. Fortunes, honors, ambitions, comforts—what are they? Fire balloons that children send up with shouts and eager cries into the darkness, they burn and blaze, and then drop in swiftly-falling sparks, and the silent stars are left shining on far above in the hollow of the night.

## CHRIST'S VALUATION OF MEN.

Christ's interest in the humblest and the basest men shows us what their real worth is. Travelling along the old beaten way of human experience he discovers to us that which we could never find out for ourselves. As he looks upon some commonplace sinner he kindles into interest. Our wonder is excited; "what," we say, "can he see there?" And he makes us look with him until we see what he sees. So he stopped before the poor Samaritan woman with whom he talked at Jacob's well. What can he see in her? A soul—that is it; behind the dullness, the coarseness, the vacuity and the viciousness, an immortal soul. He walks through the gallery of the world and stops before this or that common man or woman; and suddenly we see what God sees; not the station, the manners, the culture, the genius—these are not a soul. What I really am is not my present dullness or brightness, but what it is in me to become, the mysterious capacity for likeness to God, the deep soil of spiritual being that can bear the bloom of heavenly graces, angelic affections, holy tempers. This is what really makes a soul. And this Christ saw. As if one should take up an ugly pebble and divine its heart, should brush off the mud and cut through the dull surface, until the flash shot forth, and so find a diamond. That is the heavenly valuation of a man. That is Christ's valuation of you.

But is this real? Is there not something exaggerated in such a reading of men? Will it bear the test? Can you make it practical? This brings up the whole question, on what scale are men to be measured? If this world is the whole; if the grave ends all, then Christ's valuation of men is not a real one; it is exaggerated, unpracticable. If the worth of a soul is its use here, what it contributes to the common stock of knowledge, culture, service, then the bulk of souls are poor, cheap things. One Joshua would outweigh a million Achans on that scale.

This shows as by a lightning flash what an immense depreciation of value men would be subject to if once it became an article of common belief that there was no future life. If when a man dies that is the end of him, if the three-score years exhaust the soul then every man must be rated at what he is here and now. It is of no use to talk about what he might be, of the depths of capacity in him; there are no depths; but only a thin skim of intelligence and emotions that this one life uses up. On such a scale men would dwindle, that is the mass of men. They would be worth almost nothing, they would be only bubbles; let them float down the stream and break.

But Christ sees beyond; he justifies his deep interest in men by the immortality he has brought to light. Every human soul to his eye is something vast, immeasurable, because back of it lies eternity; "*for the joy that was set before him, he endured the cross.*" What joy? "*That he might bring many sons to glory.*" Every poor narrow human life was to him an open portal through which he looked on an endless vista of blessedness or of shame. He saw all men in the light of their eternal being.

What a vision, then, there is in a human soul; what a gallery of pictures is folded away in each—the undying succession, ever brightening or darkening, that is to come out of each petty life. This is what he sees as he bends over me and says "What shall a man give in exchange for his soul?"

## CONSECRATION.

To many minds consecration is a word full of a strange awe. It seems impossible to attach it to the common every-day world. It suggests an abandonment of all that is usual, a solitary experience. It is a going out from among men into the desert to be alone with God. It means shutting up the store, bidding farewell to society, turning one's back on politics. But I am sure all this comes from a wrong idea of what holiness really is; as if it were shut up to certain specific acts. We are hardly escaped out of the primer of Judaism where the childish mind of the race was taught the deep idea of holiness by having it attached to certain places, persons, animals, vessels. But even Judaism might teach us that it is not the thing, the occupation, that makes holy; but the fact that it is given to God.

The priest was told to make a certain ointment, and that was holy; he who used it for common purposes was to be cut off, the same as though he had blasphemed God's name. What did that teach? Why that the commonest thing, an apothecary's oil, the making of it, the use of it, could be an act of consecration as pure as the service and sacrifice in the tabernacle. It was not the oil that was holy; it was its dedication to God's service. And whatsoever you give to God—your laughter and tears, your soothing of a child's grief, your manly struggle to provide for your family, your cheerfulness under trial—all, all is spiritual, holy, consecrated.

There are those who shrink from having religion extend too far. They are willing to be religious up to a certain point. The Sabbath, the church, the closet, the time of Lent, the sacramental season—these are for God; but eating and drinking, going on a journey, voting at the polls, selling calico, going into society—these are for me. And when the presence of God, the idea of consecration, is brought in there, it is felt to be an intrusion. We want religion to be to us as the stately cathedral, the secluded cell, the meeting for prayer; not as the atmosphere that enfolds all. Many a man who will go cheerfully to church, take the sacrament, say grace at table, and even pray in public, stops short when he hears of carrying his devotion to God down to his office, out into the market, off into the fields, up on the bench. "This is too much: business is one thing, religion another; politics is one thing, serving God quite another; society is one thing, consecration altogether another; everything in its place." Yes, by all means, everything in its place; but where is the place from which you will shut out God? What is there does not belong to him? What can you do that has not in it the stamp of right or wrong? Will you shut out God from his world? for it is all his—this great rich web of life, with its interests and gains, its joys and sorrows. Will you shut out from the feast the Giver of that feast? Will you blot the painter's name from his work? He is a part of it, and to say, "We will have life, its joys and toils, the wonder and glory of it; but we will not have God in it; except in our devotional hours, our church days," is like saying, "We will live, but we will have the sun only in a few fenced-off fields."

The blessedness of life is to feel the Divine Presence

ever pressing on us as the atmosphere, ever kindling our hopes, cheering our failures, like the sun. This shrinking from the companionship of God in the common hours of life is nothing but the secret conviction of our wrong living coming to the surface. It is the child shrinking from the Father's presence because it has been breaking the Father's law.

## CHRIST'S KNOWLEDGE AND LOVE OF MEN.

The marvel is that knowing men as he does, Christ neither despairs of human nature nor despises it. He goes on his calm persistent way, enduring men, bearing with them, hoping for them, believing in them, saving them. And this, after all, is the only really inextinguishable hope for human nature, for men, for ourselves. His calm, penetrating, hopeful vision of men makes it possible for us to believe in them.

His vision goes deeper than the outward crust of dullness, of coarseness, of deceit, and sees what is really valuable underneath. This vision was ever before the Saviour's eye. He loved men. He loved the priceless jewel of humanity in each, for that meant to him not merely a certain nature interesting in its gifts, its present condition, but a divine possibility. He loved a human soul because it was of God and had inherent in it a likeness to God, a capacity for spiritual beauty and nobleness. He saw mirrored in each poor narrow nature that spread its uncleanness before him, a picture of heaven and the heavenly condition. As one looking into a road-side pool sees presently in the muddy depth a picture of the stainless blue and snowy clouds above, so Christ's penetrating love sees in every human soul a possible heaven, and this is the love that breaks through the barriers of sin and deadness.

Nothing so assures us that the great divine love of Jesus is a practical thing, a force commensurate to the hard facts of human nature, as this calm penetrating vision of men in their actual condition that everywhere in the Gospels goes with it. There can be no transforming power in any affection that has not truth for its core. Now, Christ's love is founded on reality; it is no mere burst of sentiment. It knows us just as we are; it does not see us at our worst or at our best, but altogether in that completeness of what we are and what we may become. It goes to the bottom of us, leaves nothing out, and so it cannot die. There is nothing in you to be yet revealed to his searching eye. Surprises in the future of your soul's history, doubtless there are for you; but none for him. Do not be afraid that the long stretch of unfolding faults, of unsuspected meannesses suddenly blossoming out of the dark places in your heart shall ever change him. He has known you to the roots of your being before you knew him.

If there is one thing above all others to rest on in our Saviour's love, it is this assurance that he is not blind to our faults. He sees the gangrene in the soul, and behind the gangrene he sees the possibility of health and soundness that his touch can call into reality. The very truthfulness of Christ's vision of us gives the measure of his love. To know that he has read me, to hear him say, "Ye seek me because ye did eat of the loaves and were filled," and then to see his eye still bent on me in pity and in love, is to carry a thrill of hope into the soul. Have you ever thought of the deep meaning in that saying, "He knew what was in man?" At first it looks like a cynical saying, as if to emphasize the paltriness and baseness of men, by showing how Christ read them. But that is the surface meaning only. Keep it in mind as you read of Christ's intercourse with common men and women, with the woman of Samaria, the ten lepers, the hungry multitude. You see his pity, his patience, his tenderness. Knowing all man's sin, and hardness, and spiritual stupor, he looks deeper than we can see, he sees another world opening below that bad inner nature.

"He knows what is in man:"—the deep mystery we can never understand of the heavenly capacity in the soul, of its slumbering likeness to God. And so he talks to the dull greedy crowd of *the meat which perisheth not*, of the *bread which came down from heaven*, of *eternal life*. He is reaching down after the deeper nature he knows is in them, the essence of humanity which is the likeness of God, the indestructible capacity for heaven and sainthood, and all the blessedness of righteousness. Christ sees that. He sees it in you. And the vision is one of the secrets of his power; for by his persistent belief in our better possibility, he makes us believe in it ourselves.

## INDIVIDUALITY THROUGH CHRIST.

Christ realizes for us our individuality; he makes us feel each for himself his own separate worth, the weight and value of life in each as a unique quality. He brings out that inward craving for recognition of our individuality which is so deep and real, and yet of which we are often so ashamed, and stamps it as legitimate. He shows us that our sense of separateness from all others is not merely our fancy about ourselves, but that it is a real distinction. We see it projected as a solid image on the mirror of his knowledge and valuation of us.

In this respect Christ only brings to completeness what the Bible does throughout: he fulfills what the Law does in rude beginnings. For the religion of the Bible is an individualizing religion. It is always seeking to deal with men, not in masses, but in separate personalities. It sets each man alone before God.

And this sense of the separateness of men, of the worth and responsibility of the individual, has gone on increasing as Christianity has penetrated human nature. You have only to think how it has worked in changing the relations of the citizen and the state, in the release of men to freedom and personal contact with God in the Reformation, in the fixing of the right of private judgment, and even the diseased forms of self-consciousness which mark its extravagant development in modern civilization, to feel how individualizing a force is the religion of Christ.

Let us see, then, how Christ meets the craving we all feel for individual recognition, our desire for distinctness. At first we may feel that this desire is wrong, and that we can only look for Christ to condemn it. Ought we to crave recognition for our peculiar quality of life—ought we to wish to have a separateness from the mass? It is clear that this craving does, in its sinful development, become the root of a whole class of sins, some of them the most fatal to a life with God—vanity, pride, egotism, self-assertion, ambition. The politician straining for a higher pedestal on which to display his astuteness, the writer posturing and grimacing for originality, the preacher searching for strange themes and determined to make men hear him: how we blame them, scorn them, laugh at their egotism! Then there are the lower forms of this craving, the ridiculous, the terrible forms: the man who parades his family descent, the criminals who, rather than be unknown, write their names in deeds that make men shudder. What are all these doing but trying to extract themselves from the slough of oblivion, to rise above the sense of being forgotten, effaced? But what a pitiable thing it is to feel that whether they make men attend to them or not, they are all missing the mark! If they only knew what that craving was that drove them on to such efforts, and how there was One who knew and valued the true separate self in every one of them!

For in Christ this craving has its fulfilment. He gives it its true, pure scope. The satisfaction of our individuality is in Christ's recognition of us; in his personal reading of our heart, and his definite, separate knowledge of us. Observe how, for instance, in the case of Nathaniel, Christ's eye singled him out, defined him, made him feel in a sound, healthful way his real separateness, when he said: "Behold an Israelite, indeed, in whom is no guile." Nathaniel saith unto him, "Whence knowest thou me?" Jesus answered and said unto him, "Before that Philip called thee when thou wast under the fig-tree, I saw thee." And Nathaniel's experience is only a vivid illustration of Christ's habitual way of dealing with men. Think of all the men and women he met, and how at his touch they start out from the indistinguishable mass, figures, ever since Jesus looked at them and heard them, apart, unique. Take the family at Bethany, an humble obscure group as ever made a household, the type of myriads of homes unknown in the shadows of seclusion, and how as we read, "Now Jesus loved Martha, and her sister, and Lazarus," the figures start into distinctness; how individual, how portrait-like they stand before us! Think of the poor widow who came one day to the temple—what crowds of widows there were in Jerusalem, to the carnal eye all alike in their weeds of mourning, in their lowly insignificance—but Jesus is sitting there, he reads her heart, and with a word he draws her out of the crowd, sets her apart, and forever she stands before the ages a singular soul, the widow with the two mites, the most generous spirit that visited the temple that day. Even out of the depths of infamy and sin, he draws men in whom wickedness seems to have blurred every feature, and by a word re-chisels the soul into uniqueness. How like all other thieves was that poor wretch who hung by his side on the cross: one of the millions degraded, blunted, corrupted into indistinguishableness. But Christ is near him; the subtle influence of the Divine man goes to this man's heart; he says his few words of confession, of rebuke to his fellow thief; he breathes his short prayer; and Christ's word stamps again the impress of individuality on the poor defaced soul, and he goes away into Paradise, a figure unmistakable, like no other that ever lived, forever. So through innumerable instances Christ might be shown, flooding the light of his recognition on one and another soul before indistinguishable, but henceforth marked, vivid to all time.

What mere ciphers they all were until Christ turned his light upon them! What vivid portraits of separate men and women ever since! He comes to our withered individualities, blighted in the shade of men's ignorance of us, and he says as he did one day in the synagogue to the man with the withered hand, "Stand forth!" and then we are set apart, each known, marked as himself. What a wonderful gift of God to us is this; the personal, searching, vivifying knowledge

Christ has of us! The omniscience that gathers all souls in its wide glance, to whom there is nothing hid, nothing forgotten, nothing too small—the omniscience that comes out of the vagueness and blankness of the divine attribute, and consecrates itself in the glance of a personal Saviour on each one, and sets him apart in its knowing, its appreciation, its love, as it first set him apart in its creation!—no wonder St. Paul prayed for the Ephesians that they might be "able to comprehend with all saints, what is the breadth and length and depth and height; and to know the love of Christ which passeth knowledge."

What a picture it sets before us, too, of the great human family! What a vitality and light as from a new day bursting upon the toiling masses of men, does it bring, to think that all these are to one eye as individual as our children are to us! Is there not something dreary and oppressive in the impression a great throng of unknown men produces—the spectacle of the crowds that pour through the streets of a strange city? Like a flood they pour along, as indistinguishable as the drops in a river. And as we think of the millions all alike, the drops in the human sea, our hearts sink: so many, so indistinguishable, a million hearts beating like one, and nothing but obscurity for all: what a sad place is a strange, great city! How the multitudes roll over our imagination, like waves drowning our hope and sympathy! But that is only our weakness of vision. If Christ stood by us, as each soul came by, his look and word would touch an invisible spring, and out of the blank monotony would spring an individual portrait: every soul is solitary, separate, to him.

This, I am sure, is the solution of the problem how we shall satisfy our longing for an individual recognition, appreciation, and not fall into a life of self-assertion and egotism. It is to carry this hunger to Christ. But we must remember that the individuality he recognizes, and whose claims he satisfies, is a moral individuality; the separation in our life that he will stamp as real, is one of character, not of circumstances, gifts, manner, intellect, accomplishments.

# SCATTERED THOUGHTS.

## THE CHRISTIAN PILGRIMAGE.

"Get thee out of thy country, and from thy kindred, and from thy Father's house unto a land that I will shew thee," thus the call comes to one after another, and one after another goes forth a stranger and a pilgrim. We do not hear it in visions of the night, in solemn voices from heaven, as haply Abraham heard it; it is only the still small voice speaking within; but it bids us forth and we go. We do not, like Abraham, gather our goods and families and journey to strange lands; we do not, like the hermits of early ages, bid farewell to wife and brother and child and hie to the desert to sojourn a pilgrim till the end comes; we do not, as the pious in later times, sell all and shut out the world by the convent door, waiting in the cold cell the summons to go home—but the inward separation is made. We are pilgrims in our houses, strangers among our friends, the solid mansion is only a tent, the familiar scenes are only a foreign land. It is borne in on us that we are not home. We are separated by the widest of all separations, the wandering of the heart. Our heart is in heaven; for our treasure is there. We sojourn as in a strange country.

## BENEFITS OF RESTRAINT.

There never is a time when we can afford to be set wholly free, to feel that now we may do just as we please, that no one sees us, that we shall not be called to account. From the cradle to the grave we are set by God's providence in angles of observation where the light always falls on us, where the sense of accountability bites in on the conscience and reason, and we are made to feel more or less "for this, too, I must give an answer."

Men talk a great deal, especially in these days, of the nobility of freedom, of the servility of a religion that always has a sense of restraint, a taste of the bitterness of dread in it. We are told that a man should be a law unto himself, that goodness should be spontaneous. And there is a measure of truth in it. Perfect love does cast out fear. A sanctified man, an angel in heaven, a saint in glory, will not need to be sensible of being watched; he will have the law in himself. That is a noble, a grand state; but it is the state of heaven, of a perfection far beyond us. But even that does not dispense with the element of accountability. Perfect love casts out fear, not because it gets rid of the idea of being under observation, with God's eye on it, but because it has got rid of all the lawlessness, the hidden veins of evil, which make God's eye a menace and terror.

## SUFFERING.

"It is the misfortune of kings," said a German statesman, "that they have no one to tell them the truth." Everything is softened and colored not to offend them; and so they live in an unreal world. And it is so with us when we are not subjected to suffering. God's gifts act like non-conductors; wealth, and health, and success, all make a world in which we live, on the outside of which is God. Now distance from God is distance from strength and heat and spiritual reality; just as distance from the sun is distance from warmth and force. And now comes the crashing blow that breaks down the palace wall, scatters the courtiers, tears away the silken curtains. The king is dethroned, and he walks forth to face the realities of things. And trouble comes, wealth flees, health fades, all the springs in the oasis are dry, and the desert is eating its parched way up to the man; he must perish! No, there is one deep well that never dries; it is the being of God; it is the presence of the Divine brooding Spirit. Then the soul does one of two things; it finds out the hollowness of its pretended faith; it realizes that it never knew God at all, but that its Divinity was success, happiness, the flow and gladness of mere existence; or it rises up through throes and agonies that cleave down to the bottom of the spirit, and reaches out and touches God. It finds that man can live without riches, or friends, or strength of body, if only he clasps God. And this is a real knowledge.

It is a coming nearer to the sun. What a profound word of Job that is, after the storm of his trials had passed and he returned to his rest in God: "I have heard of thee by the hearing of the ear; but now mine eye seeth thee."

## LISTENING TO GOD'S VOICE.

"Speak, Lord, for thy servant heareth." In those few words of Samuel lay the secret of his great life. The wisdom of Samuel throughout all his acts was that the touch of God's hand was constantly felt on his heart. And this must be the secret of our lives. If they are to deepen and widen and go on increasing in strength and holiness till at last they appear before God, then they must forever be feeling his touch. Not in our activities undertaking great things, not in our gifts that charm and convince men, not in our keen feelings and raptures and delightful visions of the spiritual world—in none of these things is the power of the religious life; but in this that at every turn we are listening to catch the still small voice, which when heard and followed makes life success. How simple the problem of life becomes with this key. It is only this, that we are constantly led of God.

Often, however, our souls are deaf to God's voice, because they are pre-occupied. This pre-occupation makes every voice speak with an earthly meaning. God's voice is intercepted by the roar of the world, in which we are struggling. It finds no ear in us, let it speak never so tenderly, urgently.

Would you have this gift, that began with Samuel's childhood, and went with him to old age? Would you hear God speaking to you? That very longing is the voice of God to you: you hear it dimly, as one half awakened; it is God speaking in your soul, saying, "open thine ear, and I will speak a word for thee!" But you do not know how to listen, how to get where the voice shall reach you. You must go into your closet; you must shut the door; you must call for God; you must wait for him; you must keep listening, looking, waiting. He is there. You do not hear him, but he is speaking; his thought and wish for you are going forth; they will reach you. But you must wait on the Lord. Strain your vision into the thick darkness; hold your ear to that awful silence, and sooner or later out of the darkness a form will grow, a face will shine, a voice will sound. God will speak to you, and tell you all you need to know. You shall hear him more and more continually through all the roar of the world. Life will be full of his voice; all voices will be his.

## THE CLOSEST FRIEND.

What a refuge from a cold world is the thought of Christ's knowledge of us. There are times when life wears a hard and lonely aspect even to the most favored. We taste the strange bitterness of the separateness in which each soul is set. At such times the nearest do not seem to touch us; and while we shrink from the prying attempts of man to get at our secret thoughts, yet we long for a knowledge that can read all our inward life, appreciate its perplexities, burdens, wishes, and bring the touch of sympathy. But think: there is One that knows. Not a thought, not a wish, not a vague impalpable yearning rising like a dim mist in the depth of your heart, but is seen of him. Think of it in the lonely hour when you cry "all have forsaken me." Think of it in the silent night watches when the rush of thought grows oppressive. Think of it in the great crowd where the thousand unknown faces make the sense of your solitude strike in like a winter chill. Think—there is One that knows you, reads you, answers you.

## GRACE TO BEAR SUFFERING.

Suffering when it first meets us seems the strongest thing in the universe, but when we find that there is something stronger, God's might and grace, we have made a great discovery. It is the opening of a new world. I ask you, ought we not to praise God more for grace to bear our sorrow than for sorrow's removal? In the one case God only puts out his hand and takes off our load; in the other he comes into the soul and bears the load with us. Then we are made partakers of the Divine nature, we are one with him, we feel the beating of the Divine heart against our own, and we stagger on, weak, yet oh, how strong! I would rather have God come into my life and help me carry my load, than have him send an angel to take it off. In the one way we only get rid of pain; in the other we are filled with God.

## THE TRUE PATH IN LIFE.

There is a rule of life, very popular in these days, that every man may find his right career mapped out for him in his favorite tastes: what you like to do, what you incline to naturally, that is your calling. But that, it seems to me, is a very short-sighted rule. Its fault is that it takes no account of any life but this; it leaves God and his individual and personal guidance of each one of us out of the question. To say that to succeed one must only do what he naturally inclines to, seems to me utterly pagan. It makes life to be measured only by the happiness of the hour, by the results that appear here, while Christ teaches us that life is to be measured by its eternal results. But even for results here, it is not true that only the work we have a natural bent for is fruitful work. How many lives that are useful and blessed of God and man travel in shadow and with constraint through the whole arc of life here; but we know they travel truly, and when the circle is complete beyond it will lie at last in light. St. Augustine was educated for a rhetorician, and he loved the splendor and excitement of his conspicuous place in Rome. But he was called to be a preacher of the Word: it seemed to him that he could not take the office, and it was in spite of tears and reluctance that he was ordained. But once called, he followed. He went forward cheerfully and with his whole heart; and what an impress he has left on the Christian Church!

Do not complain, then, of your life and its duties. Do not waste your strength and freshness in dreaming of what you might have done. You may not be in the path most congenial to you; you may seem to yourself to be wasting your best powers; but if God's providence has turned your steps that way, it is your path, you must tread it: there is no other way for you. Only listen for God's voice; at every turn wait for his whisper. You shall be directed and the hard path prove to you the true path.

## THE SOUL'S VALUE.

We are continually saying that men think too highly of themselves; and they do, of what they are, of their wit and grace and skill and power. But of what they may be, of the hidden treasures of their spiritual being, they think almost nothing at all; as if a man should value the curious ugliness of a lily bulb and make nothing of the lovely flower that is to come out of it. You do not think enough of yourself. You do not value your real self as highly as Jesus does. He died for it; you fling it down in the dust; you sneer at its heavenly instincts; you are tempted at times to sell it for a bauble, a bit of worldly tinsel, that soul of which he is asking you "What shall you give in exchange for it?"

## THE CURE FOR EGOTISM.

A great writer has said that vanity can never be cured; that a man once an egotist is one always, whether saint or sinner. That may be true of all mere self-culture. But there is a cure in Christ; it is the cure that comes from the vision of God, eclipsing the vision of self; it is the cure for the dazzle of the lamp by the rising of the sun. The soul that is hidden in the vision of God's great glory is hid away from egotism.

## PRAYING ALWAYS.

Discipleship to Jesus is not something that can be put on and taken off as our convenience and necessity may require. If we follow at all, we must follow always; if we are Christ's at any time, we must be his at all times. Religion is not a business of Sundays and prayer-meetings, of closet hours and revival seasons only; it is a business of every day and every hour of the day, of every place and every engagement of life.

So Jesus tells us, that we ought "always to pray," and we read of Cornelius that he "prayed to God always." If he prayed to God always, then he did not pray formally a set prayer, for then would he have prayed only on the festivals, in the morning and in the evening, and possibly, if very exact and punctilious, like Daniel, at noon. But we are told that he "prayed always;" then he did not only pray merely when he was in trouble. The burdens of sorrow, and pain, and bereavement, will often set men to praying, and they are very earnest while the goad pricks and the wound is yet sore: but it is not always night, even in this dark world; sunny days come, hours of joy and rest; then the prayer which sorrow indited ceases, as the summer brooks stop running when the storm is over. But Cornelius prayed always. How could he do it? He was a busy man, with many worldly cares. Is it possible to obey the Apostle when he tells us to "pray without ceasing?" Yes, when prayer is the free spontaneous lifting up of the spirit to God, and not the mere repetition of a form, or the forcing of a reluctant mind and heart into the presence of a neglected God—then, we can "pray without ceasing." To pray always, it is not necessary to be always *saying* prayers, or framing the heart's desires into palpable petitions. The fountain shoots its tall column heavenward; it would send the silvery shaft, with its musical sheeny spray upward forever; but a stone is laid on its mouth, and the column falls, but the spring, the joyful leap is *there*, though shut down; take but away the repressing stone, and again it leaps upward, with its feathery spray and quivering dart of gladness. So, in the child of God is the fountain of prayer; his heart leaps up to the blessed God; he wakes in the morning to send the beautiful shaft of his petitions and praises to Jesus;

but the necessary, lawful cares of his home, his business, his weariness, his very duties of religion, lay a stone on the mouth of the fountain, and he seems not to pray; but deep within, the strong spring and mighty leap of the heart's desire wait only for the care to be taken off, the business to be laid aside, and again will the soul go up to its God. The fountain would play forever, the soul would pray without ceasing; that is praying always.

## RELIGION.

The religion of Christ is in its final aim—in its highest and perfect form—a personal relation, and not a service. Religion is a state of heart towards God. Sin is spoken of in the Scriptures as a state of alienation from God: this seems to sum up all its guilt and misery—this fathoms the depth of its ruin, and exposes the very essence and lowest foundation of its nature. Religion, then, is no more than a reversal of this—it is the resumption of that first ordained relation between God and the soul, of love and harmony; and it is a great mistake to take its first crude forms for its last mature life. Now so many Christians never get beyond the first stage of religion, namely the stage of service, that it is easy for one looking over the church, and judging of the divine life by those who are but imperfectly living it, to suppose that *service* is the highest form of godliness. One might as well walk through a forest where the oaks had been stunted and dwarfed, and say oak trees were never intended to grow tall. Consider now what the divine life, in its ripened, perfected form, is intended to be. I say it is a life, not of *service primarily*, but of *love;* service is included in its broad sweep, but not as its chief end and aim. Service means work done for wages, but Christian living is not for compensation; it may take that shape at first—the believer may honestly take Christ as a Saviour, and not as a Friend; this is the first crude form; but the higher final form is that of *love*, and then service comes, not first, but in the train of love as a handmaid. Then the Christian serves Christ as a friend.

## FAITHFULNESS IN SMALL THINGS.

I fear sometimes we are slack to till our plot in the vineyard because it is not a conspicuous place. We want to do work that shall shine; well, yes, and so we ought to wish; but shine in whose eyes? in that of our fellow-workmen, or in those of the Master? Is it the applause of men we crave—to be known as a conspicuous church, an influential church, a stately, cultured, popular church? Or, is it the praise of the great Judge who accounts that one greatest, man or church, who serves most faithfully and unselfishly? One man builds the spire in the sight of all eyes, and another lays the foundation deep out of sight. But the spire-builder is no greater in the final fame of the temple than the foundation-layer.

It is a shame to think of our work as a small work, or to complain that what we do is hid away in a corner. There are no corners to God. "The darkness and the light are both alike to him." Let the pastor toiling in the lonely hamlet with his parish scattered over the hills, remember that. He is set to purify the fountains. He toils among the roots of things. There are no shouts for his work now among those silent valleys, but some day it will appear in its solid fruit. And let our home mission work go on planting the church of Christ in far-off and forgotten places. We need not be discouraged because no flourish of trumpets accompanies this toil; its flourish will come when the end crowns the work.

## THE GREAT DAYS OF GOD.

It is in our age as it has always been, the great days of God come, and to many who live in them they seem only poor, flat, empty days; they complain of the insipidity of life. It was so when Jesus lived on the earth; it was so when the Apostles were converting the Roman Empire; it was so when Luther thundered at the gates of Rome. In every stirring age there were men yawning over the dull days, and women killing the weary time by frivolous devices. And it is so now. The century is pouring into the ear of history a new story of Christian heroism and achievement; and in all our churches there are men and women who are gaping for very weariness, and praying for some new sensation in religion, while the critics are vaporing about the decay of faith and the decline of Christianity. Were the Master to speak, would he not say to us as he did to the poor, weary, old religionists and the sneering critics of his day, " *Ye can discern the face of the sky ; but can ye not discern the signs of the times?* "

## THE COMMON SENSE SCHOOL OF PHILOSOPHY.

Great as its virtues are, the common sense school has this defect, it insists on explaining everything: everything in the universe must be as plain as the multiplication table; no haze on its horizon, no dimness in its sky. But, then, the horizon on which there is no haze is a very contracted one, and the sky that has no dimness is not the illimitable vault that unrolls itself above us every night. The trouble with the common sense school, from Aristotle down, is that it has no place for the infinite, the mysterious, that sense of unfathomableness and awe which come to us with the glimpses which both nature and the Bible give us of being and truth, distinct enough for us to form some idea of, to be impressed and inspired by, but too vast for us to comprehend or explain. Now Lutheranism does not belong to the school of common sense; it is Platonic, and not Aristotelian. It has its bright, luminous centre, Christ, the Incarnate Son, the brightness of the Father's glory and the express image of his person, in whose light we can walk unperplexed; but, then, from him the universe natural and spiritual, melts away into infinite gradations of being, the last of which is but a faint mist on the illimitable horizon.

## CHRISTMAS.

It is a very wonderful thing, when we stop to think of it, that eighteen hundred years after the poor peasant child was born in that dim Eastern land, the great civilized world should be celebrating his birth-day with such pomp and holiday; celebrating it more splendidly and elaborately every year. Out of that rude age of semi-barbarism, from that uncultured peasant home, the gentle Teacher stretches out his hand and lays it on the history, the holidays, the literature and art, the religion and morality, of the world's finest civilization, and says, "These are mine;" and men, whether they acknowledge him or not, have to answer, "Yes, Jesus of Nazareth, they are thine." That, I think, is the ever-growing marvel of Christmas. Over and over again as the season comes round, though all the year men have been arguing against him, rejecting him, deriding him, the world gathers about the manger and honors the Babe of Bethlehem. All the year men tug at the chain which binds them to his throne, and then on Christmas day acknowledge that, somehow or other, Jesus of Nazareth has won a greater sway over human lives. Is that not a marvel?

## CHRIST'S INFLUENCE ON THE WORLD.

It is not too much to say that Christ has transformed the conscience, the affections, the very passions of the race. The modern sympathy for animals, the sense of responsibility for wealth and power, the conviction that national strength gives no justification for aggression, the quick compassion for all classes of the weak and suffering, the growing abhorrence of violence and impurity, the deepening estimate of the value of truth—these wonderful signs of the Christian spirit are found almost as much outside the church as within; and what does their appearance indicate but the growing power of Christ over men's thoughts and feelings? Men do not see him; and yet they are moulded by him. The very wishes of their souls are being transformed under the touch of hands invisible to them: they are the hands which clung to Mary's breast that first Christmas morning in Bethlehem. I cannot open a great novel or poem, or read a respectable newspaper, but I hear the Christian accent sounding in every sentence. There is not a great statesman but must, if he would keep the respect and confidence of the nation, at least profess allegiance to the great principles of truth, human brotherhood, sympathy for the oppressed, which are the very birth-mark of Christianity. The age is Christian, and growing more Christian. Some of its great thinkers, it is true, vehemently disclaim the name of Christ. Be it so. They may refuse to march under his banner, but fight his battles they must.

## NEARNESS TO CHRIST.

The personal element in religion is the last to ripen. Christ is clear to us as a Teacher, a Redeemer, a King, long before he is vivid as a personal Friend. How shadowy, far-off, does this Saviour often seem! What shall bring him closer? The "faith which worketh by love." Obedience is the skilful artist who, touch by touch, year after year, is bringing out the features, the smile, the deep look of the eyes, into reality. Every deed done for him, every sacrifice made in his name, every sorrow cheerfully taken because he sends it, is adding a clearness to the vision of his presence.

## A CHRISTMAS THOUGHT.

The repetition of those words, "Unto you is born this day a Saviour," should be like coming back to look at the portrait of a friend that is being painted for us; every Christmas we should find it nearer perfection.

When we turn to this portrait this year can we say, "Ah, how much more life-like, more real he is than last year?" Then our Christmas days are steps climbing up from earth to heaven. Each year we are mounting higher; each year the face that looks down on us is more vivid, clear, near. What an incomparable gift from Christ to us is it, if on this Christmas morning we can say,

"I see Him still nearer whom always I see."

## SORROW THE CURE OF SHALLOWNESS.

Can a human soul be truly great and deep that does not taste, yes, drink deeply, of the bitterness of life? Who can read the histories of the noblest characters of the Bible, who can trace the steps of the one perfect man, learning obedience by the things which he suffered, and not feel that it is possible to be too happy—yes, too innocently happy?

A life happy, and only happy, is like a virgin prairie: it is bright with verdure and flowers, but it never yields a harvest worth garnering. For that the ploughshare must tear it up, turn under its green and purple and gold, and bring the under mould to the corrosion of wind and rain; then comes the rich grain.

Mere happiness, the delight of living, leaves us shallow. That is what the Bible is repeating over and over. "It is good for me that I have been afflicted; that I might learn thy statutes!"—there it is. The writer of that had been a happy boy, wandering among the fields, drinking in the delight of mere living: what a blessed thing the sunshine was, how gay the flowers, how intoxicating the fresh breeze, his liberty, his sensation! But if he goes on wandering through the sunshine, he will never be anything but an unthinking boy. "Before I was afflicted I went astray;" that is, he had no purpose, he was out of the path, he made no progress. Then came the shadow, the storm, the fear, the anguish of life; these drive him out of the happy fields into the school; then he begins to ponder; he opens the book of life and learns the meaning of things; he is miserable, he is suffering, and his misery takes him below the surface of things; thought deepens, feeling intensifies; he is learning God's statutes. He says, "Oh, how unhappy I am!" Yes, but how much larger he is.

There are three directions in which sorrow enlarges our horizon. Of course there is nothing in sorrow itself that necessarily deepens or expands character: suffering withers, contracts, embitters a bad will, even while it acuminates it. But we are speaking now of a right will, of a Christian soul, and what sorrow does for it.

Sorrow expands *downward*, and *outward*, and *upward*.

It takes us down into ourselves. It is all very well for children to be unconscious of themselves, but there is something feeble in the life of a man that has never turned in on itself and pondered the meaning of its own existence. There is an unconsciousness, a losing of self in a greater, higher life, which does restore to us the beautiful simplicity of childhood; but that comes only when we have gone through the knowledge of ourselves, and then committed self to the keeping of God. But for a life to be truly deep and great, the soul must first explore itself. What words of experience those are, "I thought on my ways, and turned my feet unto thy testimonies;" and that picture of the prodigal son—"he came to himself." Well, the sorrow of life takes us by the hand and leads us down out of the sunshine into the deep chambers of the soul; it brings us to ourselves.

It opens outward as well as inward, for it interprets to us what is within men: once walk in the shadow, know the bitterness of bereavement, disappointment, pain, the nameless melancholy of dejection, and it is as though the figures about us had become transparent; we look through them; we see the world of fears, hopes, joys, pains, that make each man's life: how the horizon has widened! God has struck the chord of anguish in us, and all around us; from human hearts we hear the answering vibration: we know men; we have entered into the complexity of the inner life. How deeply interesting that makes the world of humanity! What a yearning toward our suffering brethren comes with our own experience of pain; what an extinction of old aversions and repulsions sorrow brings! We learn to love suffering men because we have suffered.

Most precious of all, it opens our vision upward. It has sometimes been questioned whether a perfectly happy man would ever think of God.

A life where the sun of happiness never sets has no beyond. It is sweet—but so narrow! Now, God will not have us narrow. We are his children, and something of the sweep and vastness of his being he will have us discover. He will reveal to us the immeasurable greatness and glory of himself, and so he draws aside the veil of our happiness which hides him. He makes it dark; loved faces fade in the shadow, bright scenes grow dim, the gloom enters the soul, and then we throw up our faces, and lo! God shines out through the abysmal depths of our night. "When he slew them, then they remembered that God was their Rock."

## PENTECOST.

### THE GIFT OF THE SPIRIT.

Pentecost is an experience that must be enacted in every disciple's experience. How many there are in our churches, honest, well-meaning souls, who, if they put their experience into words, would have to say with those St. Paul questioned at Ephesus, "We have not so much as heard whether there be any Holy Ghost." They are not un-Christian, but only blindly Christian. They know of a Saviour; they have read of him in the Gospels, they have heard of him by the hearing of the ear, and they painfully strive to conform their lives to what they understand to be his will; but they have never known him as a present, realized Saviour. Feebly they grasp him and hope to be saved by him, as certainly they may be; but they have never felt the strong grasp of Christ upon them, that conviction of life from him and in him which makes a man forget his old questions about whether he shall be saved, in the strong, clear consciousness of a present salvation in a justifying and life-giving Saviour. Now it is one great work of the Spirit, his first Pentecostal work, to do this for us. He changes our "Lord, I believe, help thou mine unbelief," to the grander word "I know whom I have believed."

It is the experience of Pentecost that gives individuality and originality to the religious life. Dr. Alexander, in one of his charming books, complains of the tameness and monotony of the mass of Christian lives. The souls in a church seemed like the houses in a city street where

> "The houses are all alike you know:
> All the houses alike in a row."

That is the result of a groping faith which has failed to appropriate vigorously a Saviour brought within by the work of the Spirit. When the Spirit comes he does for the soul what the sun does for the flowers: in the dark cellar all the plants wear a pallid monotony, but put them in the sun, and out of each the sun draws into distinctness its appropriate color, no one like another. For what the Spirit does is to bring the things of Christ to the soul, that each may embrace the Saviour as its own particular Saviour. But Christ realized in the life of each soul is appropriated according to the soul's natural bent: Christ in St. Paul did not give the same type of character and turn of thought as in St. John or St. Peter. But in each one Christ realizes and brings out the individual bent of the man. To be the more deeply and intimately rooted in Christ, then, is to be the more particularly and individually ourselves.

Would we have our religious experience written, not over another man's copy, but in the fresh lines of our own individuality? Then the Holy Spirit must take the pen from our hands and show us what is our own style.

## THE HOPE OF EASTER.

The Easter idea may be given in one word, one of the greatest of Christian words, *Hope*. It is this which runs like a golden thread through St. Paul's chapter on the resurrection, the great Easter-day chapter of the New Testament. "If Christ be not risen, then is our preaching vain—if Christ be not raised, your faith is vain. If in this life only we have hope in Christ, we are of all men most miserable. But now is Christ risen from the dead, and become the first fruits of them that slept." How the trumpet sounds through these great words; nothing of melancholy, of doubt, of timidity here, but the inspiring breath of one of the greatest of truths. The apostle stands by the unfathomable chasm of the tomb, into which for ages the race has been vanishing with not a whisper to tell of what is beyond, or if there be any beyond at all; he looks into the impenetrable dark, that darkness which has swallowed up so many brave and beautiful souls, which seems to swallow in its dumb abyss not only all souls, but the very worth and dignity of the soul itself; and when the trembling cry comes from his companion, "O Paul, is there any hope?" his answer comes back clear, firm, like the blast of God's trumpet—"Hope? Yes, hope in abundance; an eternal hope: Now is Christ risen from the dead—as in Adam all die, even so in Christ shall all be made alive. The trumpet shall sound, and the dead shall be raised incorruptible—for this corruptible must put on incorruption, and this mortal must put on immortality." That, I say, is the voice of hope. Over the broken tomb in the garden, then, we are to read in letters of gold, one word, *hope;* in the sweet light of the Easter morn we are to see shining that one word, *hope;* in the accents of the angels, "he is not here; he is risen," we are to hear but one word, *hope!* That is the Easter message; the Easter idea.

And, now, ever since the stone was rolled away from the tomb on that first Easter morn, a flood of light has been pouring from that open sepulchre upon the world. First it streamed upon Mary Magdalene, and lit up her trembling soul. Then it fell upon others of the weeping women, and turned their despair into triumph. It rose higher; it filled the apostolic band, the little company of the disciples. It poured out on the world; the darkness that hung like a pall on the Roman Empire fled before it. Into the wide human heart, suffocating with despair in that long night of decaying courage and dying faith, was born a wonderful hope. From the wrecks of ancient greatness came the sigh of the race, "If a man die, shall he live again?" and then out of Joseph's tomb came the answer which made the decrepit nations young again, "Because I live, ye shall live also." And so through all the Christian centuries the light of that hope has gone steadily shining till men have almost lost the power to conceive what the darkness was before Christ died and rose again. How hard it is for us, who were born and bred in this hope, to realize its brightness.

This hope is not a part of the nature of things. It is the light which Christ brought with him from the grave. Close the tomb of Joseph, efface from history the events of that first Easter morn, and night will settle again in the human heart. Do you ask what it is a hope of? I answer, it is a hope of two things combined, of life forever, and that forever a growing into Christ's perfection. We must never, as we stand before the open tomb on the Easter morn, let these two be separated. Men are always trying to satisfy themselves with the one without the other. At one time they emphasize the truth that we are immortal; as though *any* immortality would be blessedness. But how unreasonable that is: to live forever growing worse, farther from God—more hopeless, more unloving—that would not be a boon. It was not such an immortality that Christ brought to light when he rose from the grave.

On the other hand, men have urged that the true blessedness brought to light by Christ is the blessedness of goodness, and that to insist upon adding to this immortality is mere selfishness. But that, too, is only a diseased fancy. What is goodness that dies in sixty years? What is the worth of this ephemeral virtue which goes out like a candle at the puff of death? Christ did not die and rise again that we should be good, and then presently be nothing. He rose to knit us in goodness to him forever: "Because I live, ye shall live also." He died and rose again that we might live with him an eternal life, an eternal life of goodness. It is true that the great end of Christianity is to make men holy, but it is that they may be holy and happy forever. As has been said, "Virtue is its own reward; but that reward is eternal."

## LONG PRAYERS.

It is not so much the length as it is the emptiness and weakness of public prayers that wearies. Excluding such protracted petitions as have long since gone out of use, and to abuse which is only to lash a dead carcass, I affirm that the tedium of any prayer we hear now is from its quality, not its quantity. Some men are always getting ready, and never reach their prayer. Some do not pray, but only preach. Others get through their real prayer, but do not know it, and go on repeating a form of words. But whenever a pious soul with ordinary gifts has a burden and prays it out, and then stops, he will edify, and his prayer prove no weariness, be it long or short.

## THE PASTOR'S COURAGE.

If we loved men more, we would not be so afraid of them. What dull, impoverished souls sit under our ministry! Let us be frank in looking this fact in the face; how narrow, how cheap, is the Christianity of men, with its contracted scope, its selfish idea of salvation, with its sickly fears, its bigotries and jealousies, its poor vision of life. That is one side, but without the other it is only a half-truth, in effect a falsehood: the Christianity of the men before us *is* narrow and cheap, but how rich and full it may be!

Men are capable of seeing and feeling and embracing the grandeur and joy of living, not for themselves, but for him that loved them, and for the souls he has redeemed. If it were not so, what a barren, heart-sickening work would this Christian ministry of ours be!

There are those divine possibilities, in the souls to which we minister, of sacrifice for Christ and his kingdom. But we fear to show men what they are in their selfishness, and what they may become in a Christian generosity and self-denial, lest they may be offended.

## CHRISTIAN IDEALISM.

Every man to be a successful helper of men must be an idealist. He must be able to look through the integument of the mean outside, the triviality, the dullness, the shabby daily living, to the soul that lies stupefied within. He must create that soul as it is to be, in his mind's eye, as the painter creates his picture from the poor model before him, before he puts it on canvas. He must bring out the real thing as God sees it. He must learn as Jesus did to see in the tricky Zaccheus "*a son of Abraham*," in his mean neighbor a child of God.

And the way to do that is to live in that large atmosphere of heavenly communion which gives the power of heavenly insight. When we think of what Jesus saw in common men, and what we see in them; and then of what his fellowship and meditation were, and what our fellowship and meditation are, all the difficulties about working for base men are plain.

## CHRIST BOTH A PERSONAL SAVIOUR AND THE HEAD OF THE CHURCH.

There is a portrait given us in the New Testament, the portrait of a divine life, a perfect human life, and at the same time a perfect expression of God. If you study that life, and approach it, and receive it into your own, it seems to me you cannot fail to have the correction of both the errors into which the Church is alternately falling. He is the Saviour of me personally; I can know him and receive him. I must be personally by my own solitary faith united to him. There can be no truth or vitality in any religion without that. That secures forever from any excess of the churchly idea. I have seen him, I know him, I live by him; and without him personally mine I am nothing. He may be a great deal more; his life may go forth in other ways; but this much is true, I am a Christian by my personal union with him. And that is universally essential. Let that be held and taught, and the idea of Christian fellowship goes at once outside of my church; it is the death of all exclusion; it sets me at liberty to work and worship with any quantity of sects whose doctrinal system is imperfect, and even in many respects erroneous. And that keeps me from unduly magnifying the ordinances and sacraments and the organic life that belong to the corporate body, the Church. Then again it is the correction of the extreme into which the personal faith idea is so apt to run. For the Christ of the New Testament is something very much greater than my personal Saviour. He is the Head of the Church; he stands in a deep, mysterious relation to the whole body of believers of all ages; and his life is not only for me, it is for the whole body. It is something outside of me and outside of all existing Christians. It is a vast complex, with its members, and orders, and ministries, and its pervading life, into which I am taken up and used.

I do not believe we shall find any other reconciliation of these opposite extremes of Christianity. One way to solve the problem is to drop out one of the factors; you may say the Church is everything; or you may say the individual is everything. But that is only giving up the problem. Christ is for me, and he is for the Church. He died for me, and he died for the Church. And if I drop out either idea, I have mutilated Christianity.

---

## THE WORLD FOR WHICH CHRIST DIED.

We are always in danger of losing that broad view of the faith which marks the New Testament. It is so natural to be narrow; such a work of grace to have breadth of sympathy. We are continually slipping into contracted notions, shutting out the distant, the foreign, and making religion a comfortable nest in *our* parish, *our* synod, *our* church. But that is death: to settle down each into a snug little Zion of his own is to begin to decay. It is worse than death; it is deserting duty and perverting the meaning of the faith. As soon as religion means only my peace and comfort and safety, I have corrupted it.

The world, the world—not myself, not my church, not my denomination, but the great, crowded, suffering, perishing world—it was for this Christ died.

There is pain in the thought; and there is joy. The pain is in feeling the weight of a great world lying in sin. What a burden, at times, it becomes; it haunts one; it oppresses one with the sense of the millions that are sinning, putting out the little light that is in them, suffering, and ever plunging downward. But there is a joy in it, too. It is the world for which Christ died. It is redeemed, and it is to be won back

The light is in it that "lightens every man that cometh into the world." We ought to think of the world thus: as faith deepens and love burns, we will. We will look further abroad, where the finger of our Master is continually pointing us.

## THEOLOGICAL CONTROVERSIES.

Perhaps if we could get away from the controversies of words, and strifes of party feeling, to the world of inner beliefs, which each good man cherishes, and in which is his real life, we should find that there these differences grew less and less; that they were nearer the one to the other than the world saw them to be; nearer, it may be, than even they thought themselves to be. How much, when death comes to strip off the veils of life, of what men held for truth may they not then find that only the intellect held, the heart never accepted; how much that the understanding stumbled at and rejected, the heart really believed! Who can tell?

## THE DANGER OF FINE CHURCHES AND ELABORATE RITUALS.

The danger is of losing the inward and spiritual in the outward and material. Let me put it more definitely. Is there no peril that, coming to apprehend God habitually through the flaming glories of the painted window, under the sensuous excitement and ecstasy of the rolling chant, that praying through the inspiring forms of a majestic ritual and meditating on his character when possessed by the mysterious influence of grand architectural forms and under a solemn religious light, so learning to depend on these sensuous veils and images for our approach to God, we shall gradually lose the power of a spiritual access, the sense of his divine presence with us face to face? A religion of times and seasons, of holy places and sacred enclosures—this is what we have to dread. It is dangerous to make the house of God so holy and awful that all other places seem by comparison only profane and desecrated. It is dangerous to pray so habitually under the inspiration of the solemn and awful imagery and shadow of the church, that the closet, the wayside, are dull and empty of the divine presence.

No one, I take it, of even moderately impressible mind, can enter into a grand and solemn pile, where the religious atmosphere prevails, and not feel how powerful is the aid it gives to the religious temper. Thoughts of devotion, snatches of praise and prayer, go mingled from the heart heavenward; but it is a dangerous inspiration. "Darkness and mystery; confused recesses of building; artificial light employed in small quantity, but maintained with a constancy which seems to give it a kind of sacredness; preciousness of material easily comprehended by the vulgar eye; close air loaded with a sweet and peculiar odor associated only with the religious services; solemn music and tangible idols or images having popular legends attached to them—these are the stage properties of superstition, which have been from the beginning of the world, and must be to the end of it, employed by all nations, whether openly savage or nominally civilized, to produce a false awe in minds incapable of apprehending the true nature of Deity."

An awe these things do produce; but it is "a false awe." A thrill and glow proceed from them that seem the very sign and presence of higher faith, a more intense religious experience; but it is only the thrill and glow of a perilous stimulant. So the wine-drinker feels his heart burn and his spirit rise within him; so come the heavenly calm, the rapturous visions of the opium-eater; but they are only the preludes to decay and death.

## HOLINESS.

What is that quality? What is the fibre without which there can be no holiness; which, when we scrutinize a godly life, is the one thing that remains though all else goes? It is the quality of righteousness—the love and choice of what is pure and true and just. Where that is, is holiness; where that is not, holiness cannot be.

We are always in danger of losing sight of this essential quality of the divine life, that its substance is *righteousness*. We are always substituting something else for it, and thinking that this something else will do. One man thinks enthusiasm and zeal will do;

and because he is full of fire and energy, and untiring in religious labors, it seems to him he must be holy. Another thinks strong feeling will do; and raptures and thrills take the place of purity, honesty, truth. It is hard not to believe that the great preacher, eloquent, ardent, with deep thoughts of God, with powerful sympathies that melt and move masses of men, is therefore a deeply holy man; his burning words, his rich doctrine, his power to sway and persuade men, we say, are the very substance of the divine life. But they are not. If he is holy, his holiness is not in his speech, nor in his labors, nor in his zeal, but in his *righteousness;* the meek, humble, loving, Christ-like temper of the soul. We have the words of an Apostle for this, or we would hardly believe it: "Though I have the gift of prophecy, and understand all mysteries, and all knowledge; and though I have all faith, so that I could remove mountains, and have not charity, I am nothing."

## TRUE GLORYING.

This raises the question, Is it wrong to glory? And to this we answer, at once, no. The sense of something high and vast before one, the throb of hope and joy that comes with the glimpse of a world and a life just unfolding full of wonder, full of power—this, that we call glorying, is not wrong. It is wrong to glory in low things when high are offered. It is wrong to go down into the mire when one may mount up into the heavens. But to glory is all right. A man cannot be fully a man who does not glory. But in what shall we take this pride? 

There is something organ-like in the grand slow passage in that melodious old prophet Jeremiah, in which he gives an answer to our question:

"*Let him that glorieth glory in this, that he understandeth and knoweth me, that I am the Lord who exercise loving kindness, judgment and righteousness in the earth; for in these things I delight.*"

That conception of the righteous Lord appealed to the old Hebrew mind more powerfully than it has ever done to any other. But even we, of these prosaic and commonplace days, can feel it. What a sublime vision it sets before us!

## THE DISTINCTIVE FEATURE OF LUTHERAN DOCTRINE.

The real distinction of Lutheranism, as a practical system of truth, is its declaration and strong emphasis of the doctrine of justification by faith, or the truth that salvation is not something to be wrought out, but a gift freely bestowed on all who will take it from Christ.

The great Lutheran doctrine, is that men "are justified gratuitously for Christ's sake through faith when they believe that they are received into favor; and that their sins are remitted for the sake of Christ."

This doctrine relieves the mind of the intolerable

burden of working out its own acceptance with God; it divests duty of its oppressiveness, and substitutes for it the enthusiasm of love.

In one word, then, Lutheranism distinctively is simply the childlike confidence of the believer in a saving God. It says: "*I know whom I have believed, and am persuaded that he is able to keep that which I have committed unto him against that day.*"

## PREACHING.

In the New Testament preaching and teaching are almost interchangeable terms: the very essence, the differential of Christian address, is its intention to instruct, to impart knowledge for the purpose of changing or directing life. Take Christ's sermons and those of his apostles, and how the thread of instruction, the imparting of divine knowledge, runs golden and shining through them all; they are full of the knowledge that persuades, knowledge that is to be built up into the life. And preachers of the gospel are to be such teachers. But how hard it is to preach doctrine, that is, to teach and to preach vitally; how far off our instruction seems for the most part from the lives of the men and women before us.

## IMITATING CHRIST.

What a treasure is the gift of one whom we can imitate and never be disappointed! We *must* imitate some one. Consciously or unconsciously, we are continually transferring the traits of other lives to our own. We are instruments sounding each his own note, and also vibrating sympathetically to lives sounding out around us. The chord of one harp vibrates, and then the next harp vibrates in unison with it. But one of the saddest disappointments of life is that we are continually finding our models fail. The sweet instrument we thought in perfect tune sounds a false note, and we can never trust it fully again. But here is one whose whole life we may listen to, from top to bottom in endless harmonies, and never a discord, never a false note. We may trust it unreservedly. "Holy, harmless, undefiled," Jesus lives before us, and, follow him from childhood to the last sigh on the cross, never shall that perfection fail us. It is a most precious quality in Christ, that among all the lives which first draw us by their sweetness, and then disappoint us by their weakness, his life comes close to us, sweet and pure and inspiring at the first, and sweeter, purer, more inspiring, to the very end. What peace it is to follow a life that never falters, never lets us feel the ache of incompleteness—to follow a star that never misleads, never grows dim, never sets.

But there is more. It is inspiring to have a perfect model; but it is more inspiring to remember this truth about his perfection, that Christ is the picture of what God intends us to be.

Jesus is a picture of what I am in God's idea of me. That seems incredible. When I think what I am in my discord, weakness, meanness, sin, it seems impossible that this lovely, glorious being can really be my portrait. But so it is. Jesus is the portrait of myself as I shall be in heaven.

What a grand aim is it to imitate Christ! Men are forever going astray, making shipwrecks of their lives, because they take such poor aim for life. To be President, to be a greater writer or speaker, to be popular, to be a shrewd, successful man of business, to be lapped in ease and comfort—what wretched aims! How contemptible, how petty they seem by this portrait of ourselves, which Jesus shows as he stands before us, and says, "Be like me; love me; follow me, and where I am ye shall be also; as I am ye shall be too."

There comes a time, I think, when the old features start out, or steal out, be it suddenly or gradually, into the very image of our perfect Saviour. Then we have his picture in our hearts; then it goes on from one glory to another. It grows on us till there is only one face, one model, one friend for us in all the universe. And then to imitate him, to be like him, is the one business of life worth living for. So St. Paul thought when he said, "This one thing I do . . . I press towards the mark. . . . that I may know him and the power of his resurrection. . . I follow after, if that I may lay hold of that for which Christ Jesus laid hold of me."

That is the true imitation of Christ.

## THE TREATMENT OF NEW CONVERTS.

The thing to be done after a revival or spiritual awakening is to turn your new force on the work of the kingdom. Just to turn your new converts loose into the congregation is like letting your water pour over a dam. It will soon all be gone, and only leave your dam the worse for the wear. What you want is a channel by which you can get it to work; a prayer-meeting, a Bible meeting, a Missionary Society, a Young People's Meeting, where the new energy and love shall find an expression and a discipline; that is what you want. Turn it into that channel, and you will save your converts from stiffening and petrifying, and turn their force into a positive power in the work of the kingdom.

Two things we need—power from above, and the utilizing of what power comes to us.

## THOU SHALT LOVE THY NEIGHBOR AS THYSELF.

In nine cases out of ten men read Christ's command in this fashion, "*Thou shalt not harm thy neighbor.*" That explains how unconsciously the whole plane of duty to our neighbor is pitched in a distinctly lower level than that set by Christ. We lower the aim and then down comes the practice. We expound "love thy neighbor" to mean, "Do not kill him, or rob him, or slander him; let him alone," and then we fall to criticising and repelling and disliking him.

We have pitched the whole level of personal relation too low. We have taken men as they are, and as we are, and never really believed there was any other feeling possible than that of drawing to what we naturally like and recoiling from what we naturally dislike. But the whole meaning of Christ and his life in us is that everything in us and our fellows is to be translated into a higher key; that even our likes and dislikes are to be transformed and shined upon till deeper colors are brought forth.

The rising of that sun over the world of our life with men brings out the true colors there. In the gray of the morning before sunrise, everything seems gray and blank; but the sun touches the hill-side and it starts into emerald, it kisses the stream and turns it to gold. It seems to me it is but a poor Christ we have found who only makes the far-off heaven glimmer, but leaves the earth as dull and common-place as before.

## SERVANTS *vs.* FRIENDS.

If you do not enjoy your religion supremely, it is your own fault. It is not because God has made it unenjoyable. If you feel, with reference to all its branches of service, its devotional duties, its charities, its restraints and labors, its communings with God, that these are rather irksome and dry, then, I tell you, it is because you are not on the highest plane of religion. You are being religious as a *servant* of Christ, and not as a *friend*. Now, I do not say you may not reach heaven as a servant. You may go all through a long life with your livery as a bearer of God's burdens, and come up to heaven's gate and knock, and God will take you in as *only* a servant; though when you get there you must become a friend. But then you must take only a servant's portion here. If you will only look on God as a master, as a pattern to be aimed at, you cannot expect that high joy of which you read in the Bible and in history as the experience of holy men. Religion is all it professes to be; it has springs of living joy that flow bright and refreshing and sufficient all through life, through sorrow and misfortune, through sickness and poverty and human neglect; but then if you would drink of them, you must climb up to where they burst out of the mountain top, and not dig yourself a muddy ditch in the valley. God can make life a joy when it is lived in him, and he will do it; but he does it by taking us into the arms of his love as friends; he lifts us up to his side and crowns us with the joy of his communion; and yet *we* must acquiesce in this—we must go up higher, and cry, "Lord, I would be a friend, and no longer a man-servant," and Christ will open his arms, and say, "Henceforth I call you not *servants*, but I have called you *friends*."

## EASTER.

There is something very piercing in the vision of the cross of Jesus; there is something marvellously inspiring in the spectacle of the risen Lord. What beams of hope they cast down into the dark shadows of earth! What secrets of eternity they unfold to us! It is good to warm our hearts in that sunshine; it is grand to rise to those eternal prospects. But Christ has something better to give us at the cross, and in the garden by the empty tomb, than the mere luxury of feeling. For John at the cross he had a special solemn duty: "Behold, thy mother;" and from that time John had a sacred ministry all his own to carry out. And for the mourners in the garden he had a work to do: "Go tell my brethren that they go into Galilee, and there shall they see me." And they went to do his bidding.

Sometimes after the season of Easter has come and gone, and the solemn vision vanishes, and we go back to our usual life, it seems as though all our emotions and bright hopes had been only a dream. The vision fades, and we are just where we were before. Well, it is because we take only half of Christ's Easter message; the message of what he has done for us, our safety, hope and joy, and not the other half which tells us of what we are to do for him, of the ministry we owe to our fellow-men, for whom he died also, their safety, joy and hope. We cannot keep the half unless we take the whole. We cannot carry a Saviour as a secret joy in our hearts, our salvation, our eternal hope, our blessed life, unless we give him to the world. Do not think to keep him all to yourself. Do not shut your eyes to the outer world. Do not stop your ears to the cry of a lost world, that you may hear him speaking more sweetly within.

The way, then, to keep the vision of Good Friday and of the Easter morn bright before us all the year, is to know Christ not only as our Saviour, but also as the Saviour of all men; to give ourselves to him, first that he may save us from our sins and fears and poverty of soul, and then that he may use us to save our fellow men from their sin and wretchedness. "He loved me," says the great apostle, "and gave himself for me." That was his first thought before the cross and the tomb; the sweet personal bond that drew him to his Saviour's heart. And then, "I determined to know nothing among you save Jesus Christ and him crucified. * * I am debtor both to the wise and to the unwise. So much as in me is, I am ready to preach the gospel at Rome also. For I am not ashamed of the gospel of Christ, for it is the power of God unto salvation." No wonder his vision of Good Friday and Easter never faded out. He kept the two parts of Christ's revelation to him ever before his soul. With one hand he grasped the cross and the risen Saviour, and with the other he beckoned to the world to come and see what a Saviour there was for them.

Who will make his crucified Saviour, his risen Lord, a selfish luxury for his own soul alone? He is the

Saviour of all men: can we ever think of him and forget that?

Let that thought shine out above the solemn cross we contemplate, wreathe with the flowers we hang about our altars in memory of the Easter morn, go with us to the communion table. "What have I done to bring Christ to men? What have I given for him who has given all for me? What have I denied myself for him who died for me?" And then go and coin the love and hope and penitence of the Easter time into the counters of a firm purpose, a self-denial, an earnest effort to bring Christ to the souls he loves.

## WHIT-SUNDAY.

What, then, is the meaning of Whit-Sunday? The symbol of the day sums it all up. When the disciples were met in the upper room, there appeared tongues of fire upon every head. Light and heat, these are the symbols of the Holy Ghost, of God entering and possessing the soul. They are more than symbols; they are the very substance of what God does for us when we receive the blessed Spirit in his fullness. He illuminates and he quickens. We see in his light; we live in his warm life. That is the whole of Pentecost.

We shall never know what Christ really is till we have had our Pentecost. The Holy Ghost must come within the soul and show him to us face to face; not the knowledge of right and wrong, of the pain of sin and the joy of goodness, but the knowledge of all these in the bright person of Christ. Indeed, we never know what God is in the blessedness of that knowledge, till the Holy Spirit gives us sight to see him in Christ. We have seen pictures in which the face of the principal figure was turned away. Christmas and Good Friday and Easter, by themselves, are just such pictures of God, with his face unseen. The form, the action, are there, but the face is hidden. Whit-Sunday shows us our Christmas and Good Friday and Easter with the face of Christ turned to us, all the features clear and strong and lovely. As an old divine has said "Christ is God made manifest, but the Holy Ghost is the eye with which we see this manifested God."

We all know what it is to live by motives drawn merely from conscience and reason, and what it is to live by the warm flush of an inspiration. The disciples at Emmaus expressed it when they said, "Did not our hearts burn within us while he talked with us by the way?" Truth glowed and melted as it fell into their souls; a divine impulse came with its touch; they could not let him who spoke so depart; they clung to him. This was what the coming of the Holy Ghost meant. He brought Christ within. All the goodness they had admired and coldly copied, all the duty they had tried to do, and often fainted under its difficulty, was fused by that touch of flame into a glad loving impulse.

What a world apart is the work we do, the sacrifice we make for right, and that we offer from love. Service without love, how cold, how hard, how sad it is! Our experience is often mirrored in that saying of the Christian to his pastor, "I know it is my duty because I hate it so." That tells of life which has had no Pentecost yet; a real, earnest, brave, true life—but so hard and sad, so cold and slow! What we need is a fire to kindle our will towards God into a wish for him. Then instead of recognizing duty by the frown in its face we shall know it by its lovely smile.

Who has not wished often that he could set a torch to his obedience and make it blaze into an inspiration? Well, Whit-Sunday is the bringing of that torch. What we are seeking is seeking us. Pentecost did for the disciples this very thing. It came to their coldness with fire. The Holy Ghost came to them. God entered their souls, and showed them Jesus, and when they saw him the light kindled into flame. I do not care to separate the two, or to tell how they are related. They cannot be separated any more than light and heat are separated in the great works of nature. To see Christ with the inward vision of the Holy Ghost; and to love him and, for his sake, all the duty he brings us to do; this is really one.

## THE READING OF THE BIBLE.

There is such a thing as reading the Scriptures, not for doctrine, not for direction, not for texts, but for inspiration and communion with God. Dr. Alexander, in one of his suggestive notes, speaks of the effect produced on his mind by reading a whole book, an epistle, or a gospel, or a historical book, as rapidly as he could, not stopping to dwell on any point, to unravel any difficulty, but skimming over the surface, as a bird flies over the landscape, so as to get one wide view, a bird's eye view, so to speak. The effect was one of great inspiration. It was like looking on a great prospect from an eminence; the breadth, the light, the sweep of thought, filled the mind with high and uplifting emotions. To say nothing of the new vision one gets of a subject from taking it in all at once so as to catch the relations of all the parts, there is an effect produced from a long sustained contact with the mind of the Spirit caught in the continual survey of a great body of Scripture. It is like being in company with a lofty and noble nature for days; one catches also the tone, the atmosphere. So, to read the Scripture in bulk, to bathe one's mind in them, as it were, is to come in contact with God, to catch his Spirit. And this is a true devotional reading.

There is another way of devotional reading; it is to select a short passage, a promise, a pregnant statement of truth, a text, and then, after finding out by careful study what it means literally, to take it into the mind and let it lie there, to meditate on it, to let it germinate, fructify, and so unfold itself to the heart. If we combine the two, now reading microscopically, taking only a text, a paragraph; and then with a wide, rapid sweep, bringing our mind quickly into contact with large bodies of the Word, as one gets the air when riding swiftly through the country, then we shall have the best of devotional reading.

But there is no dispensing with continual and large contact with the body of Scripture. There is such a thing as being imbued with the mind of Scripture, not simply knowing its facts, being familiar with its doctrines, ready in quoting texts, but a taking of its color, its tone, its spirit. For there is a spirit goes out from the sacred pages, these are the historical facts, these the great doctrines, these the line of development, these are the body. You may have each one of these and miss the spirit, the direct touch of God, as it were, in the soul.

For it is the revelation of himself; when we read his Word we not only get direction, but we may get *him;* and this is what we should seek to reach in our reading of the Scriptures—himself.

We need to learn this use of Scripture, as a revelation of God, as a mirror of his face, as an atmosphere that gives spiritual ozone to the life. And he is most Biblical, the man of the Word, not who knows the most proof-texts, or has the best system of theology, or is most familiar with the geography and antiquities, or the original text, or who has the plan of salvation readiest at his tongue's end, but he who lives in the atmosphere of the Word, communing with God there, face to face.

In one word, the Bible is a revelation not merely of doctrine about God and his salvation, but more profoundly still it is a *revelation of God himself.*

## THE TRUE RULE OF CHRISTIAN PRACTICE.

Paul would probably have been amazed could he have foreseen how slowly the great faith he was called to propagate would come to be understood and applied. Especially would it have aroused his wonder, we may suppose, could he have foreknown that certain rudimental and simple questions of Christian practice would be under discussion and unsettled to-day, just as they were in his day. The primitive church had differences about the eating of meat offered to idols; about the observance of special days—things in themselves indifferent, but in the treatment of which there was involved a living and real question.

The thing that is important for us to know and act upon, is not whether it is right or wrong to observe special days—whether an idol is anything or nothing. There is a deeper question involved. What is that?

It is the question of *love*. You are disputing, Paul says to both parties, about the right or wrong of certain practices. There is a right and a wrong in the matter, it is true; but it is a right and a wrong of a very trivial character; and it is, moreover, a question that differs according to each man's circumstances and enlightenment. There is no general law, covering all alike; each must decide for himself, and for himself alone, and not for his neighbor. But you are forgetting a great law—the law of love—compared with which all these questions of meat, and herbs, and days, are mere chaff. It is of small importance whether you eat meat or herbs—whether you keep certain days or not; but that you should not break the law of love—that is everything. You that know that all meats are clean, and all days holy, you despise your weaker brother, who does not see so clearly as you. Nay; you go farther: you exercise your knowledge, careless whether it leads your brother into an offence against his conscience or not. You are right to say all things are clean; but that right is nothing compared to the wrong you do in offending your brother's conscience and refusing to bear his weakness.

And the same law of love applies to our modern questions of whether it be wrong to put a cross on a spire, to use a liturgy, or to have a reading-desk in a church. But there is another step in Paul's treatment of these questions, and that is too generally overlooked. It is right for the strong to give way to the weak, but the weak must understand why their scruples are yielded to. It is for their building up. The strong are to give way to them not because they are right, but because they are weak. Paul, while he plainly said to the one party, "Give way," said just as plainly to the other, "You are weak, and you are to have your way because you are weak." To leave any vagueness on that point would be a real wrong to a weak brother; for it would encourage him to hug his weakness, and to glory in it as the truth.

## LUTHER.

It is true that, after all that can be said to show why a great man affects his fellows as he does, there remains an unknown quantity, a dæmonic force, so to speak, which is not to be detected or defined by any of our criticism—the original, individual quality of the man himself. The elemental force of a great man is in the last result always a mystery. But still, though we cannot discover the whole of the secret, something of it we can.

Part of the secret, then, of the vast influence Luther exerted, is to be found in his completeness. He was all around a full, a complete man. Perhaps to some that will seem a very strange thing to say about him. In his energy, his fire, his torrent outbursts, he seems a chaotic creature, the very opposite of the round, completely-proportioned man. But by completeness in a man we are not to understand polish, symmetry, rounded proportions; but the full equipment of the nature with all the great distinctive features of humanity. It is in this respect that we say Luther was a marvelously complete man. He was myriad-sided, multiform, carrying in his one individuality all the great types and features of human nature, at the top of their power.

It is of course impossible to show this in detail: we can only suggest its truth with reference to those great cardinal features which characterize human nature. A very obvious classification of this sort is that by which we distinguish men as emotional, intellectual, practical or active. Every man, we are accustomed to say, belongs by his peculiar make to one of these classes: that is, he is predominantly a man of feeling, of thought, or of activity. To be a great man is to possess, in an eminent degree, one or two of these qualities; rarely, indeed, do we find that even men who tower above their fellows unite them all harmoniously. We have only to call to mind Aristotle the unemotional, Plato the unpractical, Calvin with his cold side, and Wesley with his lack of intellectual grasp, to see how great a man may be and yet fall short of the greatest. In Luther we have the rare spectacle of a man sent into the world who was complete in his whole make. Emotionally, intellectually, practically, he was complete and justly proportioned.

## LUTHER'S REALIZING SENSE OF GOD'S NEARNESS.

It was said of Luther that in society he would often drop his conversation with those near, and be silent; when questioned, he explained that he stopped to converse with God: so real and near was his heavenly Father to him. He had a great, living, hungering heart, which nothing but God could fill; and after God he sought as a hunter seeks for game. When he found him he lived in him. Through all he says and does, that is continually present. When Luther speaks we seem to feel God close by; his intense emotional life in the love and service of this unspeakable Friend makes of God a wonderful reality. It is this that enabled him to grasp the heart of Europe of his day, and to hold it through all these centuries.

## THE REFORMATION.

We all know what that dawning day was: it was the stepping forward of the race to a new vision of God, what he was, and how man could be at peace with him. Say what men may about the decay of faith, the one question which the race can never cease pondering and seeking an answer to, is, "what is God, how can we find him, be one with him?" Darkness and almost despair had settled in the minds of men because the only answer a corrupt church gave to that question was, "God is a stern ruler; his son, Jesus Christ, is an awful judge; only by enormous labors and sorrows can you approach and appease him." The name of God was a name of dread, the thought of Christ was a terrible thought of judgment.

Then came the cheering shout of the Reformation breaking the gloom. "Not so," cried Luther, "God is our father; Christ is our elder brother, because one with us and for our salvation: it is not terrible tasks and sufferings that can make you at peace with your Maker; you have only one thing to do—to find God." And then the world listened for the magic word, "Have faith in God. Trust in him who gave his dear Son for your salvation, and you are one with him."

Luther's doctrine, which was his only in the sense that he struck open the Bible and made men hear the Word of God so long forgotten, was that the soul finds God by faith; that God has been seeking us, and we have only to fling ourselves into his arms, and trust and submit to him as the loving, forgiving, delivering Father. He told men what God had taught him, that the just shall live by faith. And then, as they took in the great thought and looked up, what a revolution came over the universe!—courage, hope, sprang up in the human heart; the race began to resume its confidence in God.

## THE SALVATION OF THE PAGAN WORLD.

The gift that will save the pagan world from its temporal evils is not money, nor manufacture, nor commerce, but the religion of Christ which teaches men how to make the most of both worlds. Every Hindoo child trained up in the faith and practice of the gospel is one more step taken towards saving India from its terrible scourge of the famine years. And what is true of the India famine is true also of almost every other temporal evil. The heathen world groans under its curse of pestilence, poverty, misgovernment, oppression, the slave trade, because it is heathen, ungodly. It is sin that breeds these almost infinite forms of misery.

It is the least of all the blessings of our faith that it is profitable for the life that now is; but it *is* profitable even to that. To introduce the gospel, is to introduce industry, thrift, temperance, forethought, prudence, and all the qualities that at last make such great calamities, as the famines and pestilences of the heathen world, next to impossible.

## OUR LIFE A DEBT.

It will be a melancholy thing for us to remember life only as a long dream of self-gratification. To spend our means, respectably and tastefully it may be, on ourselves and families—to hoard up our savings that we may leave them a barren pile to our heirs—this is to disown our debts, to refuse our responsibilities, to pervert our trust. "I should be ashamed of myself," said Bishop Butler to his secretary, "if I could leave ten thousand pounds behind me."

Nothing in the New Testament can be plainer than this: "*no man liveth to himself;*" "*ye are not your own; ye are bought with a price.*" And the truer a man is, the more deeply he becomes a Christian, the more keenly and profoundly will he feel this: My life is a debt: my time is a debt: my knowledge, my property, all is a debt. So Paul, "*I am a debtor both to the Greek and to the barbarian.*" Not a debtor only because of his apostleship to preach to the Gentiles: that is true; but deeper than that lies the sense in him that his gifts, intellectual, moral, spiritual, his vision of faith, his zeal and fire and joy, were all so many treasures committed to him in trust for others. Is the

Gospel joy and peace to me? then I owe it to every man to bring it to him. Have I any peculiar knowledge, ability to speak, to sway and rule men? this, too, is a debt I must discharge.

## THE NOBLEST DEATH.

There is nothing nobler than to die in the flush and full swing of work—for the soldier to go from the battle-shock, the minister from the pulpit, the missionary from reaping in the white harvest field—this is a worthy end of life. It tells us what a grand thing it is to live for Christ and man, what a great thing it is to die in service for them. It burns away the baseness, the cowardice, and sloth, which creep so easily over our lives. It helps us to live better to see men die so:

> "Nothing is here for tears, nothing to wail
> Or knock the breast; no weakness, no contempt,
> Dispraise, or blame; nothing but well and fair,
> And what may quiet us in death so noble."

## THE BANE OF THEOLOGY.

It has been the bane of theology that it has been too much built up on a merely intellectual basis, a foundation of ideas only. It has begun with a definition of God, a mere abstraction of which we can have only a notional idea, but no real experience, and then it has gone on to spin its wonderful web out from that centre; that may be intensely interesting, but only intellectually, not with the interest of reality. And so theology, to the great masses of men, has been something very dry. For men generally are not intellectual; that is, they do not care for ideas apart from life; truth in bodily form, in events and persons and behavior, they do have an interest in, but not in truth as a mere abstraction, an idea. In short, they want reality, not ideas.

## CHRIST'S MINISTRY.

Who can doubt that it was a pure, supreme delight to Jesus to minister? From the day in which he sat in the temple talking with the doctors and making them feel the wonder of his divine suggestions, to the last hour of his help to the suffering, what a stream of blessedness poured through his soul! Relieving pain, enlightening ignorance, soothing sorrow, inspiring courage, lighting up the flame of goodness in fallen souls—what a rich feast life must have been to him!

## GOOD FRIDAY.

Perhaps we have separated our Good Friday too widely from the rest of the year. There is always the danger, in setting apart particular times for particular events, that we shut up our remembrance of the event to that time. There are those who use the Lord's Day so: they make it a close chamber into which all the sacredness of holy things is shut up, instead of an open window through which the sweetness and sanctity of the divine communion stream down into every day of the week. It would be a sad thing to concentrate on Good Friday our deepest devotion, only when the season is over to see the vista of the year with no cross anywhere on the horizon. "The cross," says Cardinal Newman, "is the measure of all things." That, at least, it should be to the Christian. Let us use our Good Friday, then, to learn how to take this measure of things with us all the year.

Let us think first of the cross as the expiation of our guilt; but let us not stop there. We must take the cross with us all the year, to carry the sense of God's love into our inmost hearts. For what we most need to feed the divine life within is a deepening assurance that God does love us. We labor to convince ourselves that we love God, we examine our feelings, weigh our actions, and try to stir ourselves up to love him; but love never comes so. No introspection, no stirring of ourselves up, no digging about the roots, will make our spiritual affections bloom.

But there is another side to the cross. It tells of our fellowship with the divine suffering. The cross interprets, ennobles and hallows the pain of life, by showing us that it is a sharing in the divine suffering. "I," says the Apostle, "am crucified with Christ;" that is, the suffering of his life has a fellowship with Christ's suffering on the cross. They were united by the bond of a common anguish, endured for one great and holy end. How often does St. Paul allude to his suffering with Christ; and what a different face does that thought put on sorrow; what an august, solemn, holy thing does it come to be, when in the pain we can say: "I know the fellowship of his suffering." Then sorrow becomes not the barren fellowship of a universal human anguish, leading to nothing; but the blessed communion of the divine life, suffering with Jesus, that with him we may triumph over sin and reign with him in his kingdom.

I do not see how, unless we learn to suffer with the cross of Christ before us, we can ever escape from what is the worst fruit of pain, its absorption in self, its narrowness, its egotism. But Good Friday brings us before the cross, where suffering was taken voluntarily to fulfil the will of God, to bless men. It teaches us the sacredness of all suffering that says lovingly, *Thy will be done.* It shows us the beauty of suffering that grows more tender to others as its own anguish increases. That was what Adolph Monod meant, when in the long months of agony before his death he used to say to his friends, " *Cette vie crucifiée est la vie bienheureuse.*" What, could that pain and weariness be a blessing? Yea, though a "crucified life" it could be a life of peace; indeed, the element of "blessedness" in it was just this sense that it was "crucified," a suffering with Christ. At one moment, seen from the point of view of the world, it was only a tossing sea whose billows were throbs of pain. Then the vision of Calvary broke over it, and the light from the cross lay like a path of glory over those restless waves, and the "crucified life" was, to him who apprehended the meaning of the cross, the blessed life.

## THE PHYSICAL TEST OF PRAYER.*

Prof. Tyndall's test is a test of something else besides prayer: it probes the defect apparently inseparable from an exclusive devotion of the mind to the study of truths relating to physical phenomena. Stated explicitly, it is something like this: *The habit of mind at first necessary to the investigation of physical science, and afterwards fixed and intensified by this pursuit, is unfavorable to, and, when long exclusively cultivated, destructive of the power of moral and spiritual perception.* A scientific investigator is, *quoad hoc*, unfitted for the consideration, and incapable of admitting, the force of moral and spiritual principles. To this defect, in large measure, is to be assigned the else unaccountable intellectual revulsion of the scientific mind from the consideration of truths that will not be formulated under physical laws or by scientific methods.

---

*Note.—The test referred to was to make a single ward or hospital the object of special prayer by the whole body of Christians for a fixed period of years, and then at the end of the period to compare the mortality with that of similar wards or hospitals, and note the difference, if any.

## THE TRUE SOURCE OF POWER IN PREACHING.

Times change and men with them; but the change is only superficial. Under all the mutations of fashions, dialects, political and social revolutions, the great strata of human feeling, conscience, spiritual and moral need, run unchanged and unchangeable. What touched the Jew and the Greek and the Roman when the first preachers of Christianity went abroad from Jerusalem, will touch men in America now. And if anything is written clearly in every page of the history of the progress Christianity has made, it is this: Do not go to men with proofs of Christianity, but with the naked truths themselves; do not preach about the doctrines of Christ, but preach Christ himself. The dogmatic system may lose edge and weight; but the facts of Christ's life and death, the doctrine of his Person and Spirit, and the relations he brings men into to another world, when urged with the simplicity of authority, may at any time touch the old springs of human nature that never fail.

These elements of power are simply incalculable, because they have to do with what is most fundamental, yet most imponderable, in man: the sympathetic, religious nature. Again and again have the philosophers ruled it out as non-existent, because not measurable and calculable; and again and again, after being ruled out, it has unmistakably asserted itself. It may lie inert through a slumbering generation, as in

England before the Wesleyan revival; it may be overlaid and buried, as in continental Europe before the Reformation; it may be despised and counted out of the real factors of civilization, as it is by the science of this generation: but when the time of need comes, one ardent soul speaks, the old story is rehearsed, and the sleeping awake, the buried comes out of its grave, the wisdom of philosophy is confounded by a resurrection that refuses to be measured or contained.

## THE NEW MORALITY OF TASTE.

One thing is clear, that the new morality based on taste must differ from what we know by that name, by a total lack of the element of infinitude. It may be practically efficient in procuring for man the lower orders of well-being, and it may afford a certain refined and even intense pleasure; but when it has done its best it is still of the earth, earthy. What is the high end this scheme of conduct proposes? Its utmost aim is to secure the well-being of the race for its existence on the earth, meaning by well-being, physical happiness, mental satisfaction, and the gratification of the sympathies in procuring physical happiness and mental satisfaction for the race reciprocally. That is its *summum bonum*, its highest ideal of moral perfection. Now we do not hesitate to say that this end, while not wholly ignoble, is of the very essence of earthliness, and wholly inadequate to satisfy the deepest craving of man even in his present imperfect and undeveloped state. It gives aim and motive enough to keep him going after a tread-mill fashion, and so would hunger, or dislike of physical pain. But it does not give scope enough to let us feel that life is worth all the fine talk the new philosophy makes about it. It goes out to each individual with his own life; it goes out for the race with the extinction of the earth. When looked at as a whole it is a beggarly, degrading ideal of life. In one word, it is finite; and man shut in to the present state of things, never will feel any otherwise than that he is imprisoned. You may argue with him that human existence *is* only a prison, and that the best thing for the race is to make that prison as comfortable as possible till we are called out to execution; but you will never get him to believe from the bottom of his soul that comfort is his highest good; not until that in him which makes him great and original and above nature is killed out. If the new morality could succeed in establishing itself, it would be by extirpating one whole side of human nature, and that the greatest. It will get man to live by taste instead of by the Word of God when it has starved out of him all that is worth keeping alive, and not before.

The trouble with this whole new system of ethics is the same that ailed the old Ptolemaic system of the universe, *Geocentricism.* As that made the earth the centre of all things, so this makes man the centre of his universe. It really degrades him by showing him nothing higher than himself. A universe of persons with no Being who worthily commands the reverence and obedience of all is a chaotic, inadequate universe to such a creature as man. Accordingly here come in the modern substitutes for God, the Positivists' "Worship of Humanity," the Agnostics' cult of "Altruism:" we are to adore humanity in its essence; we are to live for the race. But to adore humanity is only to worship myself multiplied indefinitely; and to live for the race, if there be no one above us of whom man is the image and child, is only to live for myself repeated over and over. Now the business of living for a multiplied self may be arithmetically worthy, but it is hard to see how it can be so morally. Multiply man as many million times as you please, and you only get so many millions of men, not a sublimated, apotheosized something that is different in kind from the individual. So that, after all, the dignity of living for the race, if that race has no God and Father, is only the dignity of living for one's self contemplated in a magnifying mirror. If it is base to live for the happiness of one man, because that one is myself, it can not be noble to live for the happiness of a million men, who are only myself reduplicated indefinitely.

## "THY WILL BE DONE."

How true it is that the practical use of this petition of the Lord's Prayer is confined almost exclusively to its passive side. When we ask for that holy will to be done, we are apt to mean that we should suffer it patiently. But how full the Bible is of fingers that point us to the active side. When St. Paul is talking to the Thessalonians concerning their personal purity and honesty he tells them "this is the will of God, even your sanctification, that ye should abstain from fornication:" the active side is plain enough there. And then to the Romans he writes, urging them not to be conformed to the world, but by a transformation to give a practical exhibition of religion by a spiritual life, to prove the "*good and acceptable and perfect will of God.*" And there, too, it is something to be done, something wrought out in the active life by the co-operation of men and God, that is meant by God's will. Perhaps it is the strong light thrown on the passive side of this petition by Christ's own use of it in his agony in the garden that has given so many minds this one-sided bias. We hear him pray, "Thy will be done;" we see him submit to drink the cup—and the powerful vision burns it on our minds that the Father's will is something to be borne rather than something to be done. But if we think for a moment we will remember that those hours of submission in the garden and on the cross were only passages of suffering let into a rich, full, active life, the burden of which was the *doing* of the Father's will. His own words teach us that: "My meat is to do the will of him that sent me, and to finish his work." To live the life of obedience, to teach, to heal, to reveal God to men, and in it all to suffer, and by suffering to learn a more perfect obedience to the will of his Father—this was Christ's reading of his own petition that the will of God be done. The great thing was the active doing of the Divine will, and to that suffering was only incidental; it came in as the chafing and breaking of the stream on the opposing rocks come in to the stream's progress; but the life of the stream is not that broken passage, but the movement through that and beyond.

And what was truth for him is truth, too, for us: we suffer his will only that we may come more perfectly to do that will; even as Christ suffered on the cross, that he might perfectly work out the Father's will that all might be saved.

## PROVINCIALISM.

A man may be penetrated with the spirit of his own times, may have ceased to be provincial as regards place or nation; but may yet be provincial in his unacquaintance with other ages. He may be a skillful man of affairs, a keen reasoner, but he is for all that provincial. There is one side of culture that is not to be worked out, nor reasoned out; it comes to a man, it possesses him. It is the effect produced by viewing life and its questions, art, literature, religion, society, from many points of vision. And there is no other way of multiplying one's points of vision than by looking through other men's eyes, yielding up our natural habit of thought for the time being, and taking the stand of other ages. If I would get the look that life and its problems had to the Roman, I must stand where the Roman stood and look on it through his eyes. And what other way is there for me to get by his side and to see things as they looked to him, but by studying his literature and history, and these, too, as they were to him, not as a modern writer reproduces or describes them. In short, there is no other way of knowing how other races and ages of human beings thought and felt but by steeping ourselves in their atmosphere, that is, in their history and literature. If we do that, if we take our stand by the Roman and see with his eyes, in so far we escape from our natural provincialism, and receive a culture that is wholly unique of its kind. So, in proportion as age after age, through its literature, its art, its religion, its social life, is brought home to our familiar apprehension, this broadening process is carried on, and little by little the provincial habit is eradicated.

## THE HIGHER EDUCATION WITHOUT GOD.

The higher education has no room for so primary a work on morals as the Bible. Then it must confront the problem alone. Here is the "natural man;" he is still vicious, unaccountably fond of vile ways, with a real love for rascality, unamenable to reason, unchangeable by any kind of government or educational manipulation. All sorts of polities, social atmospheres, sanitary measures, educational remedies, have been applied to him, and nothing has ever done him any good, but religion. Even that has not restrained him much, but yet it has restrained. He changes his plan of operations, he transforms his outward appearance, but at bottom, in his heart, he is the same natural man. He is no longer a soulless Greek, given over to unnatural vices. He has got over his ferocious carnivorous mood, when he was a Roman. He is no freebooting baron of the Middle Ages. He does not drink himself under the table every night, after the style of Queen Anne's age. But here he is, the same inwardly bad fellow. He appears in all sorts of shapes: we all have something of him in us.

The whole theory of regenerating man by education is based on the assumption, that what cures a bad disposition is light. One is tempted here to repeat what the great Master of morals, of conduct, said about the effect of light on man's bad disposition—that the trouble with men was not that they had not light, but that when light came they did not want it, that they refused it, and fought against it. But no amount of information, of breadth of view, of training of the reasoning powers, and of the faculties of taste, is going to have the slightest effect by itself on man's conduct. For that is wrong not by defect of knowledge, or narrowness of outlook, or weakness of the logical faculty, or faultiness of the eye or ear; but by a positive quality. It is a positive force that will go after what it wants. And when the pagan poet said, "I see the better but the worse pursue," he described just the case we have to deal with—that of a being who goes wrong when he has plenty of light, who goes wrong because he has a force in him that nerves itself, that chooses to defy what is right.

It has been so over and over again in the history of the world. Men have had a fair start again and again; and again and again they have, despite all the *superior education* afforded them, gone steadily down. They have had it in Egypt, in Greece, in Rome, in every great country in Europe. And always an unaccountable element showed itself, a vicious element, and in spite of all efforts it conquered every time. Nothing yet has ever eliminated it: reverse the terms, put them how you will, there the bad quantity appears, not a negative, but a pressing, positive quantity; a quality that bites-in, that eats through everything, national character, literary culture, refined taste, primitive simplicity, inherited virtues.

## THEOLOGY.

Theology is the bridge that spans the gulf between heaven and earth; but it must plant a pier on either side. It springs from heaven on the one side; but it must touch the earth on the other, or men will at last decline to go over it. The great trouble is that theology has been projecting itself in the air, failing to touch life; or touching it only so remotely, so obscurely, that men have found it hard to see the connection between the doctrine taught and the life to be lived.

## THE THREE DISTINCTIVELY LUTHERAN DOCTRINES.

Among the Protestant churches the Lutheran has always been distinguished by three great lines of religious thought related to and growing out of three doctrines emphasized, not so much in her creeds and confessions, as in the theological discussions of the Church. Those lines of thought are represented by the several doctrines of *Justification by Faith, Baptism, and the Lord's Supper.*

---

## LARGENESS OF STYLE.

This is a vague expression. What, it will be said, is meant by "largeness" in such a connection? Well, perhaps it is not easy to define: but it may be possible to suggest a meaning. Apart from any sharply defined quality in a work of imagination or intellectual construction, as wit, or brilliancy, or acumen, or profundity, we are sensible of a general atmosphere that belongs to the whole production. The writer, we say to ourselves, looks at things in a small way; he sees only one side; he is a pettifogger; everything is belittled under his treatment: or, on the other hand, we say, he has a broad outlook; he sees things on a great scale; he takes us out into the open air and makes us feel the vastness of the great heavens and earth. This sort of atmosphere may be felt in a work that apparently admits of no great expansion of thought. Homer writes of the squabbles of the Greeks and Trojans and the absurd interferences of a very petty lot of celestials; and yet he has this large tone. It broadens and lifts up one's sense of things to read him. Madame Dacier, his French translator, said that after reading the Iliad everything was magnified: the men she met on the street seemed ten feet high. The largeness is not in the subject, but in the treatment; and that we refer at last to the largeness in the man. Such is the effect produced by Bishop Butler. Whether he writes of Compassion or Self-Deceit, of Resentment or the Love of God, the subject broadens and deepens under his hand. A certain grandeur invests the thoughts as they arise. The greatness of God, the dignity of man, the sweetness and excellence of piety, the miseries of sin, all appear in a strangely impressive light: the old figures come before us as the figures of life came upon the Greek stage, uplifted, made heroic, with a great carriage that overawes and expands the sensibilities. It is not that we are told anything new; but the old truth in the larger utterance has the wonder and majesty of a fresh revelation.

## SCIENCE vs. THEOLOGY.

Science fascinates the mind by its element of positiveness; and truly, apart from the matter of scientific discovery, its vast extension of the fields of knowledge, the mastery it gives man over nature, it is doing a great educating work on the intellect of the race in teaching it exactness, sincerity, love for reality. It is this new charm of apparent superior reality which is making it shine for the moment over its rival Theology. We are all for the moment taken by the wonderful feat of being able to weigh the sun and tell the number of tons it turns in the scales; it seems that to know how many millions of years it took to evolve the earth out of nebulous mist is vastly grander than to believe that "God created the heavens and the earth." It is the contrast of the sharply defined, the exact, with the mysterious, the dimly seen, the immeasurable. But that must pass. Its very charm, its positiveness, its clear cut, sharply defined outline of knowledge, becomes after awhile a weariness, for it is a limitation. The eye loves a sharp outline, a clear bounded object; but it loves even more the depth of the limitless sky; and the mind, after the definite bounds, the weights and measures of science, craves its boundless heaven, its depth of mystery fathomless, its infinite God. As Mr. Arnold says, "There are times when a reaction against religion and metaphysical discussion sets in, when an interest in physical science and the practical arts, is called *an interest in things*, and an interest in morals and religion is called an *interest in words*."

## THE REALITY OF THEOLOGY.

The cure for the disesteem into which Theology has fallen in the Church and out of the Church, is reality. By reality I mean the sense of positiveness, of vitality, which comes to us when we find that a truth really affects our lives; that it explains difficulties, throws light on the path, changes life, satisfies some need. Scientific thought makes a great deal of what it calls verification: *i. e.* the trial of a theory, a statement of truth, by experiment. Well, theology will get reality, and gather to itself the honor it once had, when it verifies itself, *i. e.* when it shows men that all its great truths are implicated in their common life.

## PASTORAL MANAGEMENT.

If, as pastors, we can find something for every man to do, can mark out each one's place, and rouse an individual interest in specific Christian work, we shall have no trouble in finding interested hearers. But simply to preach from Sunday to Sunday to a people, as one lectures to a lyceum, with no other immediate objective point than to say something fresh and stirring, is of all work the most depressing. It is no wonder that the modern minister is ever seeking some new place. There is nothing in the way of means that can freshen the pulpit like bringing it into direct contact with the coöperative work of the pews. The organizing, administrative preacher, will never be dull to his co-laborers; and his work with them, and through them, will most rapidly increase the number of those who, from an interest in the work of Christ, will find an interest in the word of Christ.

## THE COMMUNION SEASON.

The sneer indulged by many at our communion season, that there believers rejoice, and weep, and are filled with devout feeling, and then go back to their homes to plod on in the old way, is a very shallow sneer. It implies that all emotion is idle and false that does not issue in some palpable work. True, genuine religious emotion does arouse to greater religious activity; but a certain measure, a very large measure, is expended simply in the act of love, of praise—worship and love are their own end.

"Beauty is its own excuse for being;"

and the outflow of love and worship to God is its own justification. It ends in him and completes itself in glorifying him. And so our solemn sacramental seasons are justified in their deep emotion, even as the praises of the heavenly host are justified, because they are paid to God.

## THE SCRIPTURAL METHOD OF SALVATION.

The revelation of the Bible is not only to the effect that men are in danger of perishing, and that there is but a short time in which to save them, but also that there are elements which make the matter of haste in saving individuals not the first consideration. If we accept the position that the great thing about religion is to get the individual out of danger, at once then we immediately impugn the whole scheme of redemption as set forth in the Scriptures. It is there made plain enough that the immediate rescue of the individual from ruin is not the first consideration, for all the arrangements for the Gospel system are made with a deliberate and gradual preparation which to those who think only of the particular individuals must seem cold-blooded cruelty. Hundreds of years elapse between the successive steps by which the race is brought nearer the revelation and work of the Redeemer. Thousands of years roll away before the promise of salvation made on the threshold of Eden is fulfilled in the perfected salvation on Calvary. There are reasons then for doubting whether the matter of haste is so important in God's view as some others. From the slow processes by which he has unfolded his great redemption, we are led to infer that the salvation of men is not a work that can be done hurriedly. We are accustomed to say that time was requisite for the ripening of the redemptive work. St. Paul says that "when the fullness of the time was come, God sent forth his Son." Christ refuses to be hurried by his brethren to go up to Jerusalem, though they urge that if his message is really divine it ought to be proclaimed at once: "My time," answers Christ to this plea for haste, "is not yet come." All this line of thought, rather, this plain drift of revelation, seems to point us to something like this, that in the matter of salvation quickness is not so important as thoroughness. There is such a thing as making so much of the mere rescue from peril as to cheapen and really make worthless the salvation itself. What good is it to rescue a man from a burning house if to get him out you have to club him and so injure his brain that when out he is only a raging maniac? You want to get him out of the flames a whole man, and he might as well burn to death as live a lunatic.

www.ingramcontent.com/pod-product-compliance
Lightning Source LLC
Chambersburg PA
CBHW031852220426
43663CB00006B/589